THE OFFICIAL®
IDENTIFICATION AND
PRICE GUIDE TO

AMERICAN
ILLUSTRATOR
ART

THE OFFICIAL® IDENTIFICATION AND PRICE GUIDE TO

AMERICAN ILLUSTRATOR ART

ANNE GILBERT

FIRST EDITION

HOUSE OF COLLECTIBLES • NEW YORK

Important Notice. All of the information, including valuations, in this book has been compiled from the most reliable sources, and every effort has been made to eliminate errors and questionable data. Nevertheless, the possibility of error, in a work of such immense scope, always exists. The publisher will not be held responsible for losses which may occur in the purchase, sale, or other transaction of items because of information contained herein. Readers who feel they have discovered errors are invited to *write* and inform us, so they may be corrected in subsequent editions. Those seeking further information on the topics covered in this book are advised to refer to the complete line of *Official Price Guides* published by the House of Collectibles.

Cover art © Curtis Publishing Co.

© 1991 by Anne Gilbert

This is a registered trademark of Random House, Inc.

All rights reserved under International and Pan-American Copyright Conventions.

Published by: House of Collectibles
201 East 50th Street
New York, New York 10022

Distributed by Ballantine Books, a division of Random House, Inc., New York, and simultaneously in Canada by Random House of Canada Limited, Toronto.

Text design by Holly Johnson

Manufactured in the United States of America

ISBN: 0-876-37833-5

First Edition: August 1991

10 9 8 7 6 5 4 3 2 1

*To future generations of illustrators,
who will always find new ways to stretch our
imaginations in step with the twenty-first century.*

CONTENTS

FOREWORD

The art of illustration is as old as the cave paintings. Art performed a function in early cultures. It was used as body painting or as costume for rituals and celebrations, as icons and symbols to ensure a good harvest or fertility, or to appease the gods. Art was used on implements and tools as decoration.

Illustration today performs the same function. It is used in fashion, industrial design, publishing, and entertainment. The graphic image is part of our everyday lives in what we wear, use, or buy. It is our introduction to the world of books before we can read. Illustration has a powerful influence on us, yet to a great extent it is taken for granted. If one were to imagine removing all illustration from our culture, it would not take long to realize how much it influences, guides, and informs us and is a very necessary part of our lives, both literally and spiritually.

There is the misconception that illustration is not art because it is done for reproduction. A division was made between ''fine'' art and ''commercial'' art with the invention of the printing press. The separation is an illusion today, as gallery art is being reproduced and licensed on clothing, as games, cards, posters, *and* as illustrations, while art done as illustration by artists such as Arthur Rackham, Erté, or N. C. Wyeth hangs in galleries and museums. An attitude exists that since illustration is commissioned and the artist has direction or a manuscript to start from, it cannot be art. All art starts with an idea. Each artist has a unique personal expression or vision. If exactly the same direction was given to five different illustrators, five distinct interpretations would result. Any illustration is the personal vision of the artist, combining exaggeration, imagination, talent, and the personal handling of the media that results in the style and technique of the artist. As a matter of fact, many illustrators have followers or fans who recognize and collect a particular illustrator's printed work. Reproductions have a value of their own.

Illustrators themselves ''bought'' the idea that their original art had no value in itself because it was done for reproduction, and they sometimes used materials that were not permanent. Many artists assumed the client had the right to keep the original art. Companies that commissioned large amounts of illustration periodically threw it out or destroyed it to make room for more recent work. Both of these factors resulted in the loss of much of the earlier original art, making some illustrators' work rare and higher in value now.

The Society of Illustrators was formed in 1901 by a group of America's leading artists. Among its early members were Charles Dana Gibson,

William Glackens, and Everett Shinn. One reason they started the group was to clarify the fact that the artist owned the original art; he or she was selling the right to reproduce it, and the original art was returnable to them. This was important because the price paid for an illustration was much less than a comparable painting from a gallery. They won their fight in court. Today's artists are more aware of the resale value of their work.

The society's purpose is "to promote and stimulate interest in the art of illustration and give impetus toward high ideals in the art by means of exhibitions, lectures, educational programs, and social exchange." The society maintains one of the most extensive and historic collections of illustration in America, consisting of more than 1,500 pieces. It is a who's who of American illustration and includes work by Norman Rockwell, J. C. Leyendecker, Maxfield Parrish, and James Montgomery Flagg, to name a few, as well as current famous illustrators. A historic exhibition from the permanent collection travels to universities and libraries around the country. The society's library contains books on illustration and books about illustrators. It has a unique archival collection of biographical material on illustrators.

There are two public galleries, the Society of Illustrators' Museum of American Illustration, that exhibit group and one-man shows, works from the permanent collection, and theme shows. Among recent topics have been The American Beauty, *Time* Magazine Cover Art, *National Geographic*'s Centennial, and the Art of Medicine.

Each year the society sponsors an annual juried show of American illustration. Out of thousands of entries, about 500 pieces are chosen. This show represents the best of illustration across the nation, from categories such as books, magazines, newspapers, posters, advertising, television, and self-promotion. From this exhibition an annual book is produced that provides a record of that year. Looking back over thirty years of the Society of Illustrators' annuals one can see the change of style in the art as well as learn much about life, politics, trends, and fashion in America. The annuals chronicle a unique history and would prove useful to collectors.

As for careers, illustrators work on staff in advertising agencies, design studios, printing companies, television studios, and any business that might need full-time art services. The majority of illustrators work on a freelance basis. They set up their studio at home or rent space outside. A freelance illustrator works at odd hours, on holidays, weekends, and sometimes through the night. Illustration is a part of their ongoing daily existence; it is difficult to separate living from work. A freelance illustrator working predominatly in advertising, newspapers, or magazines is particularly susceptible to the pressures of deadlines.

As far as the opportunity for success in this field goes, any dedicated and talented person can get to the top of the profession. Another positive aspect is that illustrators are not forced into retirement as long as they can work.

The disadvantage of a staff position is "last hired and first fired." Our early education imparts to us that art is play after the three R's are done. This carries over into an attitude that art is least important in business. The disadvantage in a freelancer's life is an irregular income, which causes cash flow problems. Security is an illusion even in staff jobs but a freelancer's clients constantly change. There are no guarantees that an illustrator will be wealthy after many years in the field. It is a highly competitive profession, but many live a comfortable and productive life.

The following is an example of the variety of categories of illustration. It is not intended as a complete list but as an example of areas to examine when collecting. There are book covers, interior book illustration, album covers, magazine and newspaper art, greeting cards, posters, children's books, animation, textiles, cartoons, technical illustration such as rendering of machinery, charts, maps, medical art, plus fashion and industrial art.

The Graphic Artists Guild is an organization formed over thirty years ago to "promote and maintain high professional standards of ethics and practices and to establish, implement and enforce laws, policies and contracts to accomplish these ends." The guild publishes, among other things, *Pricing and Ethical Guidelines*, which is most helpful to artists as well as clients. The PEGS, as it is called, contains sections on how artwork is priced, professional practices, ethical standards, trade customs, and so on. Although pricing for the collector may be established from a different perspective, the PEGS can provide the collector with knowledge of illustration that may prove useful.

This collector's guide will offer additional information for people in the field of illustration as well as collectors and may prove helpful in pricing original art. It is exciting to see the growing interest and appreciation for the art of illustration in its many forms. There is a wealth of fine art waiting to be collected and appreciated.

Diane Dillon
President,
Society of Illustrators,
1987–1989

ACKNOWLEDGMENTS

A book of this scope couldn't be written by one person alone. Therefore, I have enlisted the help of the many experts in this field. While their backgrounds are varied—as dealers, collectors, illustrators—all have a common love and appreciation for American illustrator art.

It is always hard to sell a totally new idea, especially in the book field. Fortunately, Dottie (Dorothy) Harris, my Editor-in-Chief, saw far beyond my rough drafts to the potential for an exciting collecting category. Nudging me on past the finishing line, which I never thought I'd make, was my editor, Karen Shapiro. Without their encouragement, there would not have been a book.

To Walt Reed goes my special thanks. As the premiere historian, who was among the first to realize the importance of American illustrator art and to chronicle the names and works of many forgotten illustrators in his books and informative newsletter, he has interested a new generation of collectors. His advice and the generous use of both his past research and photos have made this very difficult task much easier. Working with his father, Roger Reed has added his expertise and helpful comments to this book, for which I am indebted.

My appreciation to the Society of Illustrators, who understand the need for this practical handbook. And to Diane Dillon, a past president of the Society of Illustrators, who has taken time from her busy schedule as an award-winning illustrator to write the foreword to this book.

Since I believed that readers would benefit by learning more about the various categories of illustrators (history, fashion, etc.) and the contemporary influences on their work, I sought out experts to write the introductory pieces. Of course, I called on Walt Reed, who knows better than anyone else how to evaluate the work of illustrators and differentiate the types of illustration.

For both written contributions and photos, as well as price estimates, my thanks to Les Mansfield, Terry Booth, Judy Goffman, Richard Marschall, Alan M. Goffman, Ray and Beverly Sacks, Benjamin Eisenstat and Jane Sperry Eisenstat, Kendra Krienke, Carl Sciortino, Michael Frost, Cathy and Mort Walker, Robert Benney, Leo and Diane Dillon, Frederic B. Taraba, Pam Sommers, David Leopold, and Thomas Rockwell.

For photos and realized auction prices, my thanks to Christie's, Skinner's, Guernsey's, Butterfield and Butterfield, Morton Goldberg Galleries, Sotheby's, DuMouchelles, Freeman Fine Arts, The Every Picture Tells a Story Gallery, Susan Theran, publisher of *Leonard's Annual Price Index of Art Auctions* and Margo Feiden Galleries. Thanks also to Christie's for supplying the line art that appears throughout the book.

For the loan of many rare photographic examples from their permanent collection, my appreciation to the Society of Illustrators. Thanks also to Trans Art studios for solving a photo crisis.

PART I

INTRODUCTION

HOW TO APPROACH COLLECTING
AMERICAN ILLUSTRATOR ART

For the first time, this book offers a price structure for collectors, dealers, and appraisers, who may be far from the major cities where most illustrator art comes to auction or is sold by specialized dealers. Equally important, this book offers beginning collectors affordable alternatives to the ultra-expensive illustrations, costing in the high thousands. Even though some superstar illustrators such as Norman Rockwell command top dollar, when compared to other areas of collecting in the art market, they are underpriced. While not everyone can afford a Joseph Leyendecker *Saturday Evening Post* cover, there are not only hundreds of original works by less familiar illustrators but also printed magazine covers, record album jackets, and book illustrations. This book gives selected examples of some of the most collectible illustrators, together with the signatures of some of the most important, to help in identification.

Because this is still a developing market, prices listed represent what various examples of original American illustrator art sold for at auctions, through dealers, in private sales, and in some instances, as discoveries at flea markets and garage sales. This accounts for the vast price fluctuations. In such a developing market, prices for the less-known illustrators can be extremely low.

Even though many illustrators are placed in the categories where they most often worked, such as fashion or business, there are overlaps. The same goes for the majority of cover artists; they often did magazine and book illustrations as well. Many artists, such as N. C. Wyeth, Howard Pyle, and Jessie Wilcox Smith, are mentioned in several sections of the book because of their importance.

Prices cover 1987 through September 1990, the cutoff date for the first edition of this book. Specialized illustrator auctions have been few. A breakthrough was the 1988 auction of the Bob Wale collection at Guernsey's auction in New York. Over 400 pierces were offered in a wide range of prices and estimates. Although prices realized were on the low side, nonetheless, it was a beginning that was widely advertised. New collectors, dealers, and museums found it an affordable opportunity to build American illustrator collections.

Illustration art has been around since 1455 A.D. But with the exception of a handful of famous examples (e.g., Norman Rockwell, Maxfield Parrish), collectors have had a rough time trying to put a price on hundreds of other collectible illustrators and their work. For the most part, collectors have had to go to a variety of sources, such as auction catalogs and exhibits, to put together prices for their collections. Collector newsletters offering illustrator art, such as the *Illustration House Newsletter*, published since the 1970s by Walt Reed, are not well known to the general public.

One of the most exciting aspects of collecting illustrations is that you never know where you'll find them. I remember well the day in 1957 when a friend showed me an oil painting signed by Haddon Sundblom. She had found it in the basement of the Chicago apartment building where she lived. It had simply been tossed away when its owners had moved. She had no idea of the value and did not know that the painting was an illustration for a magazine story nor that Sundblom had done the original Coca-Cola Santa Claus. I wonder if she knows today that it is worth thousands of dollars.

It was nearly two decades later that I discovered and bought the first two pieces of American illustrator art, which became the beginning of my collection and of a fascination with original illustrations. I had long forgotten the Sundblom painting.

My drawings were part of an estate sale in Wilmette, Illinois. It consisted of hundreds of pieces of art that had belonged to a former *Saturday Evening Post* art director. I paid $25 each for the pen-and-ink drawings of vintage cars. They were signed "Henry Raleigh" and dated in the 1920s. Since it was the last day of the sale, I can only speculate on the treasures I missed at equally low prices.

Although I checked through dozens of art books and artists, I wasn't able to find the name Henry Raleigh. I had no idea that I wasn't looking in the right books. Nor did I know that he had once been famous as one of America's top magazine illustrators. Then I came across an out-of-print copy of *The Illustrator in America* by Walt Reed, published in 1966. In it I found not only Henry Raleigh but many other illustrators, from Thomas Nast to Norman Rockwell.

It was another six months before I discovered other illustrations. A woman who had just seen my slide lecture, which included the two illustrations, told me that she had many similar pieces in her hall closet. She would sell them for $25 apiece. It seemed her late father had been a maintenance man at the *Saturday Evening Post*. He had salvaged some fifty pieces from the trash can.

As I later learned, this had been the fate of many original illustrations. Cover art had been saved, but thousands of illustrations had been dumped.

Among the illustrators rescued from that hall closet were some of the top names of the "Golden Age of Illustration" (1880–1914), Raleigh as well as Frederick Gruger, Wallace Morgan, and Joseph Clement Coll. All were pen-and-ink drawings with color wash or with Wolff pencil.

What were they worth? Not one of Chicago's top appraisers was certain of values. There was simply no information available, or at least none that I was able to come by. My next step was to contact Walt Reed. As a dealer and historian of American illustrator art, Reed was familiar with many values. He also told me about a new exhibit, "200 Years of American Illustration," at the New York Historical Society. Sponsored by the Society of Illustrators, it was the first time ever for such a massive display of American illustration art. Reed told me there were really no set prices because few of the illustrators had come to auction. The exceptions were Norman Rockwell and illustrators who were also known as fine artists.

I attended that first major Society of Illustrators exhibit and learned that many rare illustrations had been found in trash cans. Indeed, a rare pen-and-ink sketch by George Catlin (famed for Native American subjects), called "Athapasca Indians," and done in the middle of the 19th century, was found by a collector at a garbage dump. Even doodles done by Maxfield Parrish were saved from his waste basket. A former Macy's art director told me how advertising fashion art was routinely tossed out when the files were cleaned.

Why hasn't the illustration market been as high-priced or respected as, say, limited-edition prints done yesterday? One reason given is that since the 1930s art critics and collectors have maintained that illustrations aren't art but merely a commercial technique to sell products and ideas.

Even the late Norman Rockwell admitted that "there have been disadvantages to being an illustrator. Many who consider themselves serious painters look down their noses at us." Of course, Rockwell had the last laugh on his critics as his magazine cover art was taken seriously enough in the 1970s for collectors to plunk down five figures. And middle America collected anything Rockwellian, from plates to figurines. In fact, ask the average person on the street to name an illustrator, and the answer will probably be "Norman Rockwell." Yet in the 200-year history of American illustration there have been hundreds of talented illustrators. Rockwell said, "My hero was Howard Pyle. He seemed to represent to me the world of the true illustrator." Pyle is considered the "father of American illustration." A few years ago he was listed by *Arts & Antiques* magazine as one of the "25 most underpriced artists." And although he was famed as a teacher and illustrator (1853–1911; N. C. Wyeth and Harvey Dunn were among his students), few outside museum and illustrator circles know his name. Other names, such as Paul Revere, George Catlin, and John James Audubon, are familiar but not as illustrators.

That Society of Illustrators exhibit should have sparked interest in illustration art. It was a time when you could have picked up a J. C. Leyendecker cover for a couple of thousand dollars or had a choice of such illustrations as Everett Shinn's original drawing for "The Night Before Christmas" or a Stevan Dohanos oil for less than $2,000. It was an opportunity for adventurous art collectors to get in on the ground floor. Still, illustration art didn't seem to catch on except in the East. However, there were ripples. An occasional auction would have a sizable number of illustrations included with the other art.

It wasn't till 1979 that major auction galleries began to accept illustrator art. Among the first to "go on the block" were N. C. Wyeth, Maxfield Parrish, Howard Chandler Christy, Herbert Morton Stoops, W. H. D. Koerner, and Norman Rockwell.

In the last few years, major auction houses such as Phillips, Christie's, and Sotheby's have had illustrator auctions. In September 1988, Guernsey's New York auction gallery had a major collection of over 500 pieces of illustration art to offer, the Robert Wale collection. Along with the big names were many less-known illustrators. Realized prices ranged from several at a $50 low to a few in the high thousands. What made this auction different was the number of collectors who bought. Although price results weren't exactly sensational, they were up substantially from the previous year. More important, a market had finally been established with a wide range of illustrators and prices for collectors and dealers.

The time would seem right for an *Official® Price Guide to American Illustrator Art* that creates a new interest in the many long-forgotten illustrators, as well as in the continuing tradition of illustration art from the 1970s, 1980s, and 1990s. It is a time when illustrators no longer give away their art or their rights. Today's illustrators, justly proud of their works as art, have gallery shows to introduce their art to collectors.

The fact that original illustrator art is finally being appreciated and rising in monetary value is gratifying, not only for collectors and dealers but for contemporary American illustrators. After all, these artists saw and are seeing history, fashion, and social changes, and they expressed themselves in pen, pencil, oil, and other media as legitimate artists. Being accepted as serious painters was their ultimate goal; the question will always be why it took so long for today's collectors to recognize their work.

COLLECTORS' TOOLS AND TECHNIQUES

Let the regional and important national auction galleries know you are a potential buyer in the field of American illustrator art. Subscribe to a variety of auction catalogs in the category of American paintings. Sometimes this category will be combined with European paintings and works of art or listed as 19th- or 20th-century American paintings. Sometimes, as in the case of Butterfield and Butterfield Galleries, it may be listed under California Artists, which could and often does include illustrators.

Write a letter to the "expert" in American illustrators at the galleries, telling him or her what you are interested in—artist, medium, and so on. Galleries have a list of potential buyers who will be informed when something in their category is coming up. Some will send photos and color transparencies to interested buyers.

The catalogs vary in price depending on the importance of the auction and the auction gallery itself. Prices range from $15 per catalog to $175 for a yearly subscription. Always make sure that this includes the follow-up sheets of final prices. Major auction houses always add a 10 percent buyer's premium to the purchase price. Many small galleries and private art galleries do not.

A good source for sleepers is the general estate auction. Although you won't find any Norman Rockwell illustrations going unrecognized at low prices, there may be quality illustrators that aren't familiar to the gallery's experts. It does happen! By spending $100 to $200 you might increase the worth of your collection by a few thousand dollars. General auction catalogs are worth subscribing to.

Many illustrations look like fine works of art and have easy-to-recognize signatures; others may have the illustrator's instructions to the publisher and a caption that goes with the story being illustrated. This latter may not appeal to the person doing the pricing if he or she doesn't recognize the artist and feels that the caption material detracts from the art. To the collector of illustrator art this material is a plus; it may later help to identify the magazine or book the illustration appeared in. Many times, previous owners have covered the caption and art instructions with the mat. When buying at a private sale, always take the art out of the frame. Look not only for instructions but also the name of the publication and possibly the story title.

A perfect example of why illustrations should be carefully examined before making a private purchase is the Reginald Marsh watercolor I bought privately. Because it is small (10″ × 8″), it appeared relatively unimportant. It was signed R. Marsh and dated 1945. The owner had sent a photo to one of the auction galleries in New York for an estimate before offering it to me for sale. It had been photographed in the frame. In fact, the watercolor had never been removed from the frame since it was given to her by an artist friend in the 1960s. The auction estimate was under $1,500, and the gallery didn't accept it for consignment.

The first thing I did when she offered it to me was to take it carefully out of the frame. Underneath the mat were the words "frontispiece for John Dos Passos, *U.S.A.* The book was a best-seller in the 1940s. Now the watercolor had developed provenance—and several thousand dollars in value. The provenance and artist's instructions are written in Reginald Marsh's handwriting. Newly framed, they are clearly visible.

Illustrator art often shows up in Art Nouveau, Art Deco, and Arts and Crafts auctions. Again, the name of the illustrator may be an unfamiliar one, and the piece may have found its way to the auction because of the period it represents. It may be overpriced as Arts and Crafts or Art Deco.

For a further breakdown of prices at auction and information about when and where works by illustrators have been sold, a good source is *Leonard's Annual Price Index of Art Auctions*, published twice yearly. You may also want to write to The American Institute for the Conservation of Historic and Artistic Works, Suite 340, 1400 North Street, NW, Washington, DC 20036; (202) 232-6636.

SIGNATURES

Obviously, values are determined by signatures as well as other factors such as condition and popularity of the artist. What if a piece of art, such as a John Held, Jr., woodcut engraving, has only an estate stamp? Since not all artists signed everything they did, it is the custom for art dealers to have estate stamps made up to take the place of signatures. These stamps are quite acceptable substitutes for the artist's signature. They are hand-signed and dated either by a descendant of the artist or by someone, such as the art dealer, who is qualified to authenticate the art.

There can be problems with some estate-stamped pieces. Ask another expert why the artist didn't sign the piece. Perhaps the piece was unfinished or was an unsuccessful trial piece. Or perhaps the artist didn't feel it was worthy of his or her signature. If the work is priced almost as high as similar signed pieces, quality should be the deciding factor.

BUILD A TOTAL COLLECTION

Whenever possible, try to locate printed examples of your illustrations, from books and magazines and artists' preliminary sketches. When Robert Wales's collection of illustrator art came to the Guernsey auction in 1988, it had added importance because it included tearsheets with the original art.

Specialized collections ultimately have more value than helter-skelter purchases. You may wish to collect by period (e.g., Art Deco) or medium (oil, pen and ink), only book illustrations or a specific artist. Although many of the artists covered in this guide are known primarily for their work on certain subjects, they often branched out into other fields. If you decide to collect by category it is a good idea to contact dealers who specialize in certain areas (e.g., Western or history) or the various schools, such as the Brandywine. If they don't have what you are looking for, sooner or later they'll be able to find it for you. Because you are paying for their time and expertise, it will cost more than if you had found it at auction or at an estate sale. But the dealer has done all the leg work as well as the research on the art, and this is worth paying for.

Many collectors like to develop personal acquaintance with illustrators through correspondence. The illustrator's philosophy and sidelights on some of his or her work add to the value of a collection. Imagine your great grandfather having corresponded with Audubon, and now you have a collection of the artist's works, including letters telling how many hours it took him to paint one of his birds and what he went through to track it down. That's the start of building a collection.

SOME BUYING TIPS

Bigger may not be better. Many artists, such as Reginald Marsh, did some of their finest works under twelve inches. So buying by size is certainly not the best criterion, not only from the standpoint of quality but also of practicality. Supersize illustrations are great if they are museum quality, not so great if they are average examples or by a lesser illustrator.

Often you can buy original illustrator art for less than you would imagine. Preliminary studies, sketches, and drawings for a major painting, even by well-known illustrators, are available for a few hundred dollars. A Norman Rockwell might sell in the low thousands if it isn't finished art.

When you buy at major big-city auction houses, you're vying with monied collectors and dealers buying for clients. Certain subjects are more popular than others and may be priced at double the amount other subjects by the same artist will command.

Exchanging art with other collectors as well as with dealers is one way to upgrade a collection. You may want to start collecting a new category or artist, and so may another collector. You will be selling (swapping) at a wholesale level with the dealer, at auction with the collector.

WHAT TO DO WHEN ILLUSTRATIONS NEED RESTORATION AND FRAMING

Often you will come across unframed illustrations at flea markets or estate sales, or you will find one at auction that is in need of new mounting and framing. Although most dealers have their illustration art properly restored and framed, "discoveries" usually need expert attention. Consider that they may have foxing, tears, cracks, and other damage. After all, they have been lying in damp attics and basements or may even have been rescued from trash cans. When having illustrations framed, ask for acid-free museum mounting.

Unless you are an expert, never attempt restoration yourself. Since expert restoration is expensive, know something of the value of the "discovery" before buying. Say you've found an Arthur Becher charcoal drawing, done on artists' board, with cracks and a missing corner. If you have read this book, you will know that the price for a Becher illustration can range from $900 to $3,500 for a pen and ink to a high of $8,500 for an oil painting. Currently, there is no listing for your drawing, dated 1913. If you live far from a major city and have to make a quick decision on whether to buy or not, buy if the price is under $500. But ask yourself if the subject is one you want to live with. On the plus side, there aren't that many illustrators by Becher around, so the price can only go up. But expect that your drawing needs several hundred dollars worth of restoration, and take it to a restoration expert, even if you have to travel.

What if you discover an illustration that at first seems impossible to repair? Nothing is impossible for a conservator. For advice, contact the dealers listed in the back of this book. Ask painting curators in museums who does their restoration work. Many dealers also have become experts in restoration and might treat your "wounded" illustration.

HOW ILLUSTRATORS WERE SELECTED FOR THIS BOOK

If you are wondering where some obviously important names are, rest assured that they haven't been intentionally left out. Floyd Davis and Elmer Boyd Smith, for example, are important names for collectors to look for. However, they haven't come to auction or for sale in galleries frequently enough to give collectors a hint of current values. Perhaps they and many others will have evaluations by the next edition of this book.

You will also notice that with the exception of discussing such early influences as The Golden Age, Howard Pyle, and Harvy Dunn, illustrators are not divided into historical periods. Therefore, you'll find illustrators who worked in the 1950s, 1960s, and 1970s listed with earlier illustrators, by the special categories they most often worked in. As mentioned in the bibliography, there are many fine reference books that put them in historical perspective.

PART II

EVALUATING AMERICAN ILLUSTRATION

BY WALT REED
AND ROGER REED

OVERVIEW

Walt and Roger Reed are the proprietors of Illustration House, a SoHo gallery specializing in illustrative paintings and drawings of the 20th century. In 1974, Walt was a pioneer, dealing in illustration art in Westport, Connecticut. Father and son are considered the preeminent authorities in the field, Walt having written the definitive historical reference, The Illustrator in America 1880–1980, *and several others. These books provide background to the gallery, which includes works by Rockwell, Pyle, Abbey, N. C. Wyeth, Leyendecker, and many others. The Reeds have served as consultants to several museums and corporations and also appraise. They publish an informative combination newsletter and price listing of currently available original illustrator art:* The Illustration Collector, *$5 a copy or, by subscription, three issues for $12. Subscribers also can sell through the newsletter. They hold auctions in their gallery twice a year.*

Increasingly, illustrators' art is turning up in auction sales, museums, and antique shows, raising questions from art viewers. What is the status of this art form? A decade ago such pictures were seldom seen, reflecting the generally held view that illustration was not quite art.

There are two aspects to illustration: one is the reproduction, like the plate in a book; the other is the original art the plate was reproduced from. Awareness of illustration is usually confined to its appearance on the printed page. After serving their function—to enhance a text—the originals were almost never exhibited.

Certainly, the general public was not aware of the great disparity between the quality of the original and the printed image. A full-color painting might be reproduced in black and white or at one-tenth of its original size, and the high-speed press could not maintain fidelity to the original image. When the art itself is presented, framed and hanging on the wall, it often has an irresistible appeal to the general public. The exhibit "Two Hundred Years of American Illustration," held at the New York Historical Society in 1976, attracted record crowds. Ironically, it is precisely that popular aspect of illustration that makes certain curators skeptical of its acceptance in marble halls.

Illustration is hard to define and thwarts attempts at pigeonholing. Detractors have claimed that the requirements of the story and the art director so limit the content that the artist is reduced to a craftsperson. But the relationship between art and text is not that simple. Many of the best illustrators, from A. B. Frost in the 1880s to Robert Weaver in the 1980s, have had the strongest possible voice in determining the content and execution of their work. Once the artist has been chosen, the editor may simply okay the drawings or paintings.

For some illustrators, the challenge of working within the confines of a story is fascinating. Others have deemphasized the story, feeling that the painting should stand on its own, as in a gallery, after the story is long forgotten. Harvey Dunn and Walter Biggs produced work that often upstaged the fiction. Sometimes the opposite occurred: witness Sidney Paget's uninspired illustrations of the original Sherlock Holmes stories. The happiest marriage may occur when the author is the illustrator. Generations have and will enjoy Howard Pyle's *Men of Iron* and Maurice Sendak's *Where the Wild Things Are*.

The great majority of illustrators have had dual art careers, making it difficult to answer the question "When is an artist an illustrator?" Some, like Arthur Dove, Edward Hopper, and Andy Warhol, were clearly disenchanted with illustration and worked in a radically different way when moonlighting. Others, like Edwin Austin Abbey, Neysa McMein, and John Steuart Curry, produced paintings nearly indistinguishable from their commercial work.

Illustration can cover many specializations. It can be journalism, portraiture, or decoration. It can be cartoon or caricature. It can be poster design, set design, mural design, or fashion design. The lines are not clearly drawn. Both A. B. Frost and Lionel Feininger, in their different ways, produced illustrations that have been labeled cartoon art and fine art. Dean Cornwell worked as a magazine illustrator and as a muralist; he once managed to include one of his own murals as a background in an illustration! There are also no well-defined means to distinguish illustration stylistically. We find parallels in illustration of all of the art movements of our century: Art Nouveau by Will Bradley, impressionistic canvases by Cornwell and Biggs, Deco covers by Georges Lepape, surrealistic drawings by Boris Artzybasheff, and so on from expressionism to photorealism.

Illustration is equated with commercialism, sometimes rightly. When the painting includes a Coke bottle or an Oldsmobile, it is clearly an advertising piece. But when we see a well-painted picture of a girl playing, does it really matter whether it was produced as a magazine cover or as a commissioned portrait? And whether the artist was paid or not, or how well, is surely immaterial. Perhaps the most distinct quality of illustrations is that they are narrative—they tell a story, show a slice of life, or set a scene, much like genre paintings. In relating events, these pictures by no means leave the mainstream of art, which flows forward from the Old Masters who illustrated Bible stories for the church.

While there are no universally definable differences between illustration and other forms of fine art, still it does behave differently in the marketplace. More and more, major auction houses are putting on the block examples of the illustrator's art. Fifteen years ago, the few that were offered realized very low prices, reflecting the estimation of their worth. All that is changing, and yet it is still one of the most affordable fields of original art.

Pricing is typically affected by availability, and the illustrator was among the most prolific of artists, with an oeuvre numbering in the thousands. Yet once it had been photographed by the engraver, the art itself had little or no purpose—or value. Of all the illustrations ever produced, it is shocking to know that at least two-thirds have disappeared or been destroyed, sometimes by the artist's own hand. This should make their work more costly, but because the demand for illustration is still low, prices are kept down. And as any significant demand is only fifteen or so years old, it is simply not known how much exists. Every year sees more collections unearthed. Paradoxically, works by some "blue chips" like J. C. Leyendecker, Norman Rockwell, Dean Cornwell, and N. C. Wyeth are numerous and readily available on the market.

Rockwell probably exemplifies in the public mind the popular artist-illustrator. His covers for *The Saturday Evening Post* presented a home-spun, idealized version of American life that was admired by millions, yet no critic took his work seriously as art until he was "rediscovered" near the end of his career. A Madison Avenue showing of his originals introduced him as a leading illustrator to the art world. Simultaneous publication of a major book, *Norman Rockwell* by Thomas S. Buechner, then director of the Brooklyn Museum of Art, enhanced interest. At first, a few of his works were timorously accepted for auction and sold well above their estimates. Within a few short years, a boom was on. Almost every sale brought record prices. A milestone was reached with a quarter-million-dollar sale of a Rockwell *Post* cover in 1981. This price has been since surpassed several times in public and private sales.

While Rockwell was an acknowledged "star," hundreds of other excellent practitioners, many forgotten, are now being rediscovered and their works eagerly sought. Rockwell's mentor, J. C. Leyendecker, did nearly as many covers for *The Saturday Evening Post* in his dazzling painting technique. Prices for his covers have begun to climb after Rockwell's but are still below their potential. Some Western illustrators, like Charles Russell and Frederic Remington, have had prices that far surpass those of Rockwell. Works by Howard Pyle, Harvey Dunn, Maxfield Parrish, Jessie Willcox Smith, and other Brandywine artists command high prices when offered. Prices for children's book illustrators Edmund Dulac and Arthur Rackham have recently reached new highs. Auctions can still be volatile and unpredictable, however. The presence or absence of a few dealers can make or break a sale. Then the appraiser may have difficulty finding a statistical average for the scatter plot of prices.

Since so few illustrations were sold through galleries or auction houses, provenance is often unknown; but fortunately, this does not have a strong bearing on authenticity. Unless the artwork comes directly from the artist's estate, the origins of ownership can be murky. Why? In the old days, publishers and advertisers purchased the originals along with the reproduction rights. The advertising client had first claim on it but might return it on request. If the artist did not make an effort to repossess his or her work, the art director might have kept it or simply given it away. Legal title was nebulous. Periodically, publishers would accumulate too much art and throw it out for lack of storage. Admiring fans often received artwork for the asking. A great number of pictures surface in garage sales and country auctions; many have been rescued at the last moment from dumpsters!

By contrast, the determination of authenticity is relatively easy, for illustrators are unique in the art world: by definition, their entire output is usually published. That means there exists a printed record with which to compare an original. For the art dealer or historian, this provides a catalog of the artist's development and the ability to identify virtually every picture—even unsigned work, which was often reproduced with a by-line. For the conservator, it provides a document of the work before aging or damage or alteration occurred; this is especially helpful in restoration. To anyone who enjoys browsing through a library of bound magazines like *Harper's, Puck, Scribner's, Collier's, Vanity Fair, Outdoor Life, The New Yorker, Good Housekeeping, The Saturday Evening Post,* and *Fortune*, it provides a context for the artist—the cultural impact of an era through the relationships of illustration, literature, journalism, and advertising.

Above all, the published record can readily identify the forgery and the fake. For this reason and others, bogus copies and phoney attributions are uncommon in illustration—certainly as compared with other branches of painting, sculpture, and objets d'art—though on occasion we do see star names "muscled" into the works of the not-so-famous. The greatest reason for the rarity of fakes is the lack of temptation for the forger. In a field where museum-quality paintings can be purchased for as little as $2,000, there is simply not enough money to be made.

The field is, however, plagued by "innocent fakes," or copies made from the published work by admiring imitators. These come in all degrees of competence from the housewife to the fellow-illustrator. They may bear the artist's signature, the copyist's signature, neither, or both. Certain artists, notably Charles Dana Gibson, inspired legions of such "fakes." Most of them were done around the turn of the century, the period of his greatest popularity, and therefore on well-aged paper. If well done, they are difficult to identify as copies.

What does this mean for the new collector? Complexities and contradictions certainly but, above all, great excitement. Artwork turns up in unexpected places, at wildly variant prices. There are many specializations waiting to be pursued and areas not yet studied.

Exercise caution in investing; try to learn about the field first. Generally speaking, auction houses do not have expertise in this area. There are several good books in print. Or contact a reputable dealer who specializes; the Society of Illustrators in New York City can furnish names and addresses. Visit museums that have illustration collections, such as the New Britain Museum of American Art, the Brandywine River Museum, the Delaware Art Museum, the Library of Congress, and the Museum of the Society of Illustrators.*

TIPS FROM TWO COLLECTORS

Mort Walker, creator of the "Beetle Bailey" cartoon strip, and his wife, Cathy, are dedicated collectors of illustrations. As Mort Walker tells it, "I have been collecting cartoon art and illustrations since I was ten years old, mostly by asking the artists or the syndicates to give them to me. That all changed about twenty years ago as the market developed for this 'ephemeral' art. I gave most of my 3,000-cartoon collection to the Museum of Cartoon Art when I founded it."

My serious illustration collecting began when Cathy and I bought the studio of Gutzon Borglum (the sculptor of Mount Rushmore) for our new home. The stone walls and beamed ceilings cried out for American art of that period. Since Cathy and I both loved illustration, we decided to collect it for our home.

We live in an area where many illustrators and cartoonists reside, and we were able to deal personally with some of them, which kept the cost down. But for the old masters, we found we had to go to dealers or attend auctions. We started by going to Illustration House and spending hours with Walt and Roger Reed, going through their storerooms looking for choice works of art.

We found some wonderful examples of Dean Cornwell and Joseph

*Originally published by *Antique Market Report*, January 1986; revised and printed with permission of the authors and publisher.

Leyendecker. Leyendecker usually made elaborate studies of details before he painted his covers. We combined them into a single frame, along with a print of the finished cover to make a very interesting display.

We got some wonderful illustrations at a Guernsey auction in New York, including the Sundblom Santa for $3,250 and a Christy nude for $15,000 (plus $1,800 for framing and restoration).

We have seen prices escalate nicely in the six years we have been collecting. We bought a Norman Rockwell charcoal sketch for a *Post* cover for $8,000, and it is now worth about $40,000. We got a beautiful Walter Biggs for $4,000, now worth $20,000 minimum. Along with it, we have Biggs's color sketch and the printed page from the *Ladies' Home Journal*, which adds to the value. We always try to display the prints with the paintings when we can get them. We paid $7,000 for a John Clymer that should sell for $30,000.

Cathy and I are very careful to find good examples typical of an artist's work. We want the piece to stand up as a work of art by itself, with broad appeal, so that it will be a good investment. But we don't buy with the thought of selling—we have never sold anything.

We feel that illustration is more than decoration. Illustrations tell a story and evoke emotions more than ordinary artwork does. We enjoy them every day. They're fun to live with, and our guests seem to share our enthusiasm. My only regret is that we don't have more walls to add to the fun of our collecting.

Other artists in our collection include Harvey Dunn, James Montgomery Flagg, Robert McGinnis, Samuel Otis, Carl Setterberg, Al Parker, Herb Paus, Arthur William Brown, Robert Abbett, Bernie Fuchs, Bob Peak, Alex Raymond, Charles Saxon, Jon Whitcomb, Norman Price, James Flora, Rico Tomaso, Robert Fawcett, Al Hirschfeld, Saul Tepper, Richard Stone, Hal Foster, Ward Brackett, Dollie Tingle, and David Shaw.

PART III

HISTORY OF
ILLUSTRATION

IMPORTANT MILESTONES IN THE
HISTORY OF ILLUSTRATION

- The oldest known illustrated book was an Egyptian papyrus scroll produced about 1980 B.C.
- The first paged book, the codex, appeared during the second century A.D.
- Paper was invented in China, allegedly by Ts'ai Lun, about 105 A.D.
- The earliest Western European illustrated books were illuminated manuscripts such as the Vatican *Virgil*, which was probably produced in the fourth century A.D.
- Wood blocks were first used to produce illustrated books in China in the seventh century A.D.
- The earliest printed book that has been dated is the *Diamond Sutra*, produced in China in 868 A.D.
- Johann Gutenberg invented movable type about 1450 A.D. Before the year 1500, printing presses were established throughout Europe.
- The first use of woodcuts for book illustration were block books printed about 1455 A.D.
- The first illustrator who is known by name is Reuwich; his work appeared in the *Perigrinato in Terram Sanctam* by Breydenback in 1486.
- The earliest known examples of American illustration are a woodcut portrait of Richard Mather done in 1670 and a woodcut map of New England printed in 1677.
- The first magazine known to be published in America was published in Philadelphia in January 1741. Entitled *American Magazine, a Monthly View of the Political State of the British Colonies*, it had a type-metal illustration of the Philadelphia waterfront on the title page.
- The first great illustrator to travel to the West and record the life of the Indian tribes was George Catlin, whose *Notes of Eight Years Travel Amongst the North American Indians*, a two-volume work illustrated with 400 engravings from his paintings, was published in London in 1841.
- In 1851, an engraver named Langston discovered how to photograph drawings on wood. This permitted drawings to be enlarged or reduced photographically and foreshadowed the later development of photo engraving.
- The first original and creative professional American illustrator was Felix Darley, the most popular illustrator of the mid-19th century.
- Photoengraving, which developed from several inventions in photography, was first used to print illustrations in the late 1870s. It was

adopted most rapidly in America, where it supplanted wood engraving in magazine and newspaper illustrations by the beginning of the 20th century.

• In 1887, *Scribner's* became the first magazine to publish advertising. As others quickly followed, a whole new field of commercial illustration developed.

• One of the earliest-known American copper engravings is Paul Revere's pre-Revolutionary print of the Boston Massacre. Illustrations by Revere appeared in *Royal American Magazine* in 1774 and 1775.

• *Views of Philadelphia*, issued in 1800, and *The County Seats of America*, published in 1808, both copperplate illustrated books by the father and son team of William and Thomas Birch, are considered among the most artistically significant early American illustrations.

• The first important American illustrator was Alexander Anderson, who introduced wood engraving to the United States by copying and publishing Thomas Bewick's *General History of Quadrupeds* in 1802. Anderson's engraving of a panther was published in *New York Magazine, or Literary Repository* in April 1795.

• America's first major contribution to the technical development of illustration was steel engraving, first used for printing bank notes in 1810 by Jacob Perkins.

• The power-driven bed-and-platen press, invented by American Isaac Adams in 1830, led to the rise of national magazines during the mid-19th century. The American mass magazine industry grew to prominence during the 19th century, greatly increasing the field of illustration. *Godey's Magazine* was first published in 1830 and was followed by *Frank Leslie's Illustrated News* in 1848, *Harper's* in 1850, *McCall's* in 1870, *Ladies' Home Journal* in 1883, *Good Housekeeping* in 1885, and *Vogue* in 1892.

EARLY ILLUSTRATORS

The earliest illustrations in America were as primitive as the tools used to fashion them. Although printing presses had come to America with the colonists, the creating of American illustrations was laboriously done by hand, from cutting the woodcuts with gouge and chisel to placing the inked wooden blocks on the paper. By 1741 the first magazine known to be published in America, *American Magazine, a Monthly View of the Political State of the British Colonies*, carried illustration on the title page; for example, a view of the Philadelphia waterfront, using type metal. It was Paul Revere who left us one of the best-known examples of the early use of copper engraving. His pre-Revolutionary print of the Boston Massacre, though colorfully hand-tinted, was still a long way from the quality engravings produced by the beginning of the 19th century. Other illustrations by Revere were printed in *Royal American Magazine* in 1774–1775.

A less familiar name but one of the earliest American engravers is Amos Doolittle (1754–1832). A self-taught engraver of copper, he is best known for his series of four engravings of the battles of Lexington and Concord, drawn by Ralph Bird, and published by Doolittle in 1775. They are colorfully hand-tinted, and today a set is part of the New York Public Library print collection.

America's first actual illustrator is considered to be Alexander Anderson, who used the English technique of wood engraving popular at that time (c. 1802) and used by the English artist Thomas Bewick.

Considered two of the top illustrators of the early 19th century were Felix Octavius Carr Darley and John James Audubon. Audubon began early on to specialize in nature subjects, but Darley was a multifaceted illustrator, best known for American subjects.

FELIX OCTAVIUS CARR DARLEY (1822–1888) N.A.

Darley

Darley's book illustrations for such famous authors of the day as Washington Irving and James Fenimore Cooper extended to the growing field of magazines. By the time of his death in 1888, he had set the standards for the coming generation of illustrators.

Entry of Washington into New York, oil on canvas, 71″ × 106½″. $36,300

An early example of American illustrator art, "Boston Massacre, March 5, 1770." Drawn, engraved, printed, and sold by Paul Revere, Boston. Hand-colored engraving. PHOTO COURTESY OF THE NEW YORK HISTORICAL SOCIETY, NEW YORK CITY.

Shylock and Antonio from The Merchant of Venice, s., 12½″ × 10½″, charcoal pencil on blue paper. $88
Chief of The Little Osages, s., t., 7″ × 5¾″. $1,320
Return from the Hunt, drawing, s. in ink and d. 1844, 9″ × 11½″, black crayon. $330
Liberation, s. F. O. C. Darley and i. *fecit*, 15″ × 11″, ink wash and pencil on paper. $550

The Civil War created yet another type of illustrator, known as the pictorial reporter. Winslow Homer was among the Civil War artists to win early recognition for his sketches. His career as an illustrator lasted roughly from 1860 to 1875, but during the remaining years of his long life, he achieved further renown as a fine artist. His landscapes, and other subjects, come to auction regularly, for high prices.

WINSLOW HOMER (1836–1910)

The Initials, s. Homer, d. '64, lower left, oil on canvas, 16″ × 12¼″ (40.6 × 31.1 cm). $80,000

Fort Lion, i. on front, executed during Civil War period, 7″ × 10¹⁵⁄₁₆″, pencil on cream-colored paper. $24,200

Plains of Abraham, s. W. Homer, d. 1895, prov., exhib., lit., 13⅞″ × 19⅞″, watercolor, pencil, and gouache en grisaille on paper. $22,000

Cavalry Officer, inits. and d. W.H.'63; 8¾″ × 8″, charcoal on paper. $27,500

Girl on a Swing, s. Homer, d. 79, prov., sight size 16½″ × 8″, charcoal and white gouache on paper. $66,000

Girl Resting in Field, s. Homer, d. 1878, prov., exhib., sight size 6¾″ × 8″, pencil and wash on paper. $77,000

Young Girl in Woods, s. Homer, d. 1880, property of Hunter museum, Chattanooga, TN, 8¾″ × 11¼″, watercolor and pencil laid down on board. $99,000

Return to Camp, s. Winslow Homer, d. 1892, prov., exhib., 15⅛″ × 24⅜″, watercolor, gouache, and pencil on paper. $440,000

The Flock of Sheep, Houghton Farm, s. Homer, d. 1878, prov., exhib., lit., catalog cover illus., 8¾″ × 11⅜″, watercolor, brush and black ink and pencil on paper. $660,000

Building Fort Ethan Allen, South of Chainbridge, initial H, i. with t., 9⅝″ × 13⅜″, pencil and ink wash on paper. $7,150

One of the rare examples of Winslow Homer's work as artist-correspondent during the Civil War. "Cavalry Officer." Initialed and dated 1/1:W.H. '63. Charcoal on paper, 8¾ × 8 inches, $27,500. PHOTO COURTESY OF BUTTERFIELD & BUTTERFIELD, SAN FRANCISCO.

Thomas Nast was another artist correspondent. While still a teenager he became an artist for Frank Leslie's illustrated newspaper. At twenty-one he illustrated daily life in wartime Washington, although he did not actually go to the front lines. His career as a political cartoonist is discussed elsewhere in this book. (Also see *Special Notes* [1] at back of book.)

Two pictorial reporters who did stand side by side with the army, recording the action with sketches, were the brothers William and Alfred R. Waud. Although not much is known about their personal lives, many of their war sketches are in museums.

Edwin Forbes (1839–1895) was not only a field artist but continued his depictions of war scenes after the war, from memory, in etchings and paintings.

On the Confederate side, the name Conrad Wise Chapman stands out. He was wounded at Shiloh and, upon recovering, became a field artist. He drew hundreds of sketches depicting the Confederate army, but to date, only a fraction of these sketches has been found—enough, however, to form important collections. Perhaps there are many waiting to be discovered between the pages of old family Bibles and scrapbooks.

A new breed of illustrator grew along with the growth of the frontier in the early West. Known as artist-adventurers, they include George Catlin, Albert Bierstadt, and later Charles Schreyvogle, Frederic Remington, and Charles M. Russell.

George Catlin (1796–1872) was a lawyer with a successful practice when he made the decision to travel the West and record the life of the American Indian in drawings and paintings. He eventually self-published a book about his experiences. In 1841 a two-volume work with 400 engravings made from his paintings was published in London. It was titled *Notes of Eight Years Travel Amongst the North American Indians* and was published in many editions. His later *North American Indian Portfolio* contained twenty-five colored lithographs, many of which turn up periodically at auction and sell for several thousand dollars individually.

By 1870 there were weekly and monthly magazines with a readership that expected lots of illustrations along with their reading material. Harper Brothers gave them what they wanted in three magazines and innumerable well-illustrated books. By the early 1870s being an illustrator for these diverse publications had become an important profession. Among the group were Edwin Austin Abbey, Charles Stanley Reinhart, Arthur B. Frost, and the already well-known Thomas Nast.

At this time, reproduced art could achieve various gray, dark, or light tones only by the skill of the engraver, who cut tiny lines to simulate the effect.

As the number of illustrators grew, another important change took place. For decades it had been the custom for American artists to get their training in Europe. Now returning artists were surprised to find a new breed of "made in America" artists—the illustrators. The trend to paint and draw for a wide audience—the average American—had just begun.

PART IV

THE GOLDEN AGE OF ILLUSTRATION (1880–1914)

BY ALAN M. GOFFMAN

OVERVIEW

In 1974, Alan Goffman had an opportunity to visit the apartment where Howard Chandler Christy and his wife, Nancy, had lived at the Hotel des Artistes in New York City. Nancy (the original "Christy Girl") had recently died, and the furnishings, including paintings, had been untouched over the years. Goffman became fascinated by Christy's illustrations and was able to buy many of them. "There was not a great demand at the time for works by the American illustrators," he said. "Their affordability made it possible for me to successfully pursue my new interest." By 1978, his collection included works by Norman Rockwell, Maxfield Parrish, and others. He began conserving and framing each work, as no one had done previously. Today he is one of the top dealers in the works of the Golden Age of Illustration.

Independent development in several unrelated areas made possible the Golden Age of American Illustration. That these factors, which had nothing to do with art, all coincided at approximately the same time was extraordinary.

Illustration has been described as the visualizing of some event or passage in a printed text intended for mass consumption. Reaching a large audience required a sequence of achievements that began in the mid-19th century and had progressed enough by 1880 to allow the development of an American publishing industry without precedent.

These advances included breakthroughs in printing technology, innovations in the publishing business, the increase of literacy, and the growth of consumerism and advertising. Additionally, it was necessary to establish an American approach to illustration.

In the first half of the 19th century, methods of printing were greatly improved. It became possible to print a wood engraving at the same time and on the same page as the type. The speed of the presses increased from 2,000 pages per hour to 20,000. Paper was also improved, better able to reproduce the fine lines of the engravings.

Next, the web-perfecting press enabled print to be placed simultaneously on both sides of the paper, which was fed from continous rolls. In 1880, paper made from wood pulp was manufactured to be strong enough for use on the high-speed presses. This was much cheaper than the rag paper that was being used at the time.

Another great invention was photography. Prior to photography, the artist-illustrator constantly feuded with the engravers over misrepresentations of drawings and styles. Illustrators usually turned over their drawings to engravers, who then translated or copied them into wood engravings. Sometimes artists did not recognize these finished reproductions as being from their drawings and blamed the engraver.

By 1880, drawings could be photographed and the negative image transferred directly onto the wood block. The engraver's job was reduced to not much more than tracing. Photography also ended the restrictions on the size of a drawing because when photographed they could be enlarged or reduced.

Halftone reproduction was the next step on the way to the Golden Age. Previously, all work had been restricted to line drawings. Shading had to be done by finely cross-hatched lines. Now this problem was solved. Halftone allowed the illustrator to use the full range of tones between black and white.

The development of the halftone revolutionized illustration. Artists were freed from pen and ink and could work in watercolor, pastel, gouache, or oils. Color also became a possibility because separate screens could be shot for the primary colors plus black.

The public eagerly accepted the color reproductions, but they were extremely expensive for the publishers and not widely used until new techniques lowered costs. This resulted in lavishly illustrated books and magazines.

Harper's, *Scribner's*, and *Century* were the leading magazines in the 1880s but relatively expensive at 25 to 35 cents per issue. They had an elegant intellectual quality that did not appeal to the majority of readers. This led other publishers to produce a body of inexpensive periodicals and books to provide lighthearted and trivial entertainment.

The country had entered an era of prosperity and optimism. Salaries were higher than ever, creating a large middle class, and living expenses were relatively low. There was increased literacy and more leisure time for the American public in the 1880s. Education was available for all, resulting in a knowledgeable and informed reading audience. This new audience was willing to spend their time and money on these inexpensive, entertaining publications.

By 1903, the price of most of the popular magazines had dropped to 10 cents or less. This did not cover expenses, but publishers found in advertisers the perfect source for their profits. In this age of industrialization, companies needed a forum in which to display and advertise their many new products. America was in a period of rampant consumerism.

Conditions couldn't have been better for the illustrator. Their services were much in demand. By 1900, there were 5,500 different periodicals produced for the American public, not to mention illustrated books

Philip Boileau (1864–1917).
"Reflection." Oil on canvas,
30 × 17 inches. Signed lower
left, dated 1903, $5,000.
PHOTO COURTESY OF ALAN M.
GOFFMAN AMERICAN
PAINTINGS. (See *Special Notes*
[3] at back of book.)

printed in record numbers, some of them reaching sales of 1 million copies.

Illustrators became celebrities and personalities in their own right. Magazines advertised their names as prominently as the authors whose stories they delineated. They were called upon to endorse products and judge beauty contests. It was not unusual for them to receive fan mail.

Those at the top of their field were paid exceedingly well. Gibson was given $100,000 by *Collier's* to produce 100 drawings over a four-year period. At the height of his career, Harrison Fisher was paid $3,000 per cover picture by *Cosmopolitan*. Some were signed to exclusive contracts by the top magazines, providing them with the security of steady work.

The Golden Age of American Illustration reached its peak in 1918. The momentum that had built couldn't keep going after the war. Many reasons are given for its demise, all of which probably contributed.

It seems that the taste for light, entertaining literature was replaced by a liking for realism that was not as well suited to illustration. Motion pictures were becoming popular, and with the newly added sound began to replace periodicals as the prime source of mass entertainment.

Radios in every home made the articles and information printed by many of the magazines seem dated. There was an immediacy that could not be countered, and it was easier and more exciting to listen to professional actors read fictional stories over the air.

Photographic processes, which once helped the illustrator by reproducing his work more accurately, were now perfected and cheaper than drawn or painted pictures. Some have accused the illustrators of becoming greedy and complacent, not changing with the times.

Many illustrators continued with successful careers for quite a while longer, but never again did circumstances permit them to regain the position they held during the Golden Age of American Illustration: 1880–1914. (See *Special Notes* [2] at back of book.)

FRANKLIN BOOTH (1874–1948)

It was a misunderstanding of the media used in turn-of-the-century books and magazines that led Franklin Booth to develop his unique illustrating use of pen and ink. Believing that the steel or wood engravings were done line by line, he laboriously duplicated the look in pen and ink. His illustrations were used in magazines and books of poetry.

Mt. Holley College, s., pen and ink, 14½″ × 12½″, 2 drawings in one frame. $650
Princess and Dwarf, "He spake my name?" book illus., *Flying Islands of the Night*, 1913, s. and i., watercolor, pen and ink, 13″ × 8.75″. $7,500
Courtiers in Portico Archway, s., pen and ink, 10.25″ × 3.25″. $3,000
Workmen and Woman in Farmhouse Door, story illus., "The New Generation" by J. Oppenheim, *Harper's*, Feb. 1912, pen and ink, 15″ × 9.5″. $3,500
Two Gentlemen and a Lady, s., watercolor and pen and ink, book illus., c.1910, 8″ × 15″. $225
Storyteller and Horse Meet up with Medieval Band, s., pen and ink with red and gray watercolor wash, 6″ × 11.25″. $1,950
Progress and Prosperity, four scenes, init., pen and ink, 10″ × 7.5″. ..$750
A Spanish Bridge, prov., exhib., 25″ × 29¾″, oil on board. $6,050
Keep Step with Your Vision in the Simple Faith of a Child and **To the Unknown God**, both s., the second an illustration for *Good Housekeeping*, 15″ × 14¾″, first 8¼″ × 11¾″, pencil on Chinese white on board. $220
College Days and The Hikers, drawings, both s.; first, 10″ × 17″; second, 6½″ × 11″, both pen and black ink on board, the second heightened with Chinese white. $462
Woman on the Move and Mount Holyoke College, drawings, both s.; first, 7⅞″ × 15″; second, 7⅞″ × 13″, pen and ink on board. $462
Man standing by ruined columns, with carved water basin and clouds with angel, pen-and-ink drawing, 8½″ × 13¼″, s. upper left, matted. $800
Thanksgiving, s., 20″ × 15″, pen and black ink on board. $605
Eastertide, s., illustration for *Good Housekeeping* in 1917, 17″ × 11⅜″, pen and black ink on board. $825
Out of the Hills and Redwoods, drawings; first signed, second init.; first, 15″ × 11¾″; second, 16½″ × 14½″; first, watercolor and charcoal on board; second, charcoal on board. $660

Pencil drawing on board.
Medieval party. Signed
*Franklin Booth, upper right,
15 × 10¼ inches, $4,000.*
PHOTO COURTESY OF
PRIVATE COLLECTOR.

*Book illustration, Princess and
Dwarf, Flying Islands of the
Night, 1913. Watercolor, pen
and ink. Signed and inscribed
Franklin Booth, 13 × 75
inches, $7,500.* PHOTO
COURTESY OF ILLUSTRATION
HOUSE, INC.

FRANK W. BRANGWYN (1867–1956) R.A.

The name of Sir Frank Brangwyn is little known today, even though in his time he had almost as much influence on other illustrators as Howard Pyle. Very little of his original art comes on the market, and he is better remembered in his native England as a muralist. In this role, he is certainly one of the greatest of all time, although this can barely be gleaned from his American commissions: Rockefeller Center and the Harrisburg, Pennsylvania, capitol building.

The Life of St. Aiden, compositional study for the mosaics at St. Aiden's Church at Leeds, gouache and charcoal on brown paper, 9¾″ × 20½″, not signed. $1,200

Stowing the Jib, "The Life of the Merchant Sailor" by W. Clark Russell, *Scribner's*, July 1893, oil en grisaille on canvas, mounted on board, 19½″ × 29″, not signed. $1,200

Sailors, two figure studies, possibly from the Skinner's Hall mural, London, charcoal and brown conté on paper, 21″ × 14″, not signed. $375

Casting Rose Petals, oil on canvas, mounted, 15¼″ × 16″, not signed. $6,500

Medieval House, "Ditchling," 1921, etching, 12″ × 15⅜″, pencil, signed. $175

Look After My Folks, lithographed poster for WWI U.S. Naval Relief, 40″ × 28″. $175

Mural study, serving figures carrying bowls and urns, Sir Th. Pilkington's Banquet to King William, Skinner's Hall, London, c. 1904, charcoal, conté pencil, chalk, 20″ × 11″, not signed. $475

The Pirate Ship, inits., d.'92; 37½″ × 40¾″. $3,300

HOWARD CHANDLER CHRISTY (1873–1952)

Howard Chandler Christy first came to public attention as an artist-correspondent during the Spanish-American War. *Scribner's* and *Leslie's Weekly* used his drawings and paintings of the war. His famous "Christy Girl" was first used by *Scribner's* to illustrate a picture titled "The Soldier's Dream." After that he specialized in beautiful-girl pictures for magazine and book illustrations.

He was also a popular portraitist, painting such famous people as Amelia Earhart, Charles Evans Hughes, and Mrs. William Randolph Hearst.

A muralist in his later years, his most famous mural, *The Signing of the Constitution*, hangs in the rotunda of the Capitol in Washington, DC. He also painted the decorations for the Café des Artistes in New York. In 1980 he was elected to the Society of Illustrators Hall of Fame.

Awakening, s. and d., charcoal on illustration board, 39½″ × 27″, book illustration, exhibited in The Illustrator in America 1900–1965, Albany, GA, Nov. 1985. .... $7,000

Nude woman with draped material, highly colored background, s., canvas on board, believed to be one of three panels comprising Christy's famed decorative screens, framed, 48″ × 11″. $1,500

Woman Riding in a Boat, book illustration, *Lady of the Lake*, charcoal, 15″ × 10″, not signed. $5,200

A New Hat, s. Howard Chandler Christy, l.r., oil on canvas, unframed, 33″ × 27″ (83.5 × 68.5 cm). $4,400

The Same Old Yarn, s. Howard Chandler Christy, d. 1918, inscribed "To Byron and Virginia Ralston with best friendship, l.c., inscribed with title, l.r.; watercolor, gouache and pencil on board, 35″ × 25¼″ (88.9 × 64.1 cm). . $7,700

The Motorist, s. Howard Chandler Christy, d. 1922, 39″ × 29″. $27,500

On the Riverbank, s. Howard Chandler Christy, d. 1946, 35″ × 30″. $35,200

Applewood Cut and Split, s. Howard Chandler Christy, d. 1935, 20″ × 16″, oil on board. $2,310

Portrait of a Lady, s. Howard Chandler Christy, d. 1922, 50″ × 39″. $3,300

The Six Darlings on the Float, s. Howard Chandler Christy, d. 1914, © *Cosmopolitan*, 38″ × 60¼″, watercolor gouache and pencil on buff paper. $18,700

A Good Day for Skating, s. Howard Chandler Christy, d. 1923, i.; 37″ × 28″. $24,200

Woodland Bathers, prov., 72⅞″ × 83″. $26,400

Old Mills, s., d. 1935, prov., 30″ × 40″. $8,525

After the Storm, s., d. 1936, t. on stretcher, 42″ × 30″. $13,200

A Seductive Pose, s. Howard Chandler Christy, d. 1931, 39″ × 50¼″. $16,500

The Recital, s., d. 1914, sight size 37″ × 53″, watercolor heightened with gouache on board. $3,190

Nudes at the Beach, s. Howard Chandler Christy, d. 1930, prov., exhib., from the estate of Fred W. Noyes, Jr., 40″ × 50″. $115,500

Portrait of John Drew, s. Howard Chandler Christy, sight size 39″ × 29½″, watercolor on watercolor board. $192

Illustration of a Woman, s. Howard Chandler Christy, slightly soiled, sight size 10¼″ × 11⅛″, pencil on paper. $550

Portrait of a Woman, s. Howard Chandler Christy, and i. L.D.B., 4¾″ × 3½″, pen and ink and black wash heightened with white on paper. $165

Evangeline, s. Howard Chandler Christy, d. 1905, sight size 37″ × 26″, pen-and-ink wash on paper. $1,320

At the Party, study of three women and a man, exhib., sight size 39″ × 29½″, charcoal on paper. $605

Giving the News, s., d. 1921, 40″ × 30″, ink wash on paper. $1,320

Languid Dreams, s. Howard Chandler Christy, 36″ × 30″. $5,500

Pastoral Scene with Cart and Figure, s., prov., 34″ × 29″. $5,225

Oil on canvas. Wood Nymphs. Signed Howard Chandler Christy, 1926, 54¼ × 46⅛ inches, $10,450. PHOTO COURTESY OF CHRISTIE'S, NEW YORK.

Afternoon Cocktails. Signed Howard Chandler Christy, dated twice, 1912 and Nov. 27, 1912. Watercolor and gouache on buff board, 29½ × 39¾ inches, $7,700. PHOTO COURTESY OF CHRISTIE'S, NEW YORK.

Howard Chandler Christy. "Greek-American Alliance," 60 × 40 inches, signed lower left, and dated 1931, $18,000. PHOTO COURTESY OF ALAN M. GOFFMAN AMERICAN PAINTINGS.

Portrait of a Lady, s., i. L.D.R., sight size 4¾″ × 3½″, pen and ink heightened with gouache on paper. $550
Bather in Woodland Stream, s., d. 1946, prov., 34″ × 30″. $6,050
Landscape with Figure in Tree, s., prov., 29″ × 24½″. $6,600
Autumn Landscape with Stream, s., d. 1937, prov., 40″ × 50″. $6,875
Forest Landscape with Stream, s., prov., 35″ × 27″. $3,300
Blue Water Landscape with Trees, s., dedicated, prov., 29″ × 25″. $3,300
The American Dream Home, s. Howard Chandler Christy, d. 1937, commissioned by The National Lumber Assn. to be published as poster, never published, prov., 42⅛″ × 30⅛″. $3,850
Dunes, s., prov., 30″ × 25″. $2,475
Autumn Corn Field, s., prov., 23½″ × 28″. $2,475
Forest Clearing with Cottage, s., prov., 26″ × 22″. $2,200
Impressing the Lady, s., d. 1922, 30″ × 40″, charcoal on board. $2,090
Covered Bridge, s., prov., 20″ × 28″. $1,925
Meadow Landscape, s., prov., 20″ × 10″. $2,475
Portrait of Anna Fitzer with Her Terrier, prov., 51″ × 39½″. $2,750
Couple in Woods, s., 40″ × 28″, watercolor. $4,400
Margery Reed Souby, 60″ × 40″. $4,400
Landscape with Stream, s., d. 1950, prov., 29″ × 25″. $4,675
Nude on Beach, s., i., d., prov., 20″ × 16″. $4,950
Portrait of an Eight-Year-Old Cat, "Timmie," painted Aug. 8, 1935, and reproduced with article in *Washington Star* Aug. 16, 1935, s., d., and i., 30″ × 37″. $4,950

BENJAMIN WEST CLINEDINST (1859–1931)

B. West Clinedinst

Clinedinst studied at the Ecole des Beaux Arts in Paris, and his work appeared in many magazines and books. From 1903 to 1905 he was art editor of *Leslie's Weekly*. He also exhibited widely and was elected to membership in the National Academy of Design in 1898. In 1901 he was one of the original ten founders of the Society of Illustrators. He also painted portraits of several national figures of the time, including President Theodore Roosevelt and Admiral Peary.

Republican National Convention, s., c. 1898, black-and-white gouache, 16″ × 24″. $650

HARRY FENN (1838–1911)

Harry Fenn was born in England and received his early art training there as an apprentice to a wood-engraving firm. After completing his apprenticeship at nineteen, he journeyed to Canada and took a side trip to the United States. He stayed on, and in 1870 he was hired to travel and illustrate the book *Picturesque America*. He did similar illustrations for *Harper's Monthly* and other magazines.

Note: Most of the following illustrations appear to have been done for *Picturesque America*.

Perryville, Spring That Watered Bragg's Army, inits., i. with various notations, 8¾″ × 8¾″, pen and ink on paper. $275
Lookout Mountain, init., i. with various notations, 13″ × 20½″, pen and ink on paper. $330
Tai-Sham Summit, mono., 10½″ × 11¾″, ink and wash on paper. $385
The Ross House, Chattanooga, inits., i. with various notations, 9″ × 12¼″, pen and ink on paper. $440
Woodland Scene with Boys Exploring, Tree Study, and Lake Scene with Sailboat, each with conjoined inits. HF, largest 12″ × 17″, watercolor, pencil, ink heightened with white on paper mounted on board. $385
National Cemetery and Frayser's Farm, init., i. with various notations, 9½″ × 10½″, watercolor on paper. $825
Confederate Fortifications at Manassas Junction, init., i. with various notations, 7¼″ × 11½″, pen and ink on paper. $880
The Siege of Vicksburg, Explosion of the Vicksburg Mine, i. with various notations, 9¾″ × 14⅝″, pen and ink on paper. $880
The Carondelet Passing Island Number Ten, i. with various notations, 9½″ × 11¾″, watercolor on paper. $935

Battle of Belmont, i. with various notations, 8½″ × 14″, watercolor on paper.
....$935
Depot and Hotel, Corinth, MS, i. with various notations, 8″ × 12½″, pen
and ink on paper. $990
Headquarters of General Thomas Grant, Chattanooga, inits., i. with t. and
various notations, 15″ × 16″, pen and ink and wash on board. $1,320
Gunboats at Fort Donelson, i. with various notations, 10½″ × 14″, watercolor
on paper. $2,200
Lily Pond, s. H. Fenn with inits. in mono., 7″ × 21″, watercolor on board.
....$4,400
Provost Marshal's Office, Corinth Miss., i. with various notations, 6½″ ×
13″, watercolor on paper. $3,080
Wilderness Church, i. with various notations, 8¼″ × 10″, watercolor on pa-
per. $770

CHARLES DANA GIBSON (1867–1944) N.A.

[signature]

A gift for satire and an extraordinary talent with pen and ink made
Charles Dana Gibson the highest-paid illustrator of his day. His illustrations of the beautiful Gibson Girls created the fashion and feminine ideal.
His satirical depiction of the social life and mores were popular with the
average American, who could readily identify with his "Mr. Pipp" series done for the old *Life*. His illustrations also appeared in *Collier's
Weekly*, for which he received $100,000 for 100 illustrations over a four-
year period. *Century* magazine also used his work.

As president of the Society of Illustrators during World War I, Gibson
formed and became head of the Division of Pictorial Publicity under the
Federal Committee of Public Information. The best illustrators of the
day were recruited to design posters, billboards, and other publicity for
the war effort.

Note: Major works by Gibson are scarce, as the majority of them are
in the collection of the Library of Congress.

The Decision, pen and ink, 20″ × 28½″. $6,000
Suggestion to Bores, s., *Harper's Bazaar*, Sept. 1913, pen and ink, 19″ ×
28.25″. $5,200
Mr. Pipp Wants to Go Home, s., "The Education of Mr. Pipp," part 21, *Life*,
pen and ink, 22″ × 29.5″. $8,000
The Fashion Show, drawing, s., 18″ × 15″, pen and ink. $495
The Parting Wall, c. 1906, s. Charles Dana and S. Jones, 18½″, pen and ink
on paper. $192
The Dissection, s., 14″ × 19¼″, ink on paper. $605
A Sunny Afternoon, s. C. D. Gibson, 28″ × 37″. $715

Charles Dana Gibson, "The Garden of Youth." Pen and ink on paper, 22 × 28 inches, S.Lr. Reproduced in Life magazine, 1897, $7,500. PHOTO COURTESY OF ALAN M. GOFFMAN AMERICAN PAINTINGS.

The Confrontation, s. C. D. Gibson, 20″ × 20½″, pen and ink laid down on board. $1,430
Their First Quarrel, s., 15¾″ × 19¼″, ink on paper. $880
Portrait of a Lady in Red, s., from the Andy Warhol collection, 30″ × 25″. $2,310
Mourning, s., 23¼″ × 24″, pen and black ink on board. $935
A Council of War in the Days to Come, drawing, s. C. D. Gibson, prov., sight size 19″ × 26½″, pencil, pen and ink on paper. $1,980
Gibson Girl and Poison Pen Letter, s., illustration for "Senator Lambkin's Daughter Mary," *Harper's Bazaar*, Feb. 17, 1911, 18¾″ × 24¾″, pen and black ink and pencil on buff paper. $4,400
I Often Wonder Why You Never Got Married, s. C. D. Gibson, 19″ × 28¾″, pen and black ink on paper laid down on paper. $4,400
A Ride Through Central Park Zoo, s. C. D. Gibson, exhib., lit., 18⅛″ × 27¼″, pen and black ink and pencil on buff paper. $4,400
In the Meantime, Plate 9 from "The Education of Mr. Pipp," s. C. D. Gibson, prov., sight 18″ × 29½″, pencil, pen and ink on paper. $5,500
The American Girl Abroad, c. 1894, s. C. D. Gibson, orig. for reproduction by R. H. Russell, New York Life Publishing Co., sight size 10⅞″ × 26½″, ink and pencil on paper. $2,640
Big Game, s. C. Gibson, t., sight size 11″ × 15½″, pen and ink on paper. $150

The Parting Wall, c. 1906, s. Charles Dana and S. Jones, 18½″, pen and ink on paper. $192
Woman and Sea Serpent, s., 8¼″ × 11½″, pen and ink on paper. $247
Imperious Miss, sketch, 18″ × 12″, pen and ink. $357
The Would-Be Suitor, s. and i., prov., sight size 14″ × 12″, ink on paper. $440

WALTER GRANVILLE-SMITH (1870–1938)

Walter Granville-Smith was successful as both an illustrator and a painter. Born in Granville, New York, he studied at the Art Students League as well as abroad. His illustrations appeared in the *Ladies' Home Journal*, *Century* magazine, and *Truth* magazine. He also did covers for many of them. He is known for his humorous and light touch. His hunting subjects were turned into popular prints.

Grand Ball, s., d. '92, oil on canvas, 24″ × 18″. $3,800
Young woman, officer, and spectators, story illustration, s., Wolff pencil and wash, 13.75″ × 12.5″. $400
The Artists Critics, watercolor, s., d. 1893, black and white, 14″ × 17″. $850
Young Woman at a Sundial, watercolor, s., black, 18″ × 7″. $800
Afternoon Tea, watercolor on illustration board, s. lower left, d. 1894, *Truth* magazine cover, 1894; 21½″ × 19″. $7,500
Peacock and Urn, s., d. New York 1885, Public Administrator's Office, 13″ × 9″, on board. $275

Walter Granville Smith, "Afternoon Tea." Watercolor on board, 21½ × 19 inches. Reproduced: Truth *magazine cover, 1894, $7,500.*
PHOTO COURTESY OF ALAN M. GOFFMAN AMERICAN PAINTINGS.

Marine Scene, Waves Crashing on Beach, prov., 8″ × 11″, oil on canvas board. $220
The William P. Earle House, Belleport, Long Island, s., d. 1826, from the estate of Mary Earle Stanton, NY, 10″ × 14″. $1,540
Spring Landscape, s., 10″ × 13″, oil on board. $980
Summer Night, s. W. Granville Smith, d. 1934, t. on stretcher, overall crackling, prov., 30″ × 40¼″. $2,255
Woman on a Park Bench, estate-stamped verso, No. 71, gilded Arts and Crafts-style frame, relined on new stretcher, 14¼″ × 18⅛″. $1,045
Boating, s., 24″ × 30″. $1,100
The Phelps Homestead, Old Saybrook, CT, s. and d. W. Granville Smith/ 1936, 12″ × 16″, oil on canvas. $2,250
The Phelps Homestead, Old Saybrook, CT, s. and d. W. Granville Smith/ 1934; s. verso W. Granville Smith/36–5th Ave./New York; also mono., d. and t. verso, 12¼″ × 16¼″, oil on canvas backed by artist board. $2,250

ANGUS PETER MacDONALL (1876–1927)

MacDonall, who originally came from St. Louis, was one of the early artist-illustrators who moved to Westport, Connecticut. His work appeared in such magazines as *Harper's, Scribner's, Ladies' Home Journal,* and *American.* He also did covers for *The Saturday Evening Post.* For several years he did a regular double-spread illustration of human interest or social commentary for the old *Life* magazine.

Everything Comes to Him Who Waits, watercolor, s., *Life* humor magazine centerfold, July 21, 1911, black and white, 11¼″ × 18½″. $300
The Young Man Who Waits Until Tomorrow, watercolor, s., *Life* humor magazine centerfold, Sept. 12, 1912, black and white, 12¼″ × 18½″. $1,500

ALICE BARBER STEPHENS (1858–1932)

Alice Barber Stephens began her career as a wood engraver for *Scribner's.* Prior to that she got her training at the Pennsylvania Academy of the Fine Arts and at the Philadelphia School of Design. Her work can be recognized by its quality draftsmanship and the humble settings she often used. Some of her work is initialed.

Girl and Bicycle at Gate, 1909, init., pencil, charcoal, and watercolor, 25.75″ × 16″. $2,400
Reflection, s. lower left, d. '92, mixed media on paper, 26¼″ × 16½″. $19,500

Alice Barber Stephens,
"Afternoon Tea." Charcoal
and watercolor on board, 29½
× 19¾ inches, $3,850.
PHOTO COURTESY OF ALAN M.
GOFFMAN AMERICAN
PAINTINGS.

ALBERT E. STERNER (1863–1946) N.A.

Albert Sterner

Sterner was at home in a variety of media; he used pen and ink, watercolor, lithography, oils, etching monotypes, charcoal, pastels, crayon, and red chalk. He began as a scene painter, then became a lithographer and drew for engravers on wood blocks. After moving to New York in 1885, he became an illustrator for *Harper's*, *St. Nicholas*, and the old *Life*. He was president of the Society of Illustrators in 1907 and 1908. In 1934 he was elected a full member of the National Academy of Design.

Lounging, s., pen and ink, 11.25″ × 17.75″. $900
Portrait of Henry Hamilton Gaylord, Jr., s., i. Henry Hamilton Gaylord jr. *aetatis suae XXVI anno* and New York Oct. 1943; 16¾″ × 13″, pencil, charcoal, and red chalk on paper. $110
Portrait of Miss V. Tilton in Evening Dress, i. stretcher with artist's and sitter's names, prov., 87″ × 44½″. $3,300
Woman on Mule, s., d.'87; 14¼″ × 10″, pen and ink and gouache. $220
At the Restaurant, s. Albert Sterner, i. and d. 9 t. verso, 17⅜″ × 17″, pen and ink on paper. $275
Woman in Red, s. Albert Sterner, d. 1925; 15″ × 10″, pastel and pencil on paper. $308
Drawing of a Lady, s. Albert Sterner. $350
Gold Fish Bowl, s. Albert Sterner, d. 1919; 34″ × 29″. $1,650
Woman Seated Reading, drawing, s., d. 93; 12″ × 9″, ink. $220
Seated Nude, s., sight size 3½″ × 11″, red chalk on paper. $132
Getting Ready, s., d. 93; 13″ × 8″, watercolor. $138

Secrets, 16″ × 19″, pastel with Chinese white and pencil on paper. $528

Drawing of a Woman 1929, s., d. 1929, pencil and chalk. $143

Seated Female Nude, s., d. 1903, sight size 15½″ × 10½″, pastel on paper. $990

Portrait of a Woman, prov., sight size 13¾″ × 11¾″, watercolor on paper. $150

Removing Wounded from the Field, s., i. with various notations, 15¾″ × 20¾″, pen and ink on paper. $495

PART V

MAJOR INFLUENCES ON
ILLUSTRATOR ART

INTRODUCTION

Throughout the ages in art there have been the "masters" who gathered about them younger gifted artists. Often many of those in the original "circle" or "school" went on to become the masters, breaking out of the old master's style and gathering about them another generation of talented artists who at first attempted to emulate them. The same can be said in the field of American illustration. Consider the many Norman Rockwell "look-alike" illustrators, the copies of the famous Gibson Girl done by amateur and professional artists in an attempt to copy a "master," in this case Charles Dana Gibson.

Following are a few examples of influential American illustrators whose teachings and techniques influenced and resulted in creating some of the finest American illustrators. Several (e.g., Norman Rockwell) are listed in other sections (cover art), the categories they are most commonly associated with.

HOWARD PYLE AND THE
BRANDYWINE SCHOOL

by Terry Booth

Terry J. Booth is the owner of Chicago's Brandywine Fantasy Gallery. *His gallery is a leading dealer in both Brandywine Tradition art and in the more contemporary Fantasy Art, the only gallery in the country to cover both. Booth first became interested in the Brandywine Tradition artists in the 1970s, when he began what has become one of the most extensive collections of N. C. Wyeth illustrated books, magazines, and ephemera in the country. As that collection expanded, the names of Howard Pyle, Frank Schoonover, and other Pyle School artists were soon added. His interest in the reproductions soon led to collecting the original paintings as well. While Booth's book and magazine collection has been retained as an important reference library for the gallery, he promises there is no "special hoard of paintings we're holding back from sale." Some of the gallery's paintings have appeared in both the Delaware Art Museum's and Brandywine River Museum's exhibitions, and several are featured in the October 1990* Architectural Digest *article on the Golden Age of Illustration.* Brandywine Fantasy Gallery *advertises in the leading art collector magazines such as* Antiques, Art and Antiques, *and* US Art.

The Brandywine River starts in southeastern Pennsylvania and ends in Wilmington, Delaware. An early Revolutionary War battle was fought on its banks, and it was close to many historic events in the nation's history. Those who lived near it at the turn of the century felt a great sense of history and patriotism.

No one felt those patriotic ideals more than painter, author, and teacher Howard Pyle (1853–1911), who lived in Wilmington most of his life. Pyle was strongly influenced by American artists like Winslow Homer, the English Pre-Raphaelites, and such great Rennaisance artists as Albrecht Dürer. Pyle also associated with the great artists of his own day: William Merritt Chase and George Innes. Like Homer and his good friend Frederic Remington, Pyle created most of his art for publishers, for reproduction in popular magazines and books. The best magazine artists back then were like today's movie stars, and Pyle was among the most famous. His paintings are now in many great institutional collections in the United States and abroad.

Howard Pyle, "Escape from
the Witches' Chambers." Oil
on board, 16½ × 11 inches,
signed. Reproduced: Harper's
Monthly, February 1892.
Mary E. Wilkins, "The Little
Maid at the Door," p. 352,
$18,000. PHOTO COURTESY
OF LES MANSFIELD, FINE
AMERICAN ILLUSTRATIVE ART.

Because the paintings publishers reproduced could create lasting impressions among millions of American readers, Pyle felt that the publishers should find and use only the best artists and emphasize truly American themes. But he also knew that being a great artist wasn't enough—the print media required a special talent for communicating excitement and subtle emotion. Pyle's lifelong goal was to raise the overall quality of published artwork to his level.

Frustrated that no art school was willing to help in his search for excellence, Pyle finally set up his own school. During the summer it met on the banks of the Brandywine River in Chadds Ford, Pennsylvania. The rest of the year it met in Pyle's Wilmington studios. It was an exclusive and much sought after school (the first year 300 applied for twelve positions), and Pyle had his pick of the best young artists of his day. His vision and message were perpetuated as many of his students in turn taught others. This second generation of artists (the most notable being America's beloved Andrew Wyeth, taught by his father, Pyle student N. C. Wyeth) were born too late for the Howard Pyle School but clearly reflected his influence. Because they did, all three groups—Howard Pyle, Pyle's students, and those taught by Pyle's disciples—are now collectively known as the Brandywine Tradition artists.

Without Pyle's vision and his school, the quality of publisher-commissioned art would never have reached the quality of excellence it did. Almost every major American illustrator either studied with Pyle or acknowledges a strong influence. Pyle was the visionary, the leader, the teacher. Western artist Harold Von Schmidt called him "the father of American illustration"—few would disagree.

Very clearly, special significance is attached to the work of Brandywine Tradition artists. Not just the museums mentioned above, but other museums and many important collectors seek out and prize paintings by Brandywine Tradition artists. Some of them try to collect at least one work by Pyle and each of his students; others concentrate on just a few favorites. The most important and popular groupings are the following (some are listed elsewhere in this book under their special categories):

MAJOR HOWARD PYLE SCHOOL ARTISTS

Howard Pyle

Maxfield Parrish

Frank Schoonover

Jessie Willcox Smith

Stanley Arthurs

N. C. Wyeth

Harvey Dunn

W. H. D Koerner

Violet Oakley

OTHER MAJOR BRANDYWINE TRADITION ARTISTS

Andrew Wyeth

Peter Hurd

Dean Cornwell

John Clymer

Jamie Wyeth

Henriette Wyeth

Harold Von Schmidt

WESTERN OUTDOOR BRANDYWINE TRADITION ARTISTS

Wyeth, Dunn, Schoonover, Koerner, Von Schmidt, and Clymer, together with the following:

Philip R. Goodwin

Oliver Kemp

Percy Ivory

Charles DeFeo

Frank Stick

Gayle Hoskins

Allen True

Saul Tepper

WOMEN BRANDYWINE TRADITION ARTISTS

Jessie Willcox Smith and Violet Oakley, together with the following:

Anna Whelan Betts

Elizabeth Shippen Green

Ellen Thompson Pyle

Katharine Wireman

Ethel Franklin Betts

Charlotte Harding

Sarah S. Stilwell

MARINE BRANDYWINE TRADITION ARTISTS

Clifford Ashley   W. J. Aylward
Anton Otto Fischer

OTHER NOTABLE BRANDYWINE TRADITION ARTISTS

Arthur Becher   Harold M. Brett
Sidney Marsh Chase   Clyde DeLand
Douglas Duer   Walter Everett
Thornton Oakley   Howard E. Smith
Leslie Thrasher   Mead Schaeffer
Mario Cooper   Herbert Pitz

What makes any of these Brandywine Tradition artists collectible? For some collectors, any of the artists is desirable simply because he or she is part of a historically important group. Others are captured by the color, excitement, and spirit that seem to be common denominators in many of these artists' works. The more conservative-minded might view the existence of several museums that publicize this work as making them better investment risks than less publicized artists. Many Pennsylvania and Delaware residents have had a strong interest in these artists because many of them lived in the area. For most collectors, however, it is the style and work of one or a small number of the artists that make them want to own them. The more they know about the artist and the more works they own, the better they like them. Many do extensive research on their favorites and develop into independent experts.

Howard Pyle is today best understood by visiting the Delaware Art Museum in Wilmington. This outstanding regional museum was initially founded when the community spontaneously raised the funds to purchase and preserve Pyle's remaining paintings at his death in 1911. While the museum has added many great works by many other excellent artists over the years, it still retains a Howard Pyle room, full of some of Pyle's greatest work, that is open for all to see and appreciate.

And a short half-hour away in nearby Chadds Ford, Pennsylvania, nestled on the same banks of the Brandywine River where Howard Pyle used to hold his summer field trips, is the Brandywine River Museum. This wonderful gem of an art museum makes clear the quality and variety of art and artists that form the Brandywine Tradition. In its many rooms will be found outstanding examples of the work of Howard Pyle as well as the great Pyle students: N. C. Wyeth, Maxfield Parrish, Harvey Dunn, Frank Schoonover, Jessie Willcox Smith, and others. It also houses the most varied and important collection of Andrew Wyeth's work in the country, as well as important works by other members of the Wyeth family, including Andrew's son Jamie.

WHAT DETERMINES PRICES FOR BRANDYWINE ARTISTS

As with any work of art, the prices for paintings by any of these artists are extremely variable and depend on seven principal factors: collectibility of the artist, proof(s) of authenticity, general subject matter, size of the painting, quality of the original painting technique, current condition, and general appeal of the image.

If "location" is the key word in the real estate market, then "artist" is the key word in the art market. An initial idea about the collectibility of a particular Brandywine Tradition artist can be gained by referring to dealers' catalogs and to auction records. An artist whose name appears often and/or who brings high prices may usually be considered more sought after than infrequently named artists. No mention does not necessarily mean the artist is not very collectible, since the work of many sought-after artists may simply be scarce and appear only infrequently. For this reason, reference to a book such as the one you are reading or a chat with a knowledgeable collector or specialist dealer may provide better insight. In most cases, an authentic painting will be worth less if it is not signed by the artist because it is considered less typical.

Authenticity (i.e., did the artist really paint this?) is as important as the name of the artist. Any suspicion that a painting is not the artist's work will at best reduce its value and at worst may cause any collector to lose interest altogether. Unauthentic paintings appear either because someone has copied an authentic work or because someone has signed the artist's name to another person's work. Although some copies of Wyeth Western paintings have appeared, for instance, the copying problem is unusual among Brandywine Tradition artists. A more typical problem is finding a painting with a signature by Pyle or Wyeth or M.P. (which Maxfield Parrish used) that may actually be someone else's work. Finding a painting in print and comparing that reproduction with the suspect painting will help. Better yet is firm evidence (such as a sales receipt) that the painting came from the artist or a reputable source or that the painting appeared in a reputable museum's or dealer's exhibit or catalog. A written opinion from an acknowledged expert that the work is authentic, with some indication of when and for what the work was done, will also generally prove sufficient. All such documentation is called provenance, and its importance increases in proportion to price. The art world is full of buyers who bought a "bargain" Remington or other high-priced painting only to find that it is by an unknown (and therefore nearly worthless) hand. One such hard lesson of experience quickly teaches the importance of provenance.

General subject matter is important both on an overall basis and in relation to the individual artist. We all know there are more collectors interested in Western paintings than, for instance, scenes from World War I. But individual artists also make a name for themselves among many collectors because of the skill, excitement, and/or authenticity with which they do certain types of paintings. For instance, Howard Pyle pirate paintings are especially prized and sell for premium prices. Conversely, a painting of a normally desirable subject but one with which the artist was not identified will be worth less simply because it is not typical. Again, the lists in this book or a knowledgeable collector or dealer may be your best help in determining the desirability of specific subject matter.

Size is important but also relative. While most artists like Wyeth and Dunn and Schoonover typically worked on large canvases, certain others—Pyle and Parrish—often worked on a smaller scale. One must therefore consider a painting's size in relation to the artist's typical work, not to other artists. Also size is important only if the painting itself is well done and attractive—it is tougher to hide a bad big painting than a bad small one.

Quality of painting technique relates a great deal to what is typical for the artist. Finding a lot of paint on a canvas (referred to as a heavy impasto) may be important for an artist like Harvey Dunn, but many others typically painted very thinly. Other items affecting a painting's technical quality include the complexity of the design, the degree of detail, the quality of the coloring, and the overall care the artist appears to have given it. A good knowledge of the artist's manner of painting is very helpful here, as well as an understanding of whether the artist changed styles over the years.

The present condition of a painting can significantly affect value. The basic rule is that anything that happens over time to change a painting from its original appearance will reduce its value. Over the years a great many things can happen to a painting as it is exposed to smoke and dirt and changes in humidity and temperature and as it is handled and moved around. Since all paintings will get a little dirty with time, this it not by itself bad if they can be cleaned and restored by a knowledgeable professional. Cleaning is an art, however, and paintings can be more harmed than helped if improperly cleaned or restored.

The best advice is not to have a painting restored unless you absolutely know what you're doing. The materials on which the painting was done can affect its condition as well—works with many layers of paint done on paper, for instance (like some Maxfield Parrish works) tend to show cracking because paper will expand and contract differently from paint. Owners will do funny things as well—some have cut off parts of a Wyeth painting to fit it over the mantel, and others have had another artist overpaint an area the owner didn't like with something more to the owner's taste.

Last but not least is the general appeal of the painting. This is at best a subjective judgment, and there may be differences of opinion about particular paintings. Simply put, a happy family scene is a lot more appealing than one in which someone is sick. A painting with strong appeal, even though less well painted and rating less in other categories, may prove more desirable and valuable than a painting rating highly in all other categories but this.

ARTHUR E. BECHER (1877–1960)

·ARTHUR·E·
·BECHER·

One of the gifted students of Howard Pyle, Arthur Becher used a variety of techniques in his illustrations. Much of his early work was done in black and white with carbon or charcoal pencil. Many of his oils were

Arthur E. Becher (1877–1960). "The Future." Pen and ink with color wash, 17½ × 13 inches, signed and dated (1926) lower left. A bookplate used to illustrate a book of poetry by Edgar Guest, $3,500.
PHOTO COURTESY OF AUTHOR. (See *Special Notes* [4] at back of book.

Arthur E. Becher (1877–1960). "War and Peace," oil on canvas, 38 × 32 inches, signed and dated (1935) lower right, $8,500. PHOTO COURTESY OF LES MANSFIELD, FINE AMERICAN ILLUSTRATIVE ART. *(See Special Notes [4] at back of book.)*

on a large scale. On occasion he also did pen-and-ink illustrations. Collectors can often recognize his work by its allegorical themes. His work appeared in the *Ladies' Home Journal, McCall's*, pictorial reviews, and books of poetry. He also did landscapes.

Greek Scholar with Hand to Chin, heading for "Epode VI" *Odes and Epodes of Horace*, pen and ink, 3″ × 5.5″, init. $900
Washington's First Meeting with Hamilton at Harlem Heights, Sept. 1776, s., d.'09, *On the Trail with Washington*, oil on canvas, 24″ × 17″. $3,500
Indian Minstrel, s., oil on canvas, 26″ × 18″. $3,200
Scenes from "Dr. Tarr and Mr. Feather" and "A. Gordon Pym," stories by Edgar Allen Poe, each published in 1904, s. Arthur E. Becher, one d. 03, retouched, 19″ × 12″. $715
Wishing Well, s., d. 1925, i., 20″ × 40″. $1,760
On the Alert, s. lower left, init. lower right, 14″ × 24″, charcoal on paper.
.... $3,000
Halted by the Sound of Voices, s. lower left, appearance not determined but believed to be *American Boy*, 1941, 18″ × 29″, gesso on hardboard. .. $3,500

MAXFIELD PARRISH (1870–1966) N.A.

M · P

Maxfield Parrish was not exclusively an illustrator for children; most of his illustrations and their stories were intended for adults. But the impact they had on children is important; his brilliant use of color, his exquisite draftsmanship, and his innovative sense of design and inventive painting technique, which employed a series of glazes, had great appeal. The effect was dreamlike and inviting. With his rich, imaginative creations and personal love of the world of enchantment, Parrish brings a point of view abundant with charm and sophistication beyond many illustrators whose work was solely for children. The books he illustrated include L. Frank Baum's *Mother Goose in Prose* (1897), Eugene Field's *Poems of Childhood* (1904), Kenneth Grahame's *Dream Days* (1902), and *The Knave of Hearts* by Louise Saunders (1925).

He also used childhood and fairy tale themes for the many murals he did. One of his most famous, a thirty-foot wall decoration depicting "Old King Cole," can still be seen in the St. Regis Hotel in New York. Thousands of reproductions were made of his many illustrations.

Villa Gori, Siena, Italian Villas and Their Gardens by Edith Wharton, 1904, init., oil on stretched paper, 16.5″ × 11.25″, framed by Parrish, ... $28,500

Head of a Woman, artist's inits. M.P., from the collection of Andy Warhol, 5½″ × 5½″. $8,250

April Showers, inits. M.P., i. to L.C., s. Maxfield Parrish, d. 1908 on backing, prov., lit., cover illus. for *Collier's*, Apr. 3, 1909; 22⅛″ × 16⅛″, oil on paper laid down on paper. $11,000

Study for Bulletin Board at the Mask and Wig Club, s. Parrish verso, 23″ × 20½″, oil on panel. $16,500

Study for scenery for a production of The Tempest, artist's inits. MP, d. '09; s. Maxfield Parrish verso, from the collection of Andy Warhol, 16″ × 16″, oil on panel. $27,500

The Old Mill, s. Maxfield Parrish, d. 1942, s., d. again, i. with t. and No. 1348 verso, i. with t. on the stretcher lit., 22⅜″ × 18⅝″, oil on masonite. $66,000

Nude in Forest Landscape, sketch for cover of *Century* magazine, Aug. 1897, 14″ × 13″. $770

One Little Ingredient, Two Cops, and Study for St. Regis Menu Board, the first, inits.; the second s. Maxfield Parrish, prov., one pen and ink with watercolor, two pencil on paper. $3,025

The Knight, init. MP, used as the frontispiece for *Collier's* magazine Christmas issue, 1908, prov., 16″ × 12″, colored marker on paper. $4,950

Comic Cop, pencil study for the Page, and two mask studies, one s., one init., one bearing artist's notes, prov., various sizes, mixed media. $2,200

Barnyard Friends, prov., sight size 5¼″ × 9″, pencil and watercolor on paper. $1,430

Maxfield Parrish. One of two. Study for St. Regis menu board; study for a comic character. Colored marker on paper. Sight size: 6 × 6 inches, 10 × 9 inches, $2,200. PHOTO COURTESY OF BUTTERFIELD & BUTTERFIELD, SAN FRANCISCO.

Hill Top, s. Maxfield Parrish, d. copyright 1926, s. again, d. 1926, and i. with t. verso., lit. 35¾″ × 22⅛″, oil on panel. $198,000

Prometheus, s. Maxfield Parrish, prov., lit., 32″ × 21¼″, oil on board. $74,800

The Outlaws, inits. M.P., s. identified on label from the Pennsylvania Academy of Fine Arts verso, minor paint loss, retouched, exhib., 17⅛″ × 11½″, tempera and oil on board. $82,500

The Young King of the Black Isles, artist's inits. MP and d., s., d. The Oaks/ Windsor: Vermont: February of 1906 and i. on label affixed to back, lit., from the collection of Andy Warhol, 20″ × 16″, oil on paper. $96,250

Knave of Hearts, inits. M.P., s. Maxfield Parrish, d. Windsor Vermont 1924 and i. with t. verso, lit., catalog front cover illus., 20⅛″ × 10⅜″, oil on panel. $104,500

Morning, inits. M.P., d. 1922, s., d. Windsor Vermont 1922, i. with t. verso, lit., p. for the cover of *Life* magazine, Apr. 6, 1922; 19⅝″ × 15″, oil on panel. $77,000

Cadmus Sowing the Dragon's Teeth, s., d., lower left Maxfield Parrish, 1907, illus. for *Collier's*, Oct. 31, 1908, and *A Wonder Book* and *Tanglewood Tales* by Nathaniel Hawthorne, oil on canvas laid down, 40½″ × 32″ (103 × 81 cm). $110,000

HOWARD PYLE (1853–1911)

H. Pyle.

Howard Pyle is the most historically important of the artists because it was he who so significantly influenced American art and who created the Brandywine Tradition. As famous in his time as Remington or Charles Dana Gibson, Pyle achieved special recognition for his pirate scenes, his

Howard Pyle, "Coureurs de Bois." Originally appeared as a woodblock print in Harper's magazine, March 1888, for an article by C. H. Farnham entitled "Canadian Voyageurs on the Saguenay." Black and white oil on canvasboard, signed lower right, 19½ × 13½ inches, $42,500. PHOTO COURTESY OF BRANDYWINE FANTASY GALLERY. (See Special Notes [5] at back of book.)

historical American scenes (especially of the Revolutionary war), and his medieval England King Arthur stories (for which he not only drew or painted but wrote the narrative as well). Since much of his work was created before the color printing press, many of his paintings were done in black and white and shades of gray. While the uninitiated may consider a black-and-white work less desirable, true Pyle collectors consider the best of these the equal of his color work because of the subtle shadings and detail they contain. Pyle did a substantial amount of pen-and-ink work that is highly sought after as well, especially pieces from his medieval epics. Pyle's better work is considered difficult to find and is much sought after by a variety of collectors. Typical retail prices range from $3,000 to $10,000 for pen-and-ink work, $10,000 to $30,000 for black-and-white oils, and $20,000 to $50,000 for color oils. Exceptionally well done pieces and especially desirable subject matter may exceed these prices.

They Were Overtaken by Falmouth Himself, for "The Sestina" by James B. Cabell, *Harper's*, Jan. 1906, s. (*Chivalry*, 1909), also titled "In Knighthood's Day," oil on canvas, 24″ × 16″. $35,000
Conversion of the Pagans, frontispiece, *The First Christmas Tree*, 1897, s., oil en grisaille on canvas, 29.5″ × 18.5″. $18,500

Jester at Bedside, *The Line of Love* by James Branch Cabell, 1905, s., oil on canvas, 25″ × 17″. $30,000

The Sea Gull's Song, s., 7⅛″ × 11¼″, pen, black ink, and gouache on paper. $1,045

George Washington Conferring with His Generals at Newburgh, s., bears i. verso, sight size 8⅝″ × 11⅝″, gouache en grisaille on paper. $4,125

Washington Refusing the Crown, s., sight size 11⅝″ × 8⅝″, watercolor, gouache en grisaille on paper. $4,125

The Doge Sat Alone in a Great Carven Chair, s., illus. for *The Island of Enchantment* by Justis Miles Forman for *Harper's Monthly*, Sept. 1905; 25″ × 15½″. $18,150

The Duel, "Esmond and the Prince," s., oil in red and black on panel, 18″ × 12.5″. $24,000

Surrender, s., wood engraving proof, 5.5″ × 4.75″, pencil. $225

A Soldier of Fortune, by Howard Pyle, *Harper's*, Dec. 1893, s., oil en grisaille on canvasboard, 24″ × 16″. $23,000

Shipwrecked Sailor, s., wood engraving proof on tissue, 5″ × 5.25″, pencil. $225

Victims of the Witchcraft Delusion, for "The First Self-Made American" by Adele Marie Shaw, *Everybody's* magazine, June 1902, s., pen and ink, 7.5″ × 5″, inscribed "Ye Witch Christmas 1902." $3,600

Howard Pyle. One of two illustrations for a story written by Howard Pyle. Photographer and seated woman; The Romance of an Ambrotype, *Harper's, December 1896. Oil on panel, 8½ × 11½ inches, 5 × 6 inches. Framed together, initialed, $12,500.* PHOTO COURTESY OF ILLUSTRATION HOUSE, INC.

Frank Schoonover. "Deck Chatter," 20 × 15 inches. Charcoal on board with gray and "Schoonover Red" wash. Initialed lower right. "Judgement of the Steerage," Harper's, Sept. 1908, page 491, Rowland Elzea; Album of Brandywine Tradition Artists, $4,500. PHOTO COURTESY OF BRANDYWINE FANTASY GALLERY.

FRANK EARLE SCHOONOVER (1877–1972)

Frank E Schoonover

Noted for his scenes of the Canadian North and the American West, Frank Schoonover spent time early in his career in the Hudson's Bay region, and this greatly affected the appeal and authenticity of this work. Schoonover's men (especially the French Canadians and Indians) often have unique and very chiseled facial features, but his women are always attractive. Schoonover collectors always look for a characteristic "Schoonover red" that he used as a highlight in most of his paintings. In his later life he did many landscape paintings of the Delaware area that are very collectible. As with many Pyle students, a proportionately greater amount of Schoonover's best work was done early while Pyle's influence was greatest. Schoonover drawings typically retail from $2,000 to $5,000, and his paintings and landscapes range from $5,000 to $15,000. Good Canadian and Western scenes may bring more than this.

U.S. and Russian Soldiers as "Brothers in Battle," WW I poster design, 1917, s., d., oil on canvas, 36″ × 27″. $17,500

Eskimos Breaking Trail, *Scribner's*, May 1905, s., d. 1904, oil on panel, 16.25″ × 27.5″. $8,300

Landscape, Bushkill hayfields near boat landing (toward Dingman's), s., oil on canvas, 24″ × 30″. $3,500

Joan of Arc Leading Soldiers in Battle, heading for "The Broken Soldier and St. Joan," *Harper's*, pen and ink, 4″ × 7.75″, initialed, also includes several decorative initials. $1,800

Her Sister's Lunch, from a *Harper's* story in the early 1900s, s. lower left, init. lower right, 14½″ × 9″, charcoal on board with gray and "Schoonover red" wash. $3,500

Green Jacket, Red Cap, and White Owl's Feather!, mono., t. i., sight size 13⅝″ × 8⅞″, ink, watercolor, and gouache on board. $467

In the Grand Canyon, s., 12¼″ × 10″, oil on canvas laid down on board. $715

Cabin in the Woods, s. F. E. Schoonover, init. s., 14″ × 6¾″, oil on canvas laid down on board. $990

Washington, s., label verso i. Washington NO-1317-July-Aug-1924 Peace Chap 37 . . . , lit., 25⅞″ × 30″. $2,750

Wagon Train, s. F. E. Schoonover, d.'27, 20″ × 38″. $5,500

Man from the North, s., d.'20, reproduced as an illus. for a story by Laurie Y. Erskine in the Mar. 1921 issue of *American Boy* magazine, prov., 28″ × 36″. $7,700

NEWELL CONVERS WYETH (1882–1945)

N. C. WYETH

N. C. Wyeth is perhaps the most famous student of Pyle and was the oldest of the "Three Generations of Wyeth" in the painting exhibition that toured the United States and the world several years ago. He was both the father of America's most popular living artist, Andrew Wyeth,

N. C. Wyeth. "Mistress Friendly Soul," Mary Johnston; The Witch, Houghton Mifflin; frontispiece. 42 × 30 inches, oil on canvas, signed lower left, $50,000. PHOTO COURTESY OF BRANDYWINE FANTASY GALLERY.

and Andrew's primary teacher. N. C. was noted for his heroic masculine figures and scenes, his marvelous use of light, a wonderful sense of color, and outstanding compositional talents. His early work emphasizing Western subjects is considered especially desirable, as are his paintings for the famous Scribner's classics series such as *Treasure Island* and *The Boy's King Arthur*. Beginning in the 1930s he changed from painting with oil on canvas to painting with oil on a gesso board as a means to achieve more brilliant color and more detail. Some later tempera paintings also exist, but no authentic watercolors are known. Wyeth would frequently draw large pencil or charcoal sketches before doing a painting, and the sketches are also highly collectible. Wyeth sketches will typically retail for between $3,000 and $12,000; his paintings range from $15,000 to well over $50,000. Subject matter, image appeal, and quality are especially important with Wyeth because there are more than just collectors of illustration art interested in the better N. C. Wyeth paintings.

The Hidden Treasure, s., oil on canvas, 45″ × 40″; according to Virginia O'Hara of the Brandywine River Museum, this painting was one of six commissioned by the Unitarian Laymen's League c. 1920–23 for their book of parables for children; although this book was never published, these works were reproduced as Christmas cards with about 600,000 printings; this painting was also later reproduced in the book *The Parables of Jesus* by S. Parkes Cadman. *Literature:* Douglas Allen and Douglas Allen, Jr., *N. C. Wyeth: The Collected Paintings, Illustrations and Murals*, New York, 1972, p. 200 (for discussion of *The Parables of Jesus* by Cadman). $23,100

A California Mission, *Essentials of American History*, by T. Lawler, 1918, s., d. 1918, oil on canvas, 39.25″ × 26.25″ $42,000

The Ball . . . Rolled Straight Toward the Goal, "Skiffington's Pony," *Metropolitan* magazine, Oct. 1904, s., d., oil en grisaille on canvas, 34″ × 24″. $34,000

The Slaying of the Suitors, *The Odyssey of Homer*, 1929, s., d., oil on canvas, 48″ × 38.25″. $38,000

The Lost Vein, s. N. C. Wyeth, lower left, oil on canvas, 34″ × 25″ (86.3 × 63.5cm), this work was used as an illustration for an article in *All Around Magazine*, Feb. 1916. ....$12,100

Guns in Flanders—Flanders Guns! ("I had a man that worked them once!"), s., oil on canvas, 34″ × 24″; according to Douglas Allen, this painting appeared as an illustration for Vol. 27 of the Outward Bound Edition of Rudyard Kipling's works, entitled *The Years Between and Poems from History*. *Literature:* Rudyard Kipling, *The Years Between and Poems from History*, New York, 1919, p. 67, illus. $11,000

Greek Wrestling Match, "Beggar's Fight," book illustration, *The Odyssey of Homer*, 1929, oil on canvas, 48″ × 38″, not signed. $11,000

Pilgrim Thanksgiving, s., originally executed as Western Union Thanksgiving telegram logo, prov., 14⅛″ × 50″. $15,400

Bucky, s., 22½″ × 17″. $16,610

I Ain't Through with You Yet, s., executed for "The Recoil" by Raine in *Redbook*, Jan. 1909, exhib., sold by the Greenville County Museum for acquisition funds, 24″ × 26″. $20,350

Supply Wagon, s. N. C. Wyeth, d. 1905 and i., 39″, × 25¾″. .....,.. $97,400
The Lindbergh Family, s., 22″ × 42″. $14,300
The Bucking Bronco, s. N. C. Wyeth, exhib., 34″ × 25″. $66,000
The Family Farmer, d. 1945, prov., 35″ × 42″, pencil on paper. $8,800
The Moose Call, s. N. C. Wyeth, 36″ × 40″. $66,000
Chicken Soup, estate of Elizabeth Ellis of Hilton Head, SC, 24″ × 26″.
.... $6,600
Seeking the New Home, s. N. C. Wyeth, 34″ × 47″. $65,000
Confiding in Him, for "The Great Minus" by Gilbert Parker, *Scribner's*, s.
lower right, 43½″ × 31½″, oil on canvas. $75,000

HOW TO EVALUATE OTHER HOWARD PYLE STUDENTS

Other male Howard Pyle students are valued primarily for the subject matter they painted and the quality of their work. As a general rule, one would expect drawings to range from $250 to $750 and paintings to range from $1,000 up to $5,000 for particularly well done pieces with desirable subject matter. Outdoor paintings by artists like Oliver Kemp, Charles DeFeo, and Allen True would be expected to command higher values, as would Western scenes by artists like Gayle Hoskins and Percy Ivory. Good quality and good subject matter work by scarcer artists, like Walter Everett or Clyde DeLand, also may command premium prices.

CHARLES DeFEO (1892–1978)

Lounging Woman in Green Dress, s., watercolor, 20″ × 13.75″. $1,200
Two figure studies: (a) woman in gold evening dress, watercolor, 22.5″ × 15″, not signed; (b) woman in pink evening dress, watercolor, 19.5″ × 13.75″, not signed. $300

WALTER HUNT EVERETT (1880–1946)

Wary Everett

While still living on the family farm, Walter Everett studied art in Howard Pyle's composition class. He also studied at the School of Industrial Arts in Philadelphia, where he later taught illustration. Collectors can recognize his works by their poster-like style, with flattened shapes and unmodeled forms. Color and value changes define the subjects. The overall look is impressionistic.

The Lonely King, s., oil on panel, 11″ × 7.25″. $3,200

PHILIP R. GOODWIN (1882–1935)

Philip R. Goodwin -

Philip R. Goodwin achieved great recognition during the early part of this century for his authentic Western and outdoor scenes because a great many were reproduced on widely distributed calendars and prints. The prints were so popular that they often were framed, and the calendar tops and prints are still actively bought and sold as paper collectibles. Some of Goodwin's work also appeared on the cover of *Field and Stream* and on gunpowder company calendars (today just the calendars may sell for $100 or more). Goodwin paintings typically sell in the $10,000 to $25,000 range, but there are a few avid collectors willing to pay more for particularly desirable outdoor and Western subjects.

Mountaineer Marking a Tree, story illustration, "Blazing a Trail," 1905, s., d., oil on canvas, 28″ × 19″. $14,500

GAYLE P. HOSKINS (1887–1962)

Cowboy and woman, "Shure I love you," story illustration, "The Flight of the McMahons" *Cosmopolitan*, July 1913, s., oil on canvas, 21″ × 30″. ...$1,200
Black baseball players pleading with umpire, s., story illustration, oil on canvas, 26″ × 21.5″. $2,000
The Lone Trail, s., 26″ × 36″. $880
Trouble on the Mountain, s., 27″ × 36″. $1,320

PERCY V. E. IVORY (1883–1960)

Bewitched, "An Idyll of the Shadows," *McClure's*, May 1920(?), s., oil on canvas, 35″ × 26″. $1,600

W. R. JOYCE

The Piper, cover for *Life* magazine, s., d. 1910, gouache, 14″ × 10″. ...$225

FRANK STICK (1884–1966)

The best of Stick's work features dawn and sunset scenes involving hunters and campers, with the golden or blue and often misty backgrounds creating unusually pleasant moods. A goodly number of Stick's paintings are now preserved in North Carolina near where he was instrumental in establishing the Cape Hatteras National Seashore. Stick's paintings are somewhat scarcer than those of other Pyle students, in part because he stopped painting in the late 1920s to concentrate on various conservation projects. Frank Stick oil paintings will retail between $3,000 and $7,500, with particularly desirable subject matter bringing more.

In the Nick of Time, s. lower left, 37″ × 27″, oil on canvas. $9,500

WOMEN STUDENTS OF HOWARD PYLE

Pyle himself did not favor devoting much time to women artists because he expected that (as was typical at the time) most would soon abandon art to assume primary responsibility for raising a family. This appears to have happened with many, and others abandoned art early for health reasons, but artists like Violet Oakley and Jessie Willcox Smith proved him wrong. The more sought-after scarce artists include Sarah S. Stilwell and the Betts sisters (Anna Whelan and Ethel Franklin). Their paintings may range from $2,500 up to $15,000 or more for particularly fine examples. Ellen Thompson Pyle, Katharine Wireman, and Elizabeth Shippen Green (who did much of her work in charcoal and pastels and is somewhat easier to find) would range somewhat lower. (See *Special Notes* [6] at back of book.)

ANNA WHELAN BETTS

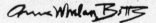

As one of Howard Pyle's promising studens at Drexel Institute, Anna Whelan Betts was among those given the opportunity to illustrate a serial story for *Collier's* magazine. She went on to work for such magazines as *Ladies' Home Journal, Century* magazine, *Harper's Monthly*, and *St. Nicholas*. Collectors can recognize her work by its delicate beauty.

Young Woman Carrying Baskets to the Beach, "Emmeline," Mar. 1908, init., oil on canvas en grisaille, 22″ × 15.25″. $3,800

ELIZABETH SHIPPEN GREEN (1871–1954)

Elizabeth Shippen Green, born in Philadelphia, studied at the Pennsylvania Academy of the Fine Arts with Robert Vonnoh and Thomas Eakins before she studied with Howard Pyle at the Drexel Institute. Her early works were for *The Saturday Evening Post, Ladies' Home Journal,* and books. She was also under exclusive contract with Harper's magazines for many years. Collectors can recognize her work by its vivid color (resembling stained-glass windows) and its bold outlines.

The Birdhouse, s., charcoal, 24″ × 15″. $450
Ariel Rising from the Sea, heading for *The Tempest* in *Tales from Shakespeare* by Charles and Mary Lamb, 1922, pen and ink, 4.75″ × 8.75″, not signed. $675
Antoine with a Wooden Soldier, "Aurélie," *Harper's Monthly,* c. 1910, init., charcoal, 6.5″ × 15″. $1,800

VIOLET OAKLEY (1874–1961)

V. Oakley

Violet Oakley achieved early recognition for her book and magazine art, but it was Howard Pyle who recognized her genius for color and composition. Pyle encouraged Oakley to work with stained glass and to do large murals, and by 1902 she was doing murals in Pennsylvania's Capitol building in Harrisburg. Other major commissions followed that occupied most of her time. While Oakley remained an active artist throughout her life, the output of publisher-commissioned work was small and is therefore rather scarce. Her charcoal sketches and drawings would start at $1,000; her scarcer color work would bring $5,000 or more.

Henry VIII and Anne Boleyn, s., charcoal study for a mural, 19″ × 37″. $8,500

JESSIE WILLCOX SMITH (1863–1935)

JESSIE WILLCOX SMITH

Jessie Willcox Smith is the most famous of Pyle's women students. She is best remembered for a series of children's books and for her *Good Housekeeping* covers, which appeared on every issue between 1919 and 1933. Working in oil, charcoal, and pastels, she was a master at capturing the innocent, intense play of children. Her work is relatively scarce and is considered highly desirable. She was commissioned to do numerous portraits of real children, but her special magic was found in the children she created in her mind, and those have proved to be most collectible. Her smaller drawings range from $1,000 to $2,500, and her paintings may bring from $7,500 up to $20,000 and over.

Jessie Willcox Smith. "The Dark."
Signed lower left, oil on board, 24½
× 15½ inches, $13,000. PHOTO
COURTESY OF SKINNER GALLERIES.

Jessie Willcox Smith. "The
Grappe [sic] Arbour." Signed
lower right, oil with charcoal
on board, 24¾ × 18¼
inches, $25,000. PHOTO
COURTESY OF SKINNER
GALLERIES.

Girl holding a book, exhibition catalog cover, "Announcing an Exhibition by J. W. Smith," reproduced *American Magazine of Art*, July 1925, pen and ink, 9.5″ × 6″, init., lower right. *Note:* This drawing is a variation of the cover design for *A Child's Garden of Verses*, 1910. .... $7,000
Rebecca of Sunny Brook Farm, s. Jessie Willcox Smith, lower left, oil and charcoal on board, 18⅜″ × 16⅜″ (46.7 × 41.6cm); this painting was used as an illus. for *Boys and Girls of Bookland* by Nora Archibald Smith, 1923. .... $16,500

SARAH S. STILWELL (1878–1939)

Sarah S. Stilwell Weber not only studied with Howard Pyle at the Drexel Institute in Philadelphia but also attended his summer classes at Chadds Ford, Pennsylvania.

Collectors can recognize her work not only by the Pyle influence but also by her exotic approach. Her work appeared in such magazines as *Collier's, The Saturday Evening Post, St. Nicholas*, and *Harper's Bazaar*. She illustrated many children's books.

Woman in Kimono, Playing Lute, cover painting, *Saturday Evening Post*, Feb. 9, 1907, s., oil on canvas, 18″ × 24″. $16,500
Love at First Sight, cover painting for *Associated Sunday Magazine*, Oct. 8, 1905, init., oil on canvas, 22″ × 18″. $22,500
Three Graces with Garland of Flowers, sketch for *Vogue* cover, June 13, 1913, watercolor, 11″ × 8″, not signed, ... $1,400

THE INFLUENCE OF
HARVEY DUNN

by Les Mansfield

Les Mansfield became interested in American illustration in 1969. With Walt Reed's help he was able to collect the work of most of the major illustrators. In January 1980, he started dealing in American illustration full time. He advertises nationally and specializes in Harvey Dunn and Nick Eggenhofer.

Like Howard Pyle, Harvey Dunn was also a teacher as well as an illustrator, whose students went on to become famous illustrators in their own right. You will find most of them listed elsewhere in this book with prices. Even though some aren't listed because of a lack of prices at this time, they are "sleepers" worth keeping an eye out for.

A partial list of Dunn students follows:

James E. Allen	Arthur Fuller	Grant Reynard
Lyman Anderson	Vernon Grant	Mead Schaeffer
Harry Ballinger	Leland Gustafson	Amos Sewell
Harry Beckhoff	Robert G. Harris	Irwin Shope
John Clymer	Albin Henning	Hal Stone
Dan Content	Don Hewitt	Frank Street
Mario Cooper	Steven Kidd	Saul Tepper
John Stewart Curry	Walt Louderback	Rico Tomaso
Curtis G. Delano	Arthur Mitchell	Harold Von Schmidt
Charlie Dye	Burt Procter	Harry Wickey
Clark Faye	Paul Rabut	Cliff Young
Nancy Faye	Ken Reilly	

HARVEY DUNN (1884–1952)

Harvey T. Dunn was born in a homesteader's house in Manchester, South Dakota. As a test for hiring a worker, his father would see if the man could plow as much land as his son Harvey could. He would work all day and sketch at night. He showed enough promise in his art to go to college in Brookings, South Dakota, and later he enrolled in the Chicago

73

Harvey Dunn. "Cattle at Rest." Oil on canvas, 15 × 35 inches. Initialed and dated 1911, lower right. Reproduced: Harper's Weekly *6/24/11, "The Nester Girl" by Dave King. $12,000.* PHOTO COURTESY OF LES MANSFIELD, FINE AMERICAN ILLUSTRATIVE ART.

Institute of Art (1902–1904). Dunn met Howard Pyle at the institute and was asked to enroll in Pyle's fall class in Wilmington.

Dunn arrived in Wilmington in the summer of 1904 and studied under Pyle until the summer of 1906. Pyle influenced Dunn more than any other artist, and it was his hope that Dunn would teach future generations of illustrators. One of Dunn's first illustrations appeared in *The Saturday Evening Post*, June 2, 1906. It marked the beginning of a long career with the *Post* and included over 900 illustrations. (See *Special Notes* [7] at back of book.)

Dunn remained in Wilmington until 1914. During this time, besides illustrating for the *Post*, he did work for all of the major magazines, including *Century, Collier's, Delineator, Everybody's, Hampton's, Harper's, Hearst's, Ladies' Home Journal, McClure's, Metropolitan, Outing, Pearson's, People's, Popular, Redbook,* and *Scribner's*.

Demand for his work was ever-increasing, and in order to be closer to the publishers, the Dunn family moved to Leonia, New Jersey, in 1914. Dunn had established himself in the field of illustration and thus felt a need to begin teaching. This dual role continued throughout his life.

With America's involvement in World War I, Dunn joined the A.E.F. artists, and in 1918 he went overseas. Several of his paintings depicting military action appeared as covers for the *American Legion* magazine.

On his return in 1919, the Dunn family moved to Tenafly, New Jersey. In 1924, he started teaching at the Grand Central School of Art and also started traveling back to South Dakota to visit friends and family and sketch the terrain for future prairie paintings that he would do in his studio in Tenafly. Another notable milestone in Dunn's life was being elected to the National Academy of Design in 1945.

Harvey Dunn was a great storyteller and philosopher. He used these skills in his paintings and in teaching. He was a great communicator. He believed that it was more important to paint from feelings than with thought, to capture the spirit of the moment rather than have everything totally factual. "Make your paintings come alive," he taught.

A wonderful colorist, he developed a swirling paint style. Standing at arm's length from his canvases, he would apply color in circular motions with bristle brushes loaded with paint. He would also apply paint with a palette knife.

Dunn made no distinction between illustration and fine art. He thought that a great painting would stand on its own long after the magazine in which it appeared was forgotten.

Mountain Men, "High Country," *Saturday Evening Post*, 1907, s., oil on canvas, 36″ × 24″. $29,000
Cavalier and Cat Quaffing Ale, "A Toast to Mr. Krebs," (Mr. Krebs was Harvey Dunn's father-in-law), 1908, init., d., pen and ink, 11″ × 7″. . $2,400
Danish Warrior Reading Paper, 1908, s., pen and ink, 4″ × 4″. $1,100
Good Men and True, inits. H.T.D., d. 09, s. again, 13¼″ × 36⅛″, oil en grisaille on canvas. $4,180
A Violent Struggle, mono. inits. and d. 15, 30″ × 24″. $2,640
Two Western Prospectors with Burros, "They drifted away through the purple haze," story illustration, "Salt of the Earth" by Peter B. Kyne, *Saturday Evening Post*, Feb. 3, 1917, s., d., oil on canvas mounted, 15.5″ × 38.5″.
.... $9,200
The Old Miner, s., with monogrammed inits. HTD and dated 24, u. r., s. Harvey Dunn, d. April 1925, and i. *Ladies' Home Journal* on reverse, oil on canvas, 30¼″ × 40″ (77 × 101cm); illus. for "Kingpin" by Tristum Tupper, *Ladies' Home Journal*, Apr. 1925. .... $8,800
Wheel of Fortune, i., on tacking edge, Harvey Dunn, relined, retouched, 38¼″ × 32¼″. $4,400
San Antonio, s. H. T. Dunn, d. 1911, prov., exhib., 30″ × 40″. $52,250

COLLECTOR TIPS

A few points should be considered when collecting Harvey Dunn paintings.

1. Dunn was one of a handful of Pyle students whose quality of work remained high throughout his life. But his style did continue to develop, and if you compare his early *Post* illustrations (1906–1922) to his later Prairie paintings (1925–1952), you will be struck with the high quality of each painting.

2. Harvey Dunn was a Westerner. Even though he lived in the East for most of his life (1904 on), he made regular trips out West. Some of his closest friends were Westerners—Gayle Hoskins, Arthur Mitchell, and Harold Von Schmidt, to name just a few.

3. Subject matter has to be an important criterion when collecting

*Harvey Dunn. "Women Having Coffee." Signed and dated lower left,
1943. Oil on canvas, $24,750.* PHOTO COURTESY OF BUTTERFIELD &
BUTTERFIELD, SAN FRANCISCO.

Dunn paintings. The highest prices paid according to subject matter are
in the following order: (1) Western (cowboys and Indians) and Prairie,
(2) genre—paintings depicting everyday life, (3) the classics (e.g., *A Tale
of Two Cities*), (4) military—World War I, (5) outside the United States—
Africa, Egypt, India, Europe, etc.

JOHN CLYMER (1907–) A.R.C.A.

John Clymer

John Clymer studied art in both Canada and the United States. His early illustrations appeared first in Canadian publications, then in American pulp magazines. After that, he worked for most of the American magazines. He did a variety of illustrations for advertising campaigns and also illustrated historic episodes for the U.S. Marine Corps.

Paddlewheeler at Dock, s., 24″ × 36″. $935
The Regatta, bears sig., 24″ × 36¼″. $990
Ships at Harbor, s., 24″.× 36″. $1,760

PAUL RABUT (1914–1983)

PAUL RABUT

Paul Rabut thoroughly researched the subjects of his illustration assignments, becoming an authority in several fields. His specialty became all phases of American history, especially Native American culture. He was also interested in other primitive societies, including African, Oceanic, and pre-Columbian. His work appeared in *The Saturday Evening Post* and other major magazines.

College Days, GM calendar illus., s., tempera, 15″ × 21″. $200
Army nurse on telephone, advertisement, *Western Electric*, s. lr, gouache, 10″ × 9.75″. $250
The Trapping of Tio, *Saturday Evening Post*, Sept. 2, 1953, s., casein on illus. bd., 12″ × 23″. $1,200
Rendezvous with Death, story by Burnham Carter, *Saturday Evening Post*, s., casein on illus. bd., 17½″ × 13½″. $900

GRANT TYSON REYNARD (1887–1968) N.A.

Reynard

After studying at the Chicago Art Institute and the Chicago Academy of Fine Arts, Grant Tyson Reynard got his first job as art editor of *Redbook* magazine (then published in Chicago). Three years later he went east to study with Harvey Dunn. Within a year he was doing assignments for *The Saturday Evening Post*, *Harper's Bazaar*, and others. Most of these early illustrations were done in charcoal. He gradually became an etcher and painter, using a variety of media. His works now hang in such major museums as the Metropolitan Museum of Art and the Library of Congress.

Emmett Kelly at the Ringling Circus, story illustration, "Waiting to Enter," s., brush and ink, 16″ × 13.5″. $700

AMOS SEWELL (1901–1983)

Born in San Francisco, Amos Sewell first studied nights at the California School of Fine Arts. He later moved to New York, where he attended the Art Students League and the Grand Central School of Art. Harvey Dunn was one of his teachers. His first assignments were black-and-white dry-brush illustrations for the pulp magazines. These jobs were followed by illustrations and covers for *Country Gentleman* and *The Saturday Evening Post*. He is known for homespun, rural subjects and children.

Small boy shooting slingshot, story illustration, "Women Are Sure Ornery," *Saturday Evening Post*, s. lr, casein on gesso panel, 16″ × 19.25″. $1,100
The Raid, gouache, 14″ × 11″, init., comprehensive study for *Saturday Evening Post* cover, Feb. 19, 1955; note in margin from Ken Stuart, art editor for the *Post* to Mr. Sewell indicating changes for the final painting, framed copy of cover included in lot. $600
The Covered Wagon, s., *Saturday Evening Post*, charcoal, 11½″ × 16″. . $60
Crowd at fire, story illustration, "Fighting the Fire," *Saturday Evening Post*, s., charcoal and red watercolor, 27″ × 35″. $850

SAUL TEPPER (1899–1988)

Saul Tepper was a native New Yorker who enjoyed a full, varied career. A student of Harvey Dunn, he went on to do illustrations not only for fiction but also for advertising. Among his advertising clients were Mobil Oil, Coca-Cola, and Packard.

Easy Money, s., i "To Frank best wishes, Saul Tepper," oil on board, 13½″ × 11″. $200
Golden Flower, story by Pearl Buck, *Woman's Home Companion*, 1939, s., d., oil on canvas, 22″ × 36″. $7,500
Taking Leave, init., blue monochrome gouache, 16″ × 15″. $500
Debutante Diplomacy, story by Maude Parker, *Saturday Evening Post*, May 21, 1927, s., d., lower left, oil on canvas, 40″ × 32″. $3,400

Saul Tepper. Factory Interior Scene. Signed, dated, '29 upper left, oil on canvas, 26½ × 40 inches, $4,700. PHOTO COURTESY OF BUTTERFIELD & BUTTERFIELD, SAN FRANCISCO.

Woman in Cobbler's Shop, "A Matter of Shoes" by Leona Dalrymple, *American*, Aug. 26, 1933, s., oil on canvas, 31″ × 44″. $3,400
Circus Elephant Parade, "Silver Spangles" by Ettie Stephens Pritchard, *Delineator*, Nov. 1934, s., red and black oil on canvas, 30″ × 30″. $2,500
Lumberjack and Girl in Boat, *Saturday Evening Post*, 1939, s., d., oil on canvas, 40″ × 28″. $4,000
Legal Matters, "Carrousel" by Fannie Hurst, *Cosmopolitan*, Oct. 1929, s., d., blue monochrome oil on canvas, 28″ × 40″. $2,000

THE CIRCLE OF EIGHT

This was an informal but important influence in illustration. It consisted of eight artists who had been trained in newspaper illustration. Newspaper artists of the late 19th century had to make numerous on-the-spot sketches of races, fires, and other important news events. This style of illustration was replaced by photography by the end of the century. The Circle of Eight included William Glackens, Everett Shinn, John Sloan, George Luks, Arthur B. Davies, Robert Henri, Robert Lawson, and Maurice Prendergast.

They went on to be recognized as fine artists, whose works currently demand many thousands of dollars. Glackens, Shinn, and Sloan did many illustrations for a variety of media, but it is as illustrators that prices for their works are listed in this book. In addition, Joseph Pennell and Reginald Marsh, who joined the Circle of Eight later on, are listed in this section.

HOW TO RECOGNIZE EXAMPLES

The style is reminiscent of the sketchiness of newspaper illustrations, emphasizing the central characters involved in the story and the overall atmosphere.

WILLIAM J. GLACKENS (1870–1938) N.A.

Glackens began by doing newspaper sketches of everything from fires and parades to public ceremonies. During the Spanish American War he was an artist-correspondent, and just before the war he had become a magazine illustrator. He was a member of the Circle of Eight and exhibited independently at the National Academy in 1908. Some of his early paintings show the influence of the Impressionist artists Manet and Renoir; they sell for $20,000 up.

Dinner Party, s. W. Glackens, l.r., pen, brush, black ink and pencil, and collage on paper, $11\frac{1}{2}$ ″ × $11\frac{1}{2}$ ″ (29.2 × 29.2cm), s. under the mat, illus. for *The Saturday Evening Post*. $2,420

Courtroom, s. W. Glackens, l.l., s. Glackens, i. "The Boss 2" on the reverse, pen and brush and black ink, pencil and Chinese white on paper, $12\frac{5}{8}$ ″ × $13\frac{1}{2}$ ″ (32.7 × 34.3cm), illus. for *The Saturday Evening Post*. $2,860

Washington Square and a Café Scene, double-sided pastel, s. W. Glackens, l.l., pastel and pencil on tan paper, sight size 10″ × 14½″ (25.4 × 36.8cm). $2,000
Family at Dinner, brush and ink, 7.75″ × 8″, not signed. $3,800
The Boss, Inspector McCue, drawing, s. W. Glackens, i. verso, ex coll., executed 1903, 11¼″ × 9¼″, ink wash on paper. $880
Mardi Gras, s. W. Glackens, exhib., 12½″ × 19⅝″, brush and black ink, pencil, gouache, and Chinese white and pencil on board. $4,180

EVERETT SHINN (1876–1953)

EVERETT SHINN /

Beginning as a newspaper illustrator, Everett Shinn influenced later illustrators as well as the field of fine art. Generally, his subjects involved the New York scene. He worked in all media and had multiple talents as actor, playwright, and inventor. He is also known for his illustrations of Clement Clarke Moore's " 'Twas the Night Before Christmas" poem.

Santa and His Reindeer from " 'Twas the Night Before Christmas," s. Everett Shinn, d. 1942, l.c., watercolor on paper, sight size 14″ × 23″ (35.5 × 58.4 cm), watercolor reproduced in the John C. Winston Company's 1942 edition of Clement Clarke Moore's " 'Twas the Night Before Christmas" as an illustration for the poem's final quatrain:
  "He sprang to his sleigh, to his team gave a whistle,
  And away they all flew like the down of a thistle;
  But I heard him exclaim, ere he drove out of sight,
  'Happy Christmas to all, and to all a good night.' " $10,450
Woman Dressing, s., sanguine on paper, sight size 16″ × 12″, prov. Graham Gallery, New York. $5,225

Everett Shinn. "Nude in Landscape." Signed, dated "E. Shinn 1912" lower left. Conté crayon on paper, 19 × 16½ inches, $750. PHOTO COURTESY OF SKINNER GALLERIES.

After the Brawl, s., d. 1904, red chalk on tan paper, sight size 15½″ × 21½″. $2,750

Hat Shopping, s., d. 1936, pencil and watercolor on paper, sight size 13″ × 10½″. $2,750

Stage Production, s. lower right, pastel on paper, 7″ × 10″. $2,500

According to the Prophet, s., *Saturday Evening Post*, Nov. 29, 1941, orange and black gouache, 15″ × 24″. $1,200

Still Life with Children's Toys, Portrait of a Young Woman Facing Forward, Portrait of a Young Woman Facing Left, and Nude Study of a Seated Woman, four drawings: first, inits E.S., d. 37; three s. E. Shinn; third d. June 21, 1947; fourth d. Aug. 28, 1940; sight size 25″ × 19″ and smaller; first, charcoal on tan paper; three, charcoal heightened with white; two on gray paper; fourth on green paper. $660

Under the New York El Train, s. Everett Shinn, d.'35, prov., exhib., sight size 15½″ × 13½″, pastel on gray paper. $37,400

Snow Storm, Madison Square, New York, s. twice E. Shinn, d. twice 98, prov., property of the Searle Collection, 22¾″ × 25⅞″, pastel and pencil on gray paper laid down on paper. $55,000

Winter Street Scene, Paris, 1910, s. Everett Shinn, d. Paris, 1910, prov., 21½″ × 25¾″, pastel on canvas. $308,000

Reclining Nude, s., d.'16, 8″ × 12″, graphite and wash on paper. $550

Perils of War, s., d. lower right 1945, watercolor, 13½″ × 9″. $900

The Prophet and the King, s., d. 1943, sight size 15″ × 24″, charcoal and wash. $715

Prayer, s., d. 1945, mat size 16″ × 15″, watercolor. $770

Prophecy, s., d. 1945, mat size 16″ × 15½″, watercolor. $825

Portrait of a Lady in a Bonnet, s. E. Shinn, sight size 7″ × 5″, pastel and pencil on paper. $880

Theatrical Subject, s., 14″ × 17″, mixed media. $220

The Golden Lancet, i. and t. affixed on two pieces of board, affixed to mat, from the collection of Mrs. Victor H. Neirinckx, 8″ × 7″, pencil, ink and watercolor on paper. $440

Illustrations from "A Christmas on the Hearth," set of four, d. 1938, 12¾″ × 9″, ink on paper. $495

Gentleman Napping in a Chair, drawing, inits. E.S., 7½″ × 13½″, pen and ink. $550

The Prophet and the King, s., d. 1943, sight size 15″ × 24″, charcoal and wash. $550

American Primavera, s. and d. E. Shinn 1911, sight size 13½″ × 12″, conté crayon on paper. $880

Goddess Among Trees, s. E. Shinn, d. 1943, 17¼″ × 14⅜″, pencil, brush, and black ink on collage board. $935

The Prophecy, drawing, s., d. 1943, sight size 7″ × 5″, pastel and pencil on paper. $990

The Sermon on the Mount, s., d. 1945, sight size 16″ × 13¼″, charcoal and watercolor. $990

Prophecy, s., d. 1945, sight size 15¾″ × 15⅛″, watercolor on paper. . $990

Punch and Judy, s. Everett Shinn, d. 1920, 13″ × 9¾″, gouache, watercolor, charcoal, and pencil on paperboard. $26,400

New York at Night, s. Everett Shinn, d. 1933, 19″ × 12″, pastel on paper. $26,400

The Roaring Twenties, s. Everett Shinn, prov., exhib., 25″ × 17½″, watercolor, conté crayon, charcoal and pencil on paper. $27,500

The Fight, s. Everett Shinn, d.'49, prov., 8¼″ × 13¼″, watercolor and ink on paper. $27,500

Vaudeville, s., d. 1949, also t. "Vaudeville" on label affixed to frame, 18″ × 23⅔″, oil on artist board. $33,000

Clown with Violin, s. Everett Shinn, prov., 12″ × 10″, oil on canvas mounted on board. $13,200

Clown Antics, s. Everett Shinn, d. 1946, 9⅞″ × 8⅛″, oil on panel. $14,300

The Black Dress, s. Everett Shinn, commissioned by Prince Matchabelli Salon, one of three studies, prov., 24½″ × 18¾″, pastel on paper. $18,700

Winter, Washington Square, s. Everett Shinn, d. 1942, prov., 10¼″ × 15½″, pastel on paper. $19,800

The Fight, s. Everett Shinn, d.'99, prov., 8¼″ × 13¼″, watercolor and ink on paper. $22,000

Lady at Doorway, s., prov., 34½″ × 20½″, pastel. $5,280

The Trapeze Artist, s., d. 1949, prov., sight size 22″ × 17½″, pastel on paper. $8,250

The Young King from The Happy Prince, s., d. 1940, reproduced as illus. for Oscar Wilde's *The Happy Prince and Other Tales*, prov., sight size 18″ × 13½″, watercolor on paper. $8,250

Windswept Street, New York, s. Everett Shinn, d. 1907, prov., exhib., 12″ × 39″, red conté crayon on paper. $11,000

Another Clown, s. Everett Shinn, d. 1947, sold after sale, 10″ × 8⅛″, oil on paper laid down on board. $11,000

Prayer, s., d. 1945, 16″ × 15″, watercolor on paper. $1,540

Sir Henry Irving as Shylock, s., i. with t., note attached to backing, sight size 28″ × 13″, pastel on paper. $1,760

Reading, prov., from the estate of Elizabeth Rosenstein, 9″ × 8″, conté crayon and pencil on paper. $2,640

A Masquerade Ball, s., 15″ × 19½″. $2,860

Winter Wind, init. S, prov., from the estate of Elizabeth Rosenstein, 7″ × 4½″, brush and blue and brown ink and charcoal on paper. $4,180

George Sand's Son Calls Chopin a Sponge, s., d. 1942, prov., from the collection of Mrs. Victor H. Neirinckx, sight size 13¼″ × 9″, watercolor and pencil on paper. $1,045

Woman on a Veranda, 19″ × 7″, pencil and watercolor wash on board. $1,210

Two Men on a Bridge, drawing, s., 1924, 11″ × 14″, watercolor. $1,320

Lady at the Door, s., prov., 12″ × 17″, red conté crayon on paper. .. $1,430

Study for a Costume Design, inits., s., d. Everett Shinn, 1940 verso, sight size 14″ × 11¼″, gouache on brown paper. $1,430

JOHN SLOAN (1871–1951)

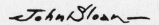

Noted for his illustrations depicting the grittier aspects of city life, John Sloan's works appeared in a variety of magazines such as *Harper's Weekly* and *Collier's*. He continued to paint the New York scene in later life, mostly for exhibitions. His etchings and lithographs are in many museums, including the Metropolitan Museum of Art in New York.

Study of a Man, s., d.'07, charcoal and crayon on paper, sight size 12½″ × 9¾″, reproduced in *King's Magazine*, July 1907. .... $1,980

The Power Salon, s. John Sloan, l.r., s. with inits. JS, d. Mch 1913, i. "To my friend William Karlin," l.l., conté crayon on paper laid down on board, 14¾″ × 19¼″ (37.5 × 48.8cm), illus. in *The Coming Nation*, Nov. 16, 1912. .... $3,850

Reddy at the Pool, s. John Sloan, l.l., oil on canvas, 20⅛″ × 24″ (51 × 61cm). $26,400

Lone Pine, s. John Sloan, l.r., s. again and i. with t. on the stretcher, oil on canvas, 24″ × 20″ (61 × 51cm), painted in 1925. .... $10,450

The Tailored Hat, s. John Sloan, s., d. 35 and i. with t. verso, 22″ × 18″, oil on board. $19,800

Twelve Apostles, s. John Sloan, painted in 1919, 20″ × 24¼″. $24,200

Philip and Schoolmates, drawing, original tissue used in making the etching illus. for W. Somerset Maugham's *Of Human Bondage*, lit., 6″ × 4″, pencil on tissue. $550

Philip and Schoolmates, drawing, executed in 1937, 7⅛″ × 4⅛″, pencil on paper. $715

I Guess These'll Do, He Said, study for *Collier's* magazine, Sept. 6, 1913, inits. J.S., 9″ × 11″, pencil on paper. $990

Recumbent Nude, s. John Sloan, exhib., 23½″ × 29″, charcoal on paper. $1,430

Girl Dressing, s. John Sloan, 15¾″ × 10″, brown chalk on paper. $1,760

Nude and Copper Cat, Fireplace, s., d. 1942, prov., 14″ × 18″, oil on board. $8,800

Nude on a Great White Pillow, s., 10″ × 8½″, oil on board. $2,420

Three Nudes Arranging Flowers, s. John Sloan, 9½″ × 10¾″, charcoal on paper. $2,420

Reclining Female Nude, inits. and d. J.S. 30, sight size 7¼″ × 9¾″, pencil on paper. $2,200

Nude and Chief Blanket, s., property of Peter Sheldon, Standish, ME, prov., lit., 26″ × 32″, oil on board. $24,200

Pancoast Sketching, s. John Sloan, d. 1907, i. XXVI, prov., exhib., 8¾″ × 10¾″, oil on board. $16,500

OTHER INFLUENTIAL
ILLUSTRATORS

ROCKWELL KENT (1882–1971)

Rockwell Kent

Rockwell Kent used his experience as an engraver and lithographer to develop his distinct "wood block" style of illustration in dramatic black and white tones. In his early work he was influenced by artist Paul Gaugin. He did illustrations for such advertisers as Marcus & Company Jewelers, Rolls-Royce, and others. Collectors should note that some of his advertising and humorous pictures are signed "Hogarth, Jr." He often illustrated his own books and those of others, such as *Moby Dick*.

Man deluged by envelopes, decorative illustration, "Love Letters," probably *Vanity Fair*; c. 1925, pen and ink, 8″ × 4″, estate-stamped, drawn in Kent's "Hogarth" style. $500

Motherhood, s. Rockwell Kent, l.r., d. 1913, l.l., oil on canvas, 32¼″ × 42″ (82 × 106.8cm); during this period, Kent was influenced by the work of Paul Gaugin and the German Expressionist Franz Marc. $22,000

Valley of the Var, s. Rockwell Kent, l.r., watercolor on paper laid down on board, 10⅛″ × 14⅛″ (25.8 × 35.8cm); according to Scott R. Ferris, "The subject of this watercolor is the valley of the River Var, in the extreme southeastern area of France; here, during the summer of 1925, Kent came to paint. $6,380

Adirondack Mountains, heading for Chapter 6, *This Is My Own*, 1939, s., brush and ink, 4″ × 5.75″ $1,000

Designs for bookplates, two-sided pencil drawing, 11″ × 8.5″, estate-stamped. $275

Drawing from Moby Dick, 5″ × 7″. $495

Policeman Stopping a Car, bears artist's estate stamp, illus. for *The New York Tribune* in 1919; 10¾″ × 15¾″, pen and black ink on board. $1,100

Christmas Eve, illus. for General Electric calendar, 12″ × 14½″, watercolor, gouache and pencil on paper. $5,500

Russian Mother, s. Rockwell Kent, d. Christmas 1943, i. "To Luis Kon," executed as a contribution to the Prussian War Relief, Inc., 13¼″ × 17″, watercolor, gouache, brush and black ink and pencil on board. $6,600

Christmas Adirondacks, illus. for General Electric calendar, executed c. 1945, certificate of authentication accompanies lot, 11″ × 15″, gouache, watercolor and pencil on board. $7,150

Generator of Jobs, s., 38″ × 44″. $23,100

Study for Marcus Jewelers, New York, stamped mono. Rockwell Kent, executed c. 1931, prov., image size 5¼″ × 6¼″, pencil on tissue mounted on board. $495

The Children's Mother, c. 1920, s., t., 14½″ × 11″, pencil on buff paper laid down on board. $660

Rockwell Kent, pen and ink, "The Course of the Future." Done for the American Export Lines, Jan. 14/1946, 8½ × 11 inches, together with the front cover for the Olana Gallery American Art Catalog, $3,000. PHOTO COURTESY OF DU MOUCHELLES GALLERY.

Tree, Illuminated Letter M, Death of Adonis, Angel Lighting Christmas Tree, and Landscape Illustration, five, all estate-stamped, pen and ink on paper. $880
Scene from Faust, sight size 7¼″ × 11″, pen and ink on paper. $1,045

REGINALD MARSH (1898–1954)

R. MARSH

Reginald Marsh began his career in 1920 as a staff artist for the New York *Daily News* and then became a cartoonist for *The New Yorker*. New York scenes and people done in the then-popular ''Ash Can'' style brought him to the attention of many magazines. He was a prolific illustrator who also did book illustrations.

Reginald Marsh. Watercolor. Frontispiece for U.S.A. by John Dos Passos. Signed R. Marsh, inscribed U.S.A., dated 1945 by artist, 10½ × 8 inches, $4,000. PHOTO COURTESY OF AUTHOR.

Man and Woman on a Bench and Four Women on the Boardwalk, a double-sided work, s. Reginald Marsh, d. 1947, l.r. recto, Chinese ink on paper, sight size each 13½" × 19¼" (34.3 by 48.2 cm). $13,200

Study of Six Women and The Josiah Macy, a double-sided watercolor, recto: s., d. 1944.5, wash and pencil on paper; verso: s., t., d. 1944, i. Standard Oil Co.—Bayone—Constable Hook, watercolor and charcoal on paper, sight size 15" × 22". $16,500

Ominous Stroll, s. Reginald Marsh, d. 1953 (lr), i. with t. and artist's name on frame, tempera on masonite, 15" × 12", prov., acquired directly from the artist's private collection, New York. $6,000

Carousel, s. Reginald Marsh, d. 1947, l.r., watercolor and brush and black ink on paper laid down on board, 22" × 30⅛" (55.8 × 76.5cm). $23,100

Two Girls on the Promenade, a double-sided drawing, s. Reginald Marsh, d.'47, l.r., s. and d. again on the reverse, brush and black ink, ink wash, and charcoal on paper, unframed, 16" × 21⅞" (40.6 × 55.5cm). $4,950

The Eugene F. Moran, Jr. and Strolling Woman, a double-sided watercolor, recto s. Reginald Marsh, d. May 30, 1937, i. with t., l.c., verso s. R. Marsh, l.r.; the first, watercolor and pencil on paper; the second, watercolor on paper, 15" × 21½" (38 × 54.5cm). $12,100

Tank Car at Siding, s. R. Marsh, d. 1936, l.r., watercolor on paper, 13½" × 19½" (34.3 × 49.5cm). $8,800

Woman Walking, a double-sided painting, recto s. R. Marsh, d. 53, l.r.; verso s. and d. again, l.r.; tempera on board, 14" × 10" (35.5 × 25.5cm), property of the Baltimore Museum of Art. $8,800

Swimming in the Hudson, s. Reginald Marsh, d.'38, prov., exhib., lit., 24" × 30", tempera on masonite. $44,000

Discussion, s. Reginald Marsh, d.'34, prov., exhib., 18" × 24", tempera on panel. $74,250

Lehigh Valley, s. Reginald Marsh, d.'38, and i. with t., prov., 14" × 20", watercolor on paper. $14,300

Girl Walking, s., d. 46, 27¾" × 22", oil on watercolor on mounted paper on board. $14,300

Varieties 1943 and Bathing Beauties, double-sided drawing, s. R. Marsh, d. 1946, stamped J. Marsh Collection, prov., 13" × 19", watercolor on paper. $15,400

On the Docks, s. Reginald Marsh, d. 1944, prov., property of the estate of Victor Rosen, Beverly Hills, CA, 22" × 30", brush and black ink and watercolor on paper. $19,800

Frolicking on the Beach, s. Marsh, d.'52, a related sketch appears on verso, prov., 24" × 30", tempera on board. $19,800

The Whirlpool at Coney Island, from the estate of Ruth Gordon, 19" × 22", oil on masonite. $22,000

Off to Work, double-sided watercolor, d. 1951 recto, s. Marsh and d. 1953 verso, sight size 28¼" × 20½", pen brush, black ink and wash on paper, recto; watercolor, pen, brush and black ink on paper, verso. $7,700

Two Girls on a Boardwalk, s. Reginald Marsh, d. 45, prov., 21" × 14½", ink wash and watercolor on paper. $6,600

New York Harbor, s. Reginald Marsh, d.'36, prov., 13⅞" × 19¾", watercolor on paper. $9,900

Woman Walking, s., c. 1946, 14" × 10", watercolor. $6,380

Women Strolling, estate of Victor Gallop, 30⅜" × 21⅞", oil wash on treated paper laid down on board. $9,900

Shipping, s., d. '28, prov., exhib., 14″ × 20″, watercolor on paper. .. $4,400
Two City Strollers, s., 16″ × 12″, oil on canvasboard. $4,675
Industrial Landscape, s., d. 1936, i. WC 36–9, prov., 14″ × 19⅝″, watercolor on paper. $4,730
Merry-Go-Round, s., i. DIV–8 and Nos. 28 and 30, executed c. 1940, 10″ × 14″, watercolor and pencil on paper. $6,050
Village Along the River, s. Marsh, sight size 8″ × 13″, watercolor on paper. $1,210
City Stroller with Red Skirt, s., prov., 5″ × 4″, oil on masonite. ... $3,575
Manhattan Skyline, s., prov., sight size 13½″ × 19½″, watercolor on paper. $2,310
Two Girls on a Corner, i. Mar 12, 1948, 10½″ × 8½″, gray wash on paper. $1,540
Street Scene with El Track, s., d. 1929, sight size 13¼″ × 19¼″, watercolor on paper. $4,125
Nude Studies, s., dedicated, 8¾″ × 11½″, pen and ink on paper. $2,860
Girl Walking, s. Reginald Marsh, '47, identified on label verso, retouched, 10″ × 8″, oil on pastel. $2,310
Circus Ride, prov., 9″ × 12″, watercolor on paper. $2,090
Off to Battle, s. Reginald Tiepolo Marsh, i., 10¾″ × 9½″, brush and black on paper. $715
Girl in a Red Skirt, prov., 7¾″ × 7″, oil on board. $825
Seated Woman, s. and d. Reginald Marsh 1951, sight size 5¼″ × 4½″, watercolr and pencil on paper. $1,100
Portrait of a Young Girl, prov., 7¾″ × 7″, oil on board. $990

JOSEPH PENNELL (1860–1926) N.A.

Architectural subjects were the main interest of Joseph Pennell while he was a pictorial reporter. Pen-and-ink drawings, etchings, and lithographs were used by such clients as *Harper's, Century,* and *McClure's.* The illustrations were of cathedrals, street scenes, and palaces, as well as panoramic views of important construction projects, among them the Panama Canal.

West Front of St. Paul's from Ludgate Hill, gouache en grisaille on paper laid down on board, 20″ × 13¾″ (50.8 × 34.9cm). $14,300
City View, Along the Water Front, s., mat 7¾″ × 9¼″, watercolor. ... $187
Eagle Tower, Carnavon Castle, s., 18½″ × 14½″, charcoal on linen board. $302
Near the Market Place, Stuttgart, s., t., sight size 13½″ × 9⅝″, India ink on paper. $550
Avignon, drawing, s., 19″ × 14″, ink. $440
Smoke and Mist Across the East River and Lower Broadway, two, first s. Jo.Pennell, i. smoke mist verso, prov.; first, 10¼″ × 13″; second, 12⅞″ × 9¾″; first, watercolor on paper; second, pastel on brown paper. $5,500

The Putney Bus and Colleoni Statue, Venice, two, both s. Jo. Pennell, second i. "48 Colleoni Venice" verso, prov.; first, 10¼″ × 7″; second, 12½″ × 9¼″; first, watercolor on paper; second, charcoal, pastel, and gouache on gray-brown paper. $6,050

Pall Mall, East London, and Charing Cross Station, London, two, both s. Jo. Pennell, prov.; first, 7″ × 10¼″; second, 10″ × 13⅞″, both watercolor on paper, the second is buff paper. $7,700

Gathering Leaves, s., d. Rome–November/10–1884, t., sight size 13⅜″ × 21″, black ink on paper. $715

New York Harbor, s. Jo. Pennell, i. "Busy Day" verso, prov., 7″ × 9⅔″, watercolor, gouache, and pencil on paper. $3,850

A Street, Indian Exhibition, s., i. with t. and indistinctly annotated in pencil, sight size 7¼″ × 8¼″, ink on paper. $715

Mont St. Michael, s. Joseph Pennell, s. and d. 1902, i. verso, exhib., sight size 25½″ × 20¼″, pen and ink on paper. $770

Light and Shadow on the City, s., prov., 11″ × 14½″, watercolor heightened with gouache on paper. $1,540

Sun Setting in Splendour, inits. of artist's wife and t. verso, view of New York Harbor, 12″ × 16″, gouache and watercolor on board. $2,750

PART VI

COLLECTING
CATEGORIES

ADVENTURE

by Frederic B. Taraba

*Frederic B. Taraba is a former curator and librarian/archivist of
the Society of Illustrators Museum of American Illustration in New
York City. A graduate of Wesleyan University, he has learned everything he knows about illustration since joining the staff of the
society in 1983. Recently, he has written articles on past illustrators
for* Step-by-Step Graphics. *Currently he is with Illustration House.*

In discussing adventure illustration art, the logical starting point is to
ask, ''What makes 'adventure'?'' To my way of thinking, the answer is
quite straightforward. A successful adventure illustration must quicken
the viewer's pulse. The pivotal moment of the story is frozen. You may
find yourself wishing the artwork could come to life and complete the
drama, much the same way as you are perhaps tempted to read the last
page of a mystery first to find out who the guilty party is.

If we agree on that point, the next question becomes ''Why collect
adventure?'' To that there are a number of viable answers. Good adventure depicted by the great illustrators typically harks back to a time when
the world was a bigger, more exciting, yet simpler place, when the con-

*Albert Beck Wenzell. Oil on board, signed lower right. Publication and date
not known, 18 × 23 inches, $1,200.* PHOTO COURTESY OF THE SOCIETY OF
ILLUSTRATORS. *(See* Special Notes *[8] at back of book.)*

frontation between good and evil was easier to discern than it often is now. If you're intrigued by classic confrontations of man versus man or man versus the elements, then adventure illustration is for you. Adventure is an escape hatch for many of us from our own safe existences as our lives begin to seem pat and predictable. If you've ever daydreamed about shooting the rapids in a kayak, taking on a horde of thugs, or jumping out of an airplane, you'll know what I'm talking about.

Howard Pyle, who is acknowledged as "the Father of American Illustration," also deserves at least partial credit for siring adventure illustration. Pyle was a renowned teacher of illustration, who greatly influenced generations to come. One can still see his hand in much of the adventure illustration created today. Many of Pyle's students became giants in the adventure field. No survey of adventure can be complete without considering the likes of Stanley Arthurs, W. J. Aylward, Harvey Dunn, George Harding, Thornton Oakley, Henry Peck, Frank Schoonover, Harry Townsend, and N. C. Wyeth; all learned at Pyle's side. In his classes, Pyle taught the picture as drama (a concept well suited to adventure commissions) and stressed the need for accurate historical detailing. Of course, it would be unfair to lay the entire mantle of responsibility for the rise of adventure illustration on Pyle's shoulders.

In 1896, publisher Frank Munsey founded *Argosy*, and the separate tradition of the pulp magazines was born. Taken as a whole, the pulps depended less on historical accuracy and more on imagination. Through their glory days, stretching into the early 1950s, pulps were an important outlet for many different kinds of writing, including science fiction, fantasy, and "true crime." Long-running success in the pulp world was enjoyed by several of Street & Smith's scores of titles; *Weird Tales* was a dominant force from 1923 through 1955. Among the illustrators who found success in the pulps are Hannes Bok, Margaret Brundage, Lee Brown Coye, Rafael DeSoto, Boris Dolgov, Virgil Finlay, Stephen Lawrence, Frank Paul, George Rozen, and J. Allen St. John.

The death of the pulp format came as a result of a complex web of historical forces, but certainly one factor that led to their waning was their very success at the newsstand. The growing market for adventure illustration shown by the impact pulps had on the reading public was not lost on the general-interest magazines. Periodicals such as *Cosmopolitan*, *The Saturday Evening Post*, and *Collier's* frequently ran adventure stories, often serializing them to create publishing's version of the cliffhanger, in much the same way that movie shorts kept audiences coming back for more. Other factors leading to the demise of the pulps were World War II paper rationing and the simple fact that there were always more of the cheap-to-produce pulps vying for space on the newsstand.

As the pulps were beginning their decline, a new market for adventure

Rudolph Belarski (1900–
1983), Synthetic Men of
Mars, *cover for* Argosy,
*1/7/1939. Oil on canvas, 36
× 24 inches, signed,
$18,000.* PHOTO COURTESY
OF ILLUSTRATION HOUSE,
INC. (See *Special Notes* [9]
at back of book.)

*Walter M. Baumhofer
(1904–1987). Cover
illustration for* Doc
Savage *magazine, May
1934,* Mystery on the
Snow. *Oil on canvas,
24½ × 21 inches,
signed lower left,
$4,000.* PHOTO
COURTESY OF THE
SOCIETY OF
ILLUSTRATORS. (See
Special Notes [10] at
back of book.)

Walter M. Baumhofer (1904–1987). Illustration for Argosy, *May 1952,*
Quick. *Oil on canvas board, 24 × 33½ inches, signed upper left, $1,500.*
PHOTO COURTESY OF THE SOCIETY OF ILLUSTRATORS. (See *Special Notes*
[11] *at back of book.)*

illustration came into play. Although paperback books had been around
for some time, it wasn't until the founding of Pocket Books by R. F. De-
Graaf in 1938 that the concept of marketing paperbacks by use of
interesting cover art really took hold. Many of the paperback publishers
that sprang up in the early 1940s, including Dell, Avon, and Popular
Library, started in the pulp magazine business. George Delacorte,
founder of Dell, summed up the rise of paperback cover art: "If you've
got a lousy book that you're stuck with, you hire your best artist to put
the finest cover on it, you have your best blurb writer put the greatest
blurb on it, and you won't lose *too* much money."*

Of course the successful paperback publishing houses played to a wide
variety of tastes; adventure was just one of many genres. Because of the
small format of paperbacks, the cover image had to be visually arresting.
This stricture led to the evolution of paperback cover art down a different
path from, for example, the artwork created for the general-interest magazines. Illustration credits varied over time and from publisher to publisher; to this day some publishers still do not credit the cover illustrators.

*Quoted from Piet Schreuders, *Paperbacks, U.S.A.: A Graphic History, 1939–1959* (San
Diego, CA: Blue Dolphin Enterprises, 1981).

Since 1939 there have been many paperback artists who have done compelling adventure work; just to name a few of my favorites, keep on the lookout for Carl Bobertz, Gerald Gregg, H. L. Hoffman, Robert Jonas, E. McKnight Kauffer, Leo Manso, Frank McCarthy, Barye Phillips, Richard Powers, Norman Saunders, Robert Stanley, and Stanley Zuckerberg.

One advantage of collecting illustration art is that, in general, it is easy, or at least *possible*, to document it, which is more difficult for artwork not created for reproduction. If you are stubborn enough and have plenty of time, virtually any tearsheet can be located through either paper dealers or libraries or by referring to any of the several books on the subject, particularly those dealing with paperback art. When buying original illustration art, be sure to check for clues on the back of the art; even the smallest notation can make your search a lot easier. This holds true even if the artwork is unsigned. So, whereas fakes are a possibility, one can closely compare the original with the printed version, which couldn't happen in other fields of collecting.

There are, of course, also disadvantages to collecting original illustration art. Foremost among these is the fact that much of illustration art was considered expendable once reproduced. Even in cases where the artwork was kept beyond its date of publication, a great deal of it still wound up in the trash heap as offices moved or companies shut down.

Matt Clark (1903–1972). Illustration for The Senorita's Choice, *American Weekly, 12/31/1950. Tempera on board, 15½ × 27½ inches, signed lower right, $1,500.* PHOTO COURTESY OF THE SOCIETY OF ILLUSTRATORS. (See *Special Notes* [12] *at back of book.*)

William A. Smith (1918–1989). Illustration for Manhattan Manhunt,
Cosmopolitan *magazine, 1943. Dissolved lithographic tusche on gessoed
panel, 23½ × 17 inches, signed lower right, $1,000.* PHOTO COURTESY OF
THE SOCIETY OF ILLUSTRATORS. (See *Special Notes* [13] at back of book.)

John McDermott (1919–1977). Illustration for Terror in the Surf,
Outdoor Life *magazine, date not known. Gouache on gessoed board, 15 ×
26 inches, signed lower left, $500.* PHOTO COURTESY OF THE SOCIETY OF
ILLUSTRATORS. (See *Special Notes* [14] at back of book.)

This problem is exacerbated by the fact that many companies did not return art to the artists, frequently buying both the rights to reproduction and the physical art itself.

Not all illustration art was relegated to the dustbin though, and that's one thing that can make the search so exciting. Materials can show up almost anywhere, from the offices of retiring art directors to estate sales of maintenance men. Rumors persist, for example, of a warehouse filled with original Street & Smith art; if anyone finds it, please let me know.

Also, because illustration was considered expendable once used and because many publishers paid poorly, artists tended to use cheap materials in creating the image, so condition is another factor to be wary of. Keep in mind that the fields of restoration and conservation are highly technical, scientific areas. I've seen countless pieces come back to life in the hands of a skilled professional. You may wish to consult a conservator before purchasing artwork that seems to have condition problems.

A list of artists who have done adventure illustration would be virtually endless. Here, however, are some of the greats you may want to watch for. Unless otherwise noted, all of the reproduced illustrations are in the permanent collection of the Society of Illustrators and consequently are *not* for sale. Prices indicate estimates for comparable images by the artists.

Loran Frederick Wilford. Illustration for The Wolf Killer *by Owen Cameron,* Collier's *magazine, 12/17/1949. Watercolor and pencil, 12 × 24 inches, signed lower left, $400.* PHOTO COURTESY OF THE SOCIETY OF ILLUSTRATORS. (See *Special Notes* [15] at back of book.)

JOSEPH CLEMENT COLL (1881–1921)

Drama in black and white was achieved by Joseph Clement Coll in his bold pen-and-ink illustrations. Beginning as a newspaper artist, he moved on to illustrate books and various magazines and periodicals. His work can be recognized by his imaginative use of pen and ink in depicting mystery stories by A. Conan Doyle and Sax Rohmer. Among the magazines using his work were *Collier's* and *Everybody's*, along with *Associated Sunday Magazine.*

Spearsmen Preparing to Attack Fortified Village, story illustration, "King of the Khyber Rifles," pen and ink, 5″ × 11″, not signed. $600
Man with Servant Bowing to Lady, 1907, s., d., pen and ink, 11.25″ × 13″ $1,500
David and The Land of Bohemia, two, both s.; first, 15³/₅″ × 11⁷/₈″, brush, pen, and black ink on black board; second, 14³/₄″ × 20¹/₂″, watercolor brush and black ink on board. $462

Joseph Clement Coll (1881–1921). Illustration for Fu Manchu *by Sax Rohmer. Pen and ink, 14¹/₂ × 12¹/₂ inches, unsigned, $1,800.* PHOTO COURTESY OF THE SOCIETY OF ILLUSTRATORS. (See *Special Notes* [16] at back of book.)

Mario Cooper (b. 1905). Illustration for Collier's *magazine, 1933. Wash on board, 16 × 9½ inches, signed upper left, $1,000.* PHOTO COURTESY OF THE SOCIETY OF ILLUSTRATORS. *(See* Special Notes *[17] at back of book.)*

MARIO RUBEN COOPER (1905–) N.A.

MARIO
COOPER

Mario Ruben Cooper was born in Mexico of Mexican-American parent-age and grew up in Los Angeles. After attending the Otis Art Institute and Chouinard Art Institute, he moved to New York, where he received instruction at the Grand Central School of Art and Columbia University. Among his teachers and influences were Pruett Carter and Harvey Dunn. His first commission for an illustration came from *Collier's* magazine.

He is known for his illustrations for adventure stories; he achieved his dramatic effects by using colored inks on illustration board.

Diamonds Are Trumps, s., gouache, 19½″ × 15″, reproduced in *American Weekly* magazine, Feb. 23, 1947. ....$250

DEAN CORNWELL (1892–1960)

Dean Cornwell worked the whole canvas in a Herculean manner, reminiscent of one of his teachers, Harvey Dunn. He also studied with Frank Brangwyn, the muralist.

This left-handed painter was a popular illustrator whose work appeared in such magazines as *Good Housekeeping*, *Redbook*, and *Cosmopolitan*. He also did many illustrations for advertisers such as General Motors Corporation (including a mural for the New York World's Fair). Among his other important works are murals for the Los Angeles Public Library and the Eastern Airlines office in Rockefeller Center.

Although Cornwell's oils sell for many thousands of dollars, there are

Dean Cornwell. Story illustration. Pirates versus Captain Blood, "Gallows Key," "Captain Blood had walked into a trap. It was too late to retreat." The Exploits of Captain Blood by Rafael Sabatini, Cosmopolitan, August 1930. Oil on canvas, orange and black, 25 × 48 inches, initialed, $24,000. PHOTO COURTESY OF ILLUSTRATION HOUSE, INC.

preliminary studies and compositions available for several hundred to a thousand dollars.

Raking the Leaves, s., oil on canvas, 29½″ × 17″. $2,640

Three Women and a Piano, story illustration, "The Proffered Advice": " 'Stand pat,' the slangy Elizabeth suggested promptly," "Kindred of the Dust" by Peter S. Kyne, *Cosmopolitan*, May 1920, s., d., u.r., oil on canvas, mounted, 28″ × 36″. $60,000

The Slave Market, story illustration, "The Robe," *Life*, 1942, s., oil on canvas, 34″ × 45″. $30,000

Men at Telephone Serving Whiskey, advertisement, c. 1946, oil on canvas, 39.75″ × 35″, not signed. $5,800

Two Men Stoking a Steel Furnace, mural study, commissioned for the New York World's Fair, "Stoking a Furnace," General Motors, 1939, s., i., Wolff pencil on glassine, 21″ × 17.5″. $1,800

Two Men in a Riverboat Wheelhouse, preliminary study, "There was a blinding flash of lightning as Captain Charlie guided the Belle between the gnarled cypress trunks," "Low Water on the Mississippi" by Ben Burman, *True*, Sept. 1952, charcoal, 9.25″ × 20.75″, not signed. $800

Two Men in a Wheelhouse, comprehensive sketch, "Low Water on the Mississippi," *True*, Sept. 1952, oil on board, 6.25″ × 13.5″, not signed. ...$1,200

Aviator Charting His Course, s., oil on canvas, 25¼″ × 29¼″. $3,025

Altercation on Shipdeck, "Off this Brig, Dutchie!" "The Good That Is in the Worst of Us" by Dale Collins, *Cosmopolitan*, 1924, d., i., red and black, oil on canvas, 24″ × 48″. $10,000

The Founding of Los Angeles, compositional study for Los Angeles Public Library mural, 1933, gouache on paper, 8¾″ × 18″, not signed. $1,600

Man in rigging, doffing hat, preliminary drawing for a calendar illustration, black, brown pencil on paper, 23″ × 20″, estate-stamped. $600

Dean Cornwell. Publication not known. Tiger, Tiger. Oil on canvas, initialed lower left, 26 × 32 inches, $8,000. PHOTO COURTESY OF THE SOCIETY OF ILLUSTRATORS.

Two Men, a Woman, a Parrot, and an Astrolabe, story illustration, "The Love Story of Jeremy Pitt," "Mr. Pitt came upon the lady of his dreams with Captain Tondeur, that man of sinister reputation," "The Exploits of Captain Blood," *Cosmopolitan*, June 1930, init., d.'30, oil on canvas, mounted, 36″ × 48″. $8,500

Portrait of Admiral Halsey (Timken Roller Bearing Series), comprehensive study, s., charcoal and colored chalk, 12¾″ × 12½″. $300

Philadelphia, s., oil on board, 24″ × 20¾″, exhib. The Illustrator in America 1900–1960, Albany, GA, Nov. 1985. Special note: Although this work has a sketch appearance, in the opinion of Mr. Wale it is a finished piece, possibly for the *American Weekly* magazine. $650

Sir Walter Raleigh and Maiden, study for the mural in the Raleigh Room at the Warwick Hotel, New York, sight size 25½″ × 35″, watercolor. ... $1,980

Holding Their Own, s. Dean Cornwell, d. 1916; 34½″ × 24″. $3,850

Man in Topper and Profile of a Man, two drawings; first, 16″ × 12¾″; second, 17⅛″ × 11⅜″; the second, charcoal and pencil on paper. $88

Color Study on Docks, inits., 14″ × 16¾″, charcoal and pastel on tracing paper. $198

Portrait of an Indian, s. Dean Cornwell, prov., 16¾″ × 13¾″, pencil and conté crayon on paper. $275

Study for a Mural and Travellers, two drawings; first, s., 22¼″ × 19″; second, 19½″ × 22¾″; first, pencil on paper; second, colored pencil, pencil, and white chalk on blue paper. $385

Colonial Soldier with Musket, 18½″ × 24″, charcoal and pencil on paper. $495

I'm Near You Because I Love You, s. Dean Cornwell, illus. for story by I. A. R. Wylkie, "Lord Bolshevic and Lady Circumstance," *Good Housekeeping*, 1921, 28″ × 36¼″. $6,050

The Carpenter and Water Carrier, two drawings; second, inits., 25½″ × 16¼″; second, 23″ × 16½″; first, crayon and chalk on tan paper; second, charcoal and red chalk on paper. $550

Study for General Motors Murals, s., d. N.Y. World's Fair, 1939, i. with t., preliminary study for General Motors murals at the 1939 World's Fair, New York, 19″ × 19″, charcoal and red chalk on paper. $660

Color Rough for Great Fisherman, 10½″ × 13½″, oil and pencil on board. $1,045

A Corner of the Studio, 23½″ × 9″, oil on board. $550

The Migration, s., book illus., *Big Fisherman* by Lloyd C. Douglas, 26⅛″ × 34⅛″. $7,150

Arab Market, mono., i., 30″ × 22″. $1,155

FREDERIC R. GRUGER (1871–1953)

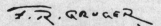

Frederic Rodrigo Gruger began his career as a newspaper illustrator for the *Philadelphia Ledger* and his career as a magazine illustrator with the old *Century* magazine. Over the years he worked for advertisers, book

Frederic Rodrigo Gruger (1871–1953). *Illustration for* The Magic of Mohammed Din *by F. Britten Austin, Redbook, August 1918. Wolff pencil on Gruger board, 12 × 18 inches, signed lower left, $1,200.* PHOTO COURTESY OF THE SOCIETY OF ILLUSTRATORS. (See *Special Notes* [18] at back of book.)

Frederic Rodrigo Gruger. *Double-page illustration of three people dining. Pencil and wash, black and white. Signed lower left, 12 × 16¼ inches, $900.* PHOTO COURTESY OF PRIVATE COLLECTOR.

publishers, and magazines such as *The Saturday Evening Post*. He developed a special effect with his drawings using a Wolff pencil rubbed with a stump of eraser, often with an underlying wash. The result was a velvety black appearance. Using the inexpensive cardboard that newspapers mounted silver prints on, he employed this technique to dramatize the many adventure stories he illustrated.

Bridal Blush, story illustration, *Collier's*, June 5, 1915, s., Wolff pencil and wash, 8″ × 11″. $175
Two men, woman having coffee on terrace, story illustration, "Three Lumps of Sugar," *Cosmopolitan*, May 1927, s., Wolff pencil and wash, 8″ × 24″.
.... $1,000

Leland Gustavson (1899–1966). Illustration for The King of Macassar, Blue. Book *magazine, 1942. Charcoal on primed canvas, 12 × 9½ inches, signed lower left, $200.* PHOTO COURTESY OF THE SOCIETY OF ILLUSTRATORS. (See *Special Notes* [19] at back of book.)

LELAND R. GUSTAVSON (1879–1966)

GUSTAVSON

Born in Moline, Illinois, Leland R. Gustavson studied nights at the Chicago Art Institute while working days at various advertising agencies, printing houses, and art services. Eventually, he moved east and studied under Harvey Dunn and Walter Biggs.

Gustavson is best known for his exciting portrayals of murder and mayhem in illustrations for *Blue Book* magazine. He also worked for *The Saturday Evening Post, Collier's, McCall's,* and *Country Gentleman.*

Dishonored, reproduced *American Weekly*, 1949, s., gouache, vignette, 13¾″ × 21¾″. $50

The Church Supper, *Country Gentleman* cover, Sept. 1947, s., oil on canvas, 34″ × 31″, copy of cover in lot. $1,200

Five story illustrations, man hitting another, with flashlight, and others, s., brush and ink, various sizes. ....:...................................... $150

The Dance, s. Gustavson, 17½″ × 22″, watercolor. $275

Soldier and a Girl Holding a Candle Approaching a Closed Door, s. Gustavson, 30½″ × 22½″. $275

WALT LOUDERBACK (1887–1941)

Walt Louderback

Walt Louderback studied at the Art Institute of Chicago. He lived in Europe during the 1920s and delivered his paintings by ship. He is known primarily for his bold illustrations depicting romance and adventure. His pirate subjects bring top dollar. He also was a successful, prize-winning painter.

Pirates Escaping Ship, story illustration, "The Burning Galleòn," 1913, s., d., oil on canvas, 34″ × 20″. $9,500

Morning Concert, s., i. with t. on stretcher, prov., exhib., winner John G. Shaffer Prize, 31¾″ × 34½″. $3,850

Under Turbulent Skies, s. Louderback, sight size 19″ × 24¾″, watercolor on paper. $220

Conversing Around the Campfire, s., d. (indistinct), 28″ × 40″. $1,980

Defendent, Judge, and Solister, three wash, s., each 12″ × 19″. $825

Walt Louderback (1887–1941). "The Burning Galleon," publication and date not known. Oil on canvas, 34 × 20 inches, signed and dated upper right, $9,500. PHOTO COURTESY OF ILLUSTRATION HOUSE, INC. *(See Special Notes [20] at back of book.)*

ROBERT McCALL (1919–)

[signature: McCall]

Aerospace and aviation are the specialties of illustrator Robert Theodore McCall. His qualifications included being a World War II bombardier instructor in the Army Air Corps; various documentary painting assignments and contributions can be seen in the U.S. Air Force art collection in Washington, DC, and Colorado Springs, Colorado.

Among his important works is the mural project done in 1976 for the National Aeronautics and Space Museum in Washington, DC. He has served as consultant on several movies, including *Star Trek* and *The Black Hole*.

McCall has designed fourteen commemorative U.S. postage stamps and published two books on space: *Our World in Space* in 1973 and *A Vision of the Future—the Art of Robert McCall*.

Lunar module launching from the moon, s., markers, watercolor, gold-leaf, 15″ × 22″. $600
Exploration of the lunar surface, s., markers, watercolor, 15″ × 22″. $800
Coming Home, double-sided drawing, s., markers, watercolor, 14″ × 21″. $500

MEAD SCHAEFFER (1898–1980)

[signature: Mead Schaeffer]

Collectors of the illustrations of Mead Schaeffer have a choice of either his early swashbuckling, theatrical, and romantic subjects or works based on realism, from Americana to World War II military service illustrations.

Schaeffer studied with Harvey Dunn and Dean Cornwell. While still in his twenties, he was offered assignments by major magazines as well as by Dodd, Mead publishers. For the latter he did a series of sixteen illustrated classics.

The second phase of his career began with an assignment from *The Saturday Evening Post* to do covers with an Americana approach. The paintings done during World War II have the ring of authenticity because Schaeffer "was there" on both submarines and aircraft.

Soldiers Interrogating Princess, story illustration, *McCall's*, 1926, init., d. lower left, oil on canvas, 27″ × 50″, reproduced, *The Illustrator in America 1900–1960s*, p. 158; exhibited, American Federation of the Arts, 1978. .... $6,200

Mead Schaeffer (1892–1980). Illustration for American *magazine, 1957. Oil on canvas, 30½ × 44½ inches, unsigned, $7,500.* PHOTO COURTESY OF THE SOCIETY OF ILLUSTRATORS. *(See* Special Notes *[21] at back of book.)*

The Moss Gatherers, s., preliminary study for *Saturday Evening Post* cover, April 5, 1947 (*Post* cover included with lot), oil on board, 11½″ × 10½″. $550

Navy PC Submarine Lookout on the Murmansk Run, *Saturday Evening Post* cover, WW II, s., oil on canvas, 43½″ × 34″. $7,500

The Swimming Hole, s., lower left, reproduced *Saturday Evening Post* cover, June 25, 1949, oil on board, 22″ × 17″. $9,000

Two Men on a Ship, s. Mead Schaeffer, 30″ × 38″. $2,250

Coral Beach, Bermuda: A Pair, prov., 14½″ × 22″, watercolor. $440

Washington's Visit to Belvoir, frontispiece for *Everybody's Washington*, Alden Arthur Knipe, 32″ × 26½″. $1,100

Lorna Doone, init., d. 30; 32″ × 26″. $1,100

Tropical Adventure, 39″ × 29″. $1,210

As High As My Heart, s. Mead Schaeffer, i. verso, 35″ × 24″. $1,760

NOEL SICKLES (1911–1982)

An early career as a newspaper artist and cartoonist influenced Noel Sickles's style when he became an illustrator. His dexterity with the

Noel Sickles (1911–1982). Illustration for The Spy Who Changed His Mind, Reader's Digest, *May 1970. Gouache on board, 10 × 14 inches, signed lower left, $800.* PHOTO COURTESY OF THE SOCIETY OF ILLUSTRATORS. (See *Special Notes* [22] at back of book.)

Noel Sickles. Illustration for The Old Man and the Sea *by Ernest Hemingway. Ink and wash on board, 8½ × 9½ inches, signed lower right, $1,000.* PHOTO COURTESY OF THE SOCIETY OF ILLUSTRATORS. (See *Special Notes* [23] at back of book.)

brush and his use of black and white with thin color washes highlight his illustrations of American historical subjects and adventure for *The Saturday Evening Post* and the *Reader's Digest* condensed books. His line and halftone drawings illustrated the *Life* magazine publication of Ernest Hemingway's *The Old Man and the Sea*. He also did a series of drawings in black ink and wash for *Life* in 1949, depicting what our first trip to the moon would be like.

There are twelve drawings in all, black ink and wash. They were executed for *Life* magazine, January 17, 1949, issue, as a projection of our first trip to the moon.

Rocket blasting off, s., 17.25″ × 14.25″.
Astronauts sleeping in bunks inside rocket, s., 9.75″ × 15″.
Booster detaching from moon rocket, 9″ × 4.75″, not signed.
Rocket in orbit, 9″ × 4.75″, not signed.
Astronauts looking out porthole at moon, 9″ × 4.75″, not signed.
Four astronauts inside capsule in spacesuits, s., 10.75″ × 15″.
Rocket nose cone, Earth behind (unpublished), 13.75″ × 15″, not signed.
Three astronauts exploring lunar crater, s., 15.25″ × 19″.
Rocket nose cone braking toward lunar surface, s., 13.75″ × 9.5″.
Astronaut climbing down ladder onto moon, 13.75″ × 9.5″, not signed.
Nose cone firing away from lunar surface, 13.75″ × 9.5″, not signed.
Return of the rocket to Earth (unpublished), s., 16.25″ × 12″.
....$6,500 as a lot
Nighttime Arrest, story illustration, "Arrest at Stakeout," *Reader's Digest*, gouache, init., 8.5″ × 11.5″. $300
Russian Intrigue, *Reader's Digest*, ink and watercolor, 11″ × 4″ not signed.
.... $600

RICO TOMASO (1898–)

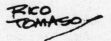

Rico Tomaso studied at the Chicago Art Institute and with Dean Cornwell, Harvey Dunn, and other noted artists. Collectors will find his style similar to Cornwell's, especially his broad brush technique. He is known for illustrations of mystery and adventure. Among the magazines he worked for was *The Saturday Evening Post*.

The Diamond Thief, *Saturday Evening Post*, s., oil on canvas, 30″ × 39″.
.... $3,500
Melee, *Saturday Evening Post*, s., oil on canvas, 26″ × 52″. $2,500
Girl with tulips, s., oil on canvas, 40.75″ × 26″. $3,000

BUSINESS AND INDUSTRY

by Robert Benney

Award-winning illustrator Robert Benney is listed, along with his works, in the "War and Military" chapter, though he was equally adept at creating illustrations for business and industry.

Orson Lowell (1871–1956). Leslie's magazine cover. Oil on canvas, 33 × 28¼ inches, $2,000. PHOTO COURTESY OF GUERNSEY'S.

There are certain conditions that the commercial illustrator must accept when creating art for business and industry. The question is it fine art or commercial art? is of little interest to the director of a large corporation that exists only to sell company products. Instead, the primary factors are, does the picture tell the story and do it with taste and the dignity becoming to the product or industry? In the case of institutional advertising, will its art or aesthetic content carry over in the public's subconscious mind the goodwill that is so much coveted?

Often, the same artist is retained for a series of illustrations, from magazine ads to the company's annual report. Many of America's most famous illustrators did some of their finest work for advertising campaigns. Among them are N. C. Wyeth, Franklin Booth, and Walter Biggs, published during the early part of the 20th century. Henry Raleigh's drawings for Maxwell House Coffee are quality works of art.

Sometimes the early-20th-century illustrators did not only the magazine cover and an inside story but a few ads as well, J. C. Leyendecker and Coles Phillips among them. In addition to magazine advertising, folders, posters, booklets, postcards, catalogs, and just about any type of promotional material was illustrated.

After World War II, public interest in travel created another opportunity for artists. Steamship lines, travel agencies, commercial airlines, and railways began aggressive advertising campaigns. Business magazines commissioned illustrators to do covers relating to business and business tycoons. However, more and more, photography took over the illustrator's work. By the end of the 1950s, jobs for illustrators in this field seemed to be sinking into oblivion. Fortunately for today's growing crop of illustrators, business and industry once again has turned to the illustrator to do what the camera can't always do—create new and exciting images using a variety of techniques and media.

JOHN ATHERTON (1900–1952)

After working at several West Coast art studios, John Atherton moved to New York, where he did illustrations for such advertising clients as General Motors, Shell Oil, and the Container Corporation of America. He also did covers for *The Saturday Evening Post*, *Fortune*, and *Holiday*. His versatility gained him equal fame as a "fine" artist, as well as awards for gallery exhibits. His love of fishing resulted in a book he authored, *The Fly and the Fish* and many illustrations on the subject.

John Atherton. "The Eclipse." Watercolor, signed. Reproduced: Ad for Metropolitan Life. Collier's 2/26/38, 14 × 13½ inches, $400. PHOTO COURTESY OF GUERNSEY'S.

Industrial Clothmaking, magazine cover design, *Fortune*, gouache on board, 13″ × 10.25″, not signed. $400

The Eclipse, reproduced, ad for Metropolitan Life, *Collier's*, Feb. 26, 1938, s., tearsheet inc. in lot, watercolor, 14″ × 13½″; 1939 *Annual of Advertising Art* award winner. $400

ROBERT FAWCETT (1903–1967)

During his long career, Robert Fawcett came to be known as "the illustrator's illustrator." Considered a superb draftsman, he received his training in drawing at the Slade School of London University. Returning to America in 1924, he began his career as an illustrator and advertising artist. Among his finest works were the series of illustrations done for *Collier's* Sherlock Holmes stories in the early 1950s. He also undertook reportorial assignments for such magazines as *Look*. Collectors will find

Robert Fawcett. Logging advertisement. Pen and ink, $750. PHOTO COURTESY OF ILLUSTRATION HOUSE, INC.

Robert Fawcett. "Jefferson at Monticello." Watercolor, 17¾ × 26½ inches, signed. Reproduced calendar illustration, $700. PHOTO COURTESY OF GUERNSEY'S.

his illustrations in a variety of media. His book, *On the Art of Drawing*, published in 1958, is still in many public libraries.

Bouquet of Flowers in a Vase, init., d. 1960, pastel, graphite, and crayon, 16.5″ × 17″. $100
Jefferson at Monticello, calendar illustration, s., watercolor, 17¾″ × 26½″. $700
In the Art Gallery, *Collier's*(?), Dec. 1955, init., gouache, 18.5″ × 14.25″. $2,500
Self-Portrait with Model, inits., exhib., illus. for *Woman's Home Companion*, Nov. 1955, 27″ × 21¾″, pen, brush, black ink, ink wash, and gouache on board. $935
Greeting the Master, inits., exhib., illus. for *The Saturday Evening Post*, 14½″ × 18½″, gouache, pen and black ink on board. $1,650

BERNARD FUCHS (1932–)

In 1975, Bernard Fuchs became the youngest illustrator ever elected to the Society of Illustrators Hall of Fame. Before that, at the age of thirty, he was named Artist of the Year by the Artists Guild of New York.

He was born in O'Fallon, Illinois, and studied at the Washington University Art School in St. Louis. He worked for a variety of Detroit ad-

*Bernard Fuchs. "Longchamps Race." Oil on canvas, 19 × 40 inches,
$7,500.* PHOTO COURTESY OF ILLUSTRATION HOUSE, INC.

vertising art studios for five years before moving to Westport,
Connecticut, where he began getting magazine assignments.

His illustrations have appeared in *Redbook, Sports Illustrated, Mc-
Call's, Cosmopolitan, TV Guide,* and other magazines. As a gallery
painter he has had one-man shows and has done official portraits of
Presidents Kennedy and Johnson. (See *Special Notes* [24] at back of
book.)

Batting Practice, "Still a Grand Old Game," *Sports Illustrated*, Aug. 16, 1976,
s., oil on canvas, 26 ″ × 25 ″. $6,800
Boxing, Entertainment and Sports Programming Network, 1980, init., oil on
canvas, 42 ″ × 28 ″. $8,500
Teeing Off, U.S. Open, Marlboro calendar, *Sports Illustrated*, June 6, 1988,
init., preliminary study, oil on canvas, 7 ″ × 14.5 ″. $2,250
Quarterback, *TV Guide* cover, fall 1981, s., oil on canvas, 32 ″ × 24 ″.
.... $5,400
Reader's Digest Books, 1983, init., oil on canvas, 23 ″ × 24 ″. $7,500
Louis Comfort Tiffany, Borden calendar, Sept. 1973, s., colored inks, 26 ″ ×
26 ″. $6,800
The Milliner's Shop, London *Reader's Digest*, 1980, init., oil on canvas, 29 ″
× 21 ″. $4,050
Still Life with Horn, calendar, Nov. 1982, init., oil on canvas, 24 ″ × 36 ″.
.... $10,500
The Real Thing, *McCall's*, June 1979, init., oil on canvas, 24 ″ × 36 ″.
.... $4,950
Venice Canal, init., oil on canvas, 40 ″ × 18 ″. $8,500
Spanish Galleon, Exxon, 1978, init., oil on canvas, 18 ″ × 53 ″. $6,800
Portrait of Dick Cavett, magazine cover, *TV Guide*, Dec. 5, 1970, s., gouache
and pastel, 20.5 ″ × 13.5 ″. $1,100
Portrait of Diane Keaton, *The New Yorker*, 1979, s., pencil, 21 ″ × 9 ″.
.... $1,200

Dan Rather, alternate *TV Guide* cover, May 30, 1981, init., oil on canvas, 24″ × 15″. $7,500
Portrait of Telly Savalas, *TV Guide* cover, Jan. 3, 1976, s., oil on canvas, 27″ × 18″. $7,500
Portrait of Ava Gardner, M-G-M calendar, Dec. 1977, init., oil on canvas, 25″ × 18″. $5,100
Portrait of James Garner, *TV Guide* cover, June 2, 1979, init., oil on canvas, 21″ × 14″. $7,500
Portrait of Barbra Streisand, for the movie *Yentl*, 1983, s., pencil, 20″ × 9″.
.... $1,200
Bridie Chance, ''The Capricorn Stone,'' *Reader's Digest Books*, 1980, init., oil on canvas, 28″ × 21″. $3,000
Patti and Sara, ''Basic Instructions,'' *McCall's*, Apr. 1979, s., oil on canvas, 24″ × 35″. $10,000
Kelly on a Swing, ''The Summer of the Yes-No Girl,'' *Redbook*, July 1975, s., oil on canvas, 17″ × 17″. $5,100
Rose and Bob on the Beach, ''Time Out of Yesterday,'' *Good Housekeeping*, May 1977, init., oil on canvas, 28″ × 28″. $6,800
Statue of Liberty, s., oil on canvas, 40″ × 30″. $13,500
Ship and Lavender Moon, Neenah Paper Co., 1982, init., oil on canvas, 36″ × 20″. $6,300

JOHN GANNAM, A.N.A. (1907–1965)

JOHN
GANNAM

John Gannam was a dedicated, self-taught illustrator. Forced to leave school at fourteen, at the death of his father, he worked at a variety of menial jobs. The turning point came early, when, as a messenger boy in an engraving house, he became interested in the work of the men who did the layouts, drawings, and lettering for the engravings. Close study and practice ripened his talents, and he began work in commercial art studios in Chicago and Detroit several years later. Upon moving to New York, he was able to sell himself as a magazine illustrator. His first assignment was for *Woman's Home Companion*, followed by continuous assignments from other magazines. However, some of his most memorable illustrations were done for advertisers such as Pacific Mills, Ipana, and St. Mary's Blankets. Collectors look for examples showing his use of watercolors, which was his usual medium, although he also used oils.

Christmas Morning, Pacific Mills advertisement, s., watercolor, 17″ × 17″.
.... $2,000
Western Couple, ''The Silver Desert,'' *Collier's*, Aug. 2, 1935, black-and-white watercolor, 13½″ × 21″, not signed. $1,100
Fiesta Time in the Southwest, illus. for advertisement for U.S. Brewers Foundation, December 1952, oil on canvas, 30″ × 33″. $1,300

Peter Helck. "Screwball on Wheels." Reproduced in True *magazine, Nov. 1955. Casein on illustration board, 15½ × 31 inches, $9,500.* PHOTO COURTESY OF LES MANSFIELD, FINE AMERICAN ILLUSTRATIVE ART.

C. PETER HELCK (1897–) N.A.

PETER HELCK

Considered one of the most important illustrators on the subjects of business and industry, C. Peter Helck's works show his attention to fine details. He studied first at the Art Students League of New York, then privately with such important teachers as Frank Brangwyn.

His illustrations have been for such advertising clients as General Electric, Mack Trucks, National Steel Corporation, and Chevrolet. His editorial work has appeared in many national magazines such as *Esquire* and *True*. (See *Special Notes* [25] at back of book.)

Frieze of Historical Figures, 8″ × 38″, pen and brush and black ink on board. $352
Two Against the Sky, abandoned factory, PA, s., oil on canvas, 24″ × 30″, exhib. "Directions in American Painting," Carnegie Institute, 1941; another version of this painting in *Famous Artists Schools* text, lesson 4, gatefold at p. 19. ....$3,000
Pilot House, s. Helck, sight size 10″ × 12″, gouache on paper. $110

EDWIN HENRY (1900–?)

Edwin Henry

Edwin Henry was an important part of the growing field of advertising illustration in the 1920s and 1930s in Chicago. Together with partners

Howard Stevens and Haddon Sundblom, he established an art service that produced advertising for Studebaker, Packard, Quaker Oats, Camel and Chesterfield cigarettes, and many others. Henry's work also appeared in major magazines, illustrating stories. Collectors can recognize his works by the fine use of color and sensitivity to the subject matter. Edwin Henry founded the famous Chicago studio with Haddon Sundblom.

Girl on Telephone, oil en grisaille on canvas, 30″ × 24″, not signed. . $400
A Gallant Rescue, s., oil on canvas, 34″ × 24″. $750
Swimmer Rescued from Cliff, story illustration, s., oil on canvas, 34″ × 24″. $900

GUY HOFF (1889–1962)

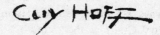

Guy Hoff began his career as a commercial illustrator for the Niagara Lithograph Company in Buffalo, New York. Moving to New York City, he did program covers for the Shubert theaters and then sold his first magazine cover to *Smart Set*. Others were done for *The Saturday Evening Post* and *Pictorial Review*. Hoff continued to do advertising art along with his magazine illustrations. Among his clients were Lux and Ivory soaps. After 1938, he did paintings and pastels for exhibition.

Blonde in blue scarf, magazine cover, probably *Smart Set,* c. 1930, s., pastel on sandboard, 20″ × 16″. $600
Cover Girl, s., d. 52, exhib. The Illustrator in America, 1900–1960, Albany, GA, November 1985, pastel on ill., 38″ × 28″. $2,000
Off the Shoulder, *Home* magazine, Feb. 19, 1946, s., pastel, 40″ × 30″. $6,800

FRANK HOFFMAN (1888–1958)

Hoffman, a lover of horses and other animals, spent his youth working and sketching around stables. In 1916, after rejection for military service because of an eye defect, he went to Taos, New Mexico, to paint. Advertisers discovered his talent, and he worked on national campaigns, eventually specializing in Western subjects, for important national magazines.

Collectors can recognize his work by the bold, broad brush work and striking colors. Since he painted more than 150 canvases in the 1940s and 1950s for Brown and Bigelow calendars, in addition to his many dry brush drawings for magazines, there are many yet to come to market.

Two Cowboys and Woman with Horses, story illustration, "Riders in the Hills," s., dry-brush and watercolor, 21″ × 19.5″. $7,500

WALTER BEACH HUMPHREY (1892–1966)

Walter Beach Humphrey graduated from Dartmouth University. The murals he later painted for the university, with nude Indian maidens, and his depiction of Eleazar Wheelock, founder and first president of Dartmouth, as a roguish rum dispenser, were a controversial subject for many years. Not always so controversial, Humphrey also did murals for the Warren Country Court at the municipal center in Glens Falls, New York.

Humphrey's career as an illustrator began in 1917, when he did illustrations and covers for magazines such as *The Saturday Evening Post*, *Collier's*, *Popular Science*, and others. His successes included advertising assignments for such clients as Brown and Bigelow Calendar Co.

Walter Beach Humphrey. "Energy." Charcoal, 18¼ × 27¼ inches, initialed, $850. PHOTO COURTESY OF GUERNSEY'S.

138

Protective, girl with raised fist has arm around little boy who is crying, Comprehensive study for an *American* magazine cover, charcoal, 18″ × 14½″, estate stamped. $50

Four American Junior Red Cross posters. $225

Starting the New Year Right, *Country Gentleman* cover (New Year 1922), s., oil on canvas, 24″ × 20″. $1,100

Industrial mural studies: (1) "The Brick Layer," init., charcoal, 27¾″ × 20¾″; (2) "The Carpenter," init., charcoal, 27¾″ × 20¾″. $550

Washington Greets Wounded Lafayette, comprehensive study for Brown & Bigelow calendar series of George Washington, charcoal, 25″ × 36″, estate stamped. $100

Friends, *American* magazine cover, January 1926, s., copy of cover included in lot, oil on canvas, 14¾″ × 11¼″. $500

Washington Crossing the Delaware, comprehensive study for calendar illustration (Brown & Bigelow Washington series), charcoal, 25″ × 36″, estate stamped. $150

Wings, s., WW II, charcoal, 13″ × 48″. $450

His Majesty, the Janitor, cover painting, *Saturday Evening Post*, Jan. 13, 1923, s., oil on canvas, 24″ × 20″. $6,000

Father Skips Church, final preliminary drawing for a *Saturday Evening Post* cover, s., charcoal on paper, 26″ × 20″. $1,100

George Washington and His Troops, inits., W.B.H., sight size 28½″ × 39½″, pencil heightened with white on paper. $110

After Dinner Music, t., s. Walter Beach Humphrey, 28″ × 18″, oil on board. $1,540

WILLIAM ANDREW LOOMIS (1892–1959)

ᴀɴᴅʀᴇɴ
ʟᴏᴏɯɪs

A visit to the studio of Howard Chandler Christy was a deciding factor that brought William Andrew Loomis into the field of illustration. Loomis had a long, successful career as both an advertising and editorial illustrator, doing covers as well as illustrations for *The Saturday Evening Post*.

Painter and model, story illustration, "Time of Learning," 1946, s. lower right, oil on canvas, 22″ × 36″. $4,800

Wings of Progress, small 3-engine passenger plane and a c. 1934 green Ford sedan with passengers, image size 18½″ × 28″. $3,025

Women Must Work, s. Andrew Loomis, t. on old lady affixed verso, illus. for *Woman's Home Companion*, 36″ × 28″. $880

Ouch, a boy sucking the thumb he has just hit with a hammer while his dog leaps to console him, s., 28″ × 36″. $880

Playtime, a boy and girl at play while their mother watches, s., 22″ × 28″ $880

William Andrew Loomis. Oil on canvas. "New Throw Rug." Black and white, signed lower right, 34 × 24 inches. PHOTO COURTESY OF DU MOUCHELLES ART GALLERIES.

Apple Kiss, Halloween clown and witch eating dangling apples, s., 30″ × 32″. $1,760
A Good Book, s. Andrew Loomis, 14″ × 20″. $2,090

FREDERIC KIMBALL MIZEN (1888–1965)

Frederic Mizen

Chicagoan Frederic Kimball Mizen excelled not only in outdoor advertising and magazine advertising illustration but also in fiction illustration for leading magazines, among them *The Saturday Evening Post* and *Cosmopolitan*. Included were magazine covers. His long-running series of advertising paintings for the Coca-Cola Company appeared in magazines, newspapers, and billboards. In his later years he did portraits.

Star-Spangled Woman, advertisement, s., oil on canvas, 32″ × 51″. . $3,200
Couple strolling at a fair, illustration, s. lower left, oil on canvas, 0.5″ × 17.75″. $2,800

Robert Riggs. "The Slave Schooner." Reproduced in Life *magazine, Sept. 3/56.* How the Negro Came to Slavery in America *by Robert Wallace, p. 56 foldout. Oil on board, 20 × 39¼ inches, initialed lower right, $25,000.* PHOTO COURTESY OF LES MANSFIELD, FINE AMERICAN ILLUSTRATIVE ART.

WILLIAM MEADE PRINCE (1893–1951)

Like many illustrators, William Meade Prince began his career in Chicago as an advertising artist. After five years he moved to Westport, Connecticut, where he was able to do illustrations for New York magazines and indulge in his love of horses and riding. He later moved to Chapel Hill, North Carolina, where he had grown up, and continued to do illustrations. In the 1940s he did a long series of ads for the Dodge Automobile Co.

German soldier pushing over the Statue of Liberty, painting for a WW I Liberty Bonds poster, "Don't let him get away with it!" s., oil on canvas, 29½″ × 20″. $1,000
Gone Fishing, two advertising illustrations for Dodge, c. 1940, s., oil en grisaille on canvas, 21.25″ × 19″. $1,800
Collecting Eggs, s., 21″ × 19″. $1,800
Dodge Brothers Coach, s., original for one of a long series of ads for the Dodge Automobile Co., oil on canvas, 19″ × 27½″. $700

ROBERT RIGGS (1896–1970) N.A.

Born in Decatur, Illinois, Robert Riggs studied at James Milliken University in Illinois and at the Art Students League in New York.

After spending two years in the army during World War I, he stayed for several months of study in France at the Academie Julian in Paris. Returning to America, he began doing sketching for the N. W. Ayer & Son advertising agency. Aside from the many advertising illustrations he did over the years, he was a successful artist in fine arts, doing his favorite subjects: clowns and prize fighting. He turned many into lithographs, which are in museum collections at the Dallas Museum of Fine Arts, the Library of Congress, and the Brooklyn Museum.

Escape with the Loot, s., egg-tempera on panel, 12″ × 28½″. $4,000
Washington arriving in New York for his Inauguration, editorial illustration, s.,reproduced *American History Illustrated* cover, April 1989, exhib. Fairfield (CT) University, 1985, oil on panel, 18″ × 36″. $4,400

CHILDREN

by Kendra Krienke

Since the age of eight, when she wrote and illustrated a book and a cartoon strip just for fun, Kendra Krienke has been involved with reading, painting, and writing. As an adult, she began collecting children's books and the original art created for them. In 1982, after dealing in 19th- and early-20th-century art, she became one of the first to sell American illustrations for children. Her specific interest, along with the better-known illustrators, has been to uncover the works of obscure illustrators and bring them to the attention of collectors. For her, "the unfamiliar always has a certain attraction." In 1989, she guest-curated an exhibition, "Childhood Enchantments," at the Museum of Cartoon Art in Rye Brook, New York.

Prior to the 19th century, illustration for children, as we know it, hardly existed. Though children's books were originally conceived to instruct, they have become, since the Victorian Age, instruments that allow children to see beyond the everyday facts to discover the fantastical "imagined nation"—a world not limited by rules. The pleasure of this discovery, though conveyed by words, is more immediately perceived by visual images created by the illustrators of children's stories.

During the last quarter of the 19th century, fantasy became the fashion. The sensibilities of the Victorian age had established children as important considerations and their interests as viable commercial enterprises. As the attitude toward children changed, so had the illustrations that proliferated their literature. Gone were the crudely printed wood-cut illustrations, grimly instructive and fearful in tone. In their place were fairies and elves, courageous lads, lively animals, and nursery rhyme characters, all recorded evidence of the land of enchantment, a child's world where nothing is demanded of you but an open mind and the belief that possibilities are endless.

Developing in tandem with the new status of children were the awesome improvements in printing. The introduction of photography allowed the use of the half-tone process, which meant that watercolors and oil paintings could be reproduced with shading rather than only simple line drawings. As photography progressed, color duplication also became possible and continued to improve as the century drew to a close. The printing advances attracted better artists.

Harold Gaze. "The Fairy Swing." Watercolor and pen and ink, 11⅝ × 8⅝ inches, signed, dated 1925, lower left. Price range for his paintings, $1,500–$5,000. PHOTO COURTESY OF KENDRA KRIENKE, CHILDREN'S ILLUSTRATIONS, NEW YORK.

Publishers were competitive by the 1890s and desired the best authors and artists for their publications. The industrialized age offered, along with its problems, greater leisure and spending ability. Children were gratified with paper toys, games, and books, and illustration increased the desirability of all. With the realization that marketable success could rest with illustration, a new era for illustrators for children and fantasy was born.

The most influential figure in changing the taste of children's illustration was Mary Mapes Dodge. With the notable exception of Felix Octavius Carr Darley (1822–1888), who illustrated Washington Irving's *Legend of Sleepy Hollow* (1848) and *Rip Van Winkle* (1849), American illustration in the mid-19th century was primitive and awkward. In 1873, the children's magazine *Our Young Folks* was sold to Scribner & Co. and integrated with the more famous periodical, *St. Nicholas*, with Mrs. Dodge as editor, and the course of illustration for children in America took a positive turn. Mary Mapes Dodge was already established in children's literature as the author of *Hans Brinker and the Silver Skates* (1865). Illustrated by Darley and Thomas Nast, this first American "classic" children's book is important because of its naturalism.

Howard Pyle (discussed elsewhere in this book) was at the center of the new American illustration. His illustrations and fairy tales reflect the nostalgic point of view in the late 19th century. His positive point of view marked a change from the earlier European-influenced, terror-inspiring fairy tales.

Characteristically American in spirit are the inventive Brownies of Canadian-born Palmer Cox (1840–1924). It was the introduction of humor, a desire to truly amuse children, that Mrs. Dodge, as editor of *St. Nicholas*, was responsible for in the late 19th century. The periodical introduced the Brownies in 1883, and the mischievous, well-meaning elfin creatures became the rage.

Written in 1900 by L. Frank Baum, *The Wizard of Oz*, an American classic, stands as one of the first important full-color children's books. Its illustrator, W. W. Denslow (1856–1915), produced characters that leapt to life with strong linear delineation on a flat poster-like plane of color.

TIPS

A signature on a work of art is reassuring but not always necessary if the provenance is legitimate and the item speaks for the artist simply in the way it's painted. (After all, a fake can have a signature!) The most important thing collectors can do is train their eye as to what is good. A name means nothing if the artwork is bad. In the field of children's illustration, there are numerous works of art—some unsigned, others signed by unlisted artists—that are artistically very fine. Look at the details of a painting. Notice the way the artist uses line and applies paint, and note the way the piece is composed. Familiarize yourself with the spirit or point of view of the artist. Register an overall response to a work of art and become acquainted with the artist's style.

Fortunately, in the area of American children's art, there are few artists bringing high enough prices to warrant faking. With the exception of some of the Brandywine artists (Jessie Willcox Smith, Maxfield Parrish), no one has much cause to forge artwork or fake signatures. That is the wonderful advantage of collecting American illustration for children and fantasy; so much is available by virtually unknown or forgotten artists at reasonable prices!

Many of the illustrations created for children are watercolors or drawings on paper or illustration board and often need special care. Proper framing is important. Only conservation materials should touch the piece, and art should never be in direct contact with glass. Protective Plexiglas can be used to guard watercolors from the harsh rays of the sun, but it is always better to hang or store works on paper away from direct light. Condition is an important consideration in buying and selling art, and while proper restoration or conservation is acceptable, it must be performed only by a professional.

Reginald Birch. "The Man in the Moon." Pen and ink drawing, 16¾ × 11⅝ inches. Price range, $300–$1,200. PHOTO COURTESY OF KENDRA KRIENKE, CHILDREN'S ILLUSTRATIONS, NEW YORK.

REGINALD BIRCH (1858-1943)

Mrs. Dodge launched the career of Reginald Birch. Always interested in quality art, she purchased a Birch illustration in 1881. The London-born illustrator had moved to this country with his family in 1870, returned to Europe for study in Munich, and eventually, in 1886, illustrated Frances Hodgson Burnett's *Little Lord Fauntleroy*, which catapulted him to fame and enslaved a generation of boys to lace, velvet suits, and long curls. A master of pen and ink, Birch's work has a graceful assuredness and delicate spontaneity. He worked prolifically for *St. Nicholas*, the old *Life*, and *Harper's*, until his death at eighty-five.

Boy in Jester's Costume Sitting, Standing Dog, "HollyBerry and Mistletoe," *St. Nicholas*, s., pen and ink, 13″ × 16″. $350
Grandma Knitting on Earth and in Heaven, story illustration for "The Scarf" by Ivy O. Eastwick, s., pen and ink, 17″ × 11.5″. $125
Fairies and Elves in Moonlight, Jonathan Bing, s., pen and ink, 17″ × 12.5″, together with two other illus. from same book. $1,000
The Pirates' Lair, cover illus. for Malcolm Douglas's *The Pirates' Lair*, 17⅛″ × 12½″, pen and black ink on paper. $88
Illustration, s. Reginald Birch, slight soiling, very slight foxing, sight size 9⅜″ × 8⅝″, pen and ink on paper. $165
Sir Charles and His Jester, drawing, s. with artist's device, illus. in *St. Nicholas*, 16⅞″ × 19″, brush and black ink and Chinese white on paper. $385
A Trusted Companion and Man Against Nature, two drawings: first, an illus. "Ask Lord Roberts," *Century* 1912, 11″ × 8″; second, for "Jeremy Tate" in *Century*, 13″ × 10″, pen and black ink on paper. $55
Too Many Spectators, illus. for *Life* magazine, 12¾″ × 18½″, pen and black ink on board. $88

GEORGE BREHM (1878-1966)

George Brehm discovered early in his career that his special talents lay in depicting children, especially boys and their fun and games. He attended the Art Students League in New York. His first illustration assignment came from *Reader's Magazine*, published in Indianapolis, Indiana. As a result of this work, *Delineator* magazine in New York gave him an assignment. After that his illustrations appeared in such magazines as *The Saturday Evening Post*.

Family Moving into "Four Winds Cottage," seven preliminary studies, *Collier's*, ink and watercolor, 11.5″ × 10.5″, 6 others, some initialed. $225
Man Struck by Snowball, story illustration, "Midwinter Madness," Mar. 25, 1926, s. lower right, oil on canvas en grisaille, 24″ × 34″. $900

Harrison Cady. "Winter in Rockport." Signed Harrison Cady lower left. Inscribed and dedicated on the reverse. Oil on masonite, 24 × 35 inches, $2,000. PHOTO COURTESY OF SKINNER GALLERIES.

HARRISON CADY (1877–?)

Cady continued the cartoon-like approach to children's illustration into the first illustrations for the 20th-century generation. His first permanent job was as illustrator for McLoughlin Brothers. Eventually, he joined the staff of the *Brooklyn Daily Eagle* and began his beetle drawings for the old *Life* magazine. Influenced by his naturalist father, his humanly ornamented beetles and other insects infected the humorous sensibilities of American children. Although he illustrated for many publications, such as *St. Nicholas* and *The Saturday Evening Post*, he is best remembered for his comical illustrations for the Thornton Burgess bedtime stories of Peter Rabbit, Johnny Chuck, and others. The creation of the Burgess characters began in 1913 and continued, along with an amiable relationship with the author, until the 1950s. Cady exhibited as a nonillustrative artist, but it is his strong sense of design and inventiveness as an illustrator for which we remember him.

Peter Rabbit and the Spiderweb, *Peter Rabbit*, 1921, pen and ink, 7.5″ × 7.25″, not signed. $250
Peter Rabbit, "He tries to educate the masses but Unc' Billy Possum proves too much for him," s., Sunday page, Oct. 17, 1920, pen and ink, 21½″ × 30″. $200

Moonlight Sonata, finely detailed bedroom scene, woman entering bathtub, man playing piano with dog watching, pencil study and drypoint, matted, 19″ × 15″. $1,200
The Adventures of Peter Cottontail, s., Shadow the Weasel chasing Squirrel, pen line and wash, 13″ × 9.5″. $900
St. Nicholas, s., pen line and wash, 13.5″ × 10.25″. $900

FANNY YOUNG CORY (COONEY) (1877–1972)

F Y C O R Y

Fanny Young Cory was one of the trail blazers at the turn of the century. She was a contributor to *St. Nicholas* and other periodicals and is best known for her simple, often humorous line and wash drawings for chil-

Fanny Young Cory. "The Babies." From One O'Cat, Schwab & Wolf, New York, 1907. Pen and ink and watercolor, 15¾ × 10½ inches. Price range, $300–$2,500. PHOTO COURTESY OF KENDRA KRIENKE, CHILDREN'S ILLUSTRATIONS, NEW YORK.

dren. Often she decorated her illustrations with borders divided into sections containing subsidiary pictures. She also had a knack of interrupting a border by using a figure that seems to be standing beyond the edge, as if about to enter the picture itself. Her pieces are usually signed with a vertical monogram. Cory created illustrations for Abbie Farwell Brown's *A Pocketful of Posies* (1902) and Josephine Dodge Daskam's *The Madness of Phillip* (1902). In addition, she wrote and illustrated three books for children, including *Little Miss Muffet* (1936). Price range for her work
.... $300–$2,500

LEO AND DIANE DILLON (1933–)

L+D DILLON

Schooled in design, typography, printmaking, woodcut art, and pochoir (the art of hand-coloring illustrations), Leo and Diane Dillon "work as one." This couple is successful in all facets of illustration. Their illus-

Leo and Diane Dillon. "Cricket Woman." Cricket magazine, 1978, cover. Pastel and watercolor, $3,000. Copyright © '78–89 L & D Dillon. PHOTO COURTESY OF LEO AND DIANE DILLON.

trations have appeared in such magazines as *The Saturday Evening Post* and *Ladies' Home Journal.* Since 1970 they have illustrated over a dozen books for children, record album covers for Caedmon, and R.C.A. Victor. They have received many awards, including the Hans Christian Andersen award in 1978. They are the subject of a book titled *The Art of Leo and Diane Dillon,* published by Ballantine Books.

GRACE DRAYTON (1877–1936)

Another early and energetic woman illustrator was the creator of Dolly Dingle and the Campbell Kids. The style of Grace Gebbie Drayton (Wiederseim) demonstrated more the aspects of caricature, but her skill was nonetheless confident and won an important place for her in the history of women illustrators. In the first years of the 20th century, she began her long-term relationship with the Campbell Soup Company. At the same time, she started illustrating and sometimes writing children's

Grace Drayton. "Dolly Dingle in India." Watercolor and pen and ink. Price range: paintings, $1,500–$6,500; pen and ink drawings, $200–$500.
PHOTO COURTESY OF KENDRA KRIENKE, CHILDREN'S ILLUSTRATIONS, NEW YORK.

books, often collaborating with her sister, Margaret G. Hays. The results over the years were the creation of such characters as Kaptin Kiddo, the Baby Bears, and later, Dolly Dimples and Bobby Bounce. The chubby little balloon-cheeked figures of her cartoons were based on her childhood drawings of herself. The February 1913 issue of *Pictorial Review* magazine announced the entrance of Drayton's "Funny Babies." Appearing for the first time in March 1913, the Dolly Dingle paper dolls were a regular feature until April 1933. Grace Drayton's illustrations appeared in many other publications of the day as well, including *Youth's Companion* (1910) and *St. Nicholas* (1913–1914). Through her two marriages and divorces (the same number as Rose O'Neill), her signature varies from V. G. Gebbie, G. G. Wiederseim, or G. G. W. (after 1900) to G. G. Drayton or G. G. D. (after 1911). Because Drayton's work was widely reproduced in books, magazine, and postcards, the collector is likely to see occasional copies. Generally drawn for amusement rather than deception, these pieces lack the sureness and fine details of the original.

Diana and Reggie Paper Dolls, illustration, s., ink and watercolor, 14.75″ × 14.5″ (Di and Reg were Dolly Dingle's English friends). $1,700

EDWARD WINDSOR KEMBLE (1861–1933)

Kemble

The humorous side of American life could not have been better illustrated by anyone than the entertaining Edward Windsor Kemble. In 1880, he joined the staff of the *New York Daily Graphic*, and in 1883, he became a staff cartoonist for *Life*. Along with Arthur Burdett Frost, he illustrated the stories of Joel Chandler Harris. Although fantasy was enjoyed in the late 19th century, so was the folklore presented in the tales from the South told by Harris in the form of a black slave, Uncle Remus. The lighthearted pen-and-ink drawings by Kemble adapted themselves well to the text (*Daddy Jake, The Runaway*, 1889). Kemble's fame originally sprang from the drawings he did in 1884 for Mark Twain's *Huckleberry Finn*. That same year he joined the staff of *Century* magazine and also contributed to its sister publication, *St. Nicholas*. His spirited renderings of black subjects and points of view kept him in the public eye, and in 1892, he illustrated Harriet Beecher Stowe's *Uncle Tom's Cabin*. His work for *St. Nicholas*, with its quality of wholesome fun, was seen and appreciated by a wider audience than many illustrators whose work was solely for children.

Old black man in naval hat, story illustration, "Isam listened," "The Hand Trigger," *Century*, s. lower right, pen and ink, 8″ × 4.25″. $650
New Laws, s., pen and ink, 6″ × 9″. $85
Old Woman with Walking Stick, s. Kemble, sight size 9″ × 7½″, pen and ink on paper. $165
The Bum, the Dog and The Pie, two drawings, framed as one, s., overall size 19½″ × 16½″, pen and black ink on paper. $198
Prayer Meeting, drawing, s., illus. for "Bathsheba" by Edith Sessions Tupper for *Associated Sunday Magazine*, Feb. 13, 1910, 6″ × 5″, pen and black ink on paper. $352
Favorate Color and The Crimson Scar, two drawings, both s.; second, d. 90; first, 10¼″ × 13⅞″; second, 13⅛″ × 12⅜″, pen and black ink on paper. $385
The Candy Country, s., i. "Rose a beautiful White figure" and with t., illustration for *Century* magazine, Nov. 1885, 12½″ × 15¾″, pen and black ink on paper. $550

PETER SHEAF NEWELL (1862–1924)

Peter Newell

Another artist who worked in a simple two-dimensional style is the author/illustrator Peter Newell, whose inventive books *The Hole Book* (1908), *The Slant Book* (1910), and *The Rocket Book* (1912) continue in the tradition of the German toy books and McLoughlin Brothers shape and pop-up books. The Newell creations were great successes and are good examples of the art of the book usurping the importance of the text.

Boy excusing himself to friends, "The Carriage Lamp," part 3, s., d. 1899, black-and-white gouache, 8″ × 11.25″. $400
Stung! William Jennings Bryan and Hearst as a porcupine, cover painting for *Harper's Weekly*, Aug 1, 1908, s., red monochrome gouache, 13″ × 12″. $2,000

ROSE O'NEILL (1875–1944)

Considered by Thomas Hart Benton to be "the world's greatest illustrator," O'Neill was not specifically an illustrator for children. Her drawings are distinctive, and her lyrical sweeping gestures and darkly delineated figures display the inimitable talents of this self-taught artist.

She is most famous for her creation of the Kewpies, who first appeared in 1909. These impish babies with turnip-shaped heads, large eyes, and

A Young Hero *By* Peter Newell

Peter Newell. "A Young Hero." Pen and ink, 9 × 11 inches. Price range, $600–$1,800. PHOTO COURTESY OF KENDRA KRIENKE, CHILDREN'S ILLUSTRATIONS, NEW YORK.

Rose O'Neill. "Kewpies Reading Lesson." Pen and ink, 11 × 17 inches. Price range for pen and ink drawings, $1,500–$4,000. PHOTO COURTESY OF KENDRA KRIENKE, CHILDREN'S ILLUSTRATIONS, NEW YORK.

plump bodies were cheerful, blundering, and helpful and were extensively reproduced in periodicals and commercial ads, such as the ones O'Neill produced for Jell-O. The highly collectible Kewpie doll was patented in 1913 and, along with all the other Kewpie items (postcards, ceramics, picture frames, etc.), made Rose O'Neill a rich woman. A flamboyant personality, she was an author, poet, and sculptor as well as an artist, and her artist range covers the cartoon-like to the highly refined.

Rose O'Neill was a regular contributor to *Puck*, where her depictions of women, blacks, and children are humorous and satirical. She also contributed a syndicated cartoon "Kewpieville," which first appeared in the *Ladies' Home Journal.*

Couple and Chaperone s., pencil, brush and ink, 16.75″ × 21.75″. . $1,900
Lady with her cook, gag cartoon, "Getting His Speed," *Puck*, June 6, 1902, s. lower left, pen and ink, dry brush, 19″ × 23″. $900

CLARA ELSENE PECK (1883–?)

Clara Elsene Peck

Clara Elsene Peck was a popular illustrator on the subjects of women and children. She worked for such magazines as *Ladies' Home Journal*. As an advertising illustrator, she worked on campaigns for Metropolitan Life, Procter & Gamble, Aeolian Company, and others.

Nymph and Pan Under a Tree, s., watercolor, 10.25″ × 14″. $1,400

MISCELLANEOUS ILLUSTRATORS

While I have tried to integrate those less known with the more famous, it is impossible to mention all of the deserving artists who produced illustrations for children.

WORTH BREHM (1883–1928)

WORTH BREHM

Some Beau, s., reproduced, *Saturday Evening Post*, charcoal, 25½″ × 16¾″. $475

BEVERLY BRODSKY

Cats Stalking Their Prey, *Secret Places*, s., watercolor, 14.25″ × 24″. $1,350

Johnny Gruelle.
"Raggedy Ann's Lucky
Pennies." Watercolor
and pen and ink. 8¹/8 ×
8³/4 inches. Price range,
$500–$4,000. PHOTO
COURTESY OF KENDRA
KRIENKE, CHILDREN'S
ILLUSTRATIONS, NEW
YORK.

Jessie Willcox Smith.
"Chicks Own Cottage"/
"A Children's Picnic."
Graphite on paper. Signed
lower left, titled within
composition. Scattered
foxing and staining,
12¹/2 × 9¹/2 inches,
$550. PHOTO COURTESY
OF SKINNER GALLERIES.

CHARLOTTE HARDING (1873–1951)

C. Harding. cc.

Woman Seated in a Train, story illustration, "I wish the entire family wouldn't insist upon doing my packing," "Identifying Anne," *McClure's*, April 1906, s., d. 1905, charcoal and conté, 10″ × 10″. $1,100

Maude Joyce at the Shrine, *Harper's*, c. 1905, charcoal and yellow gouache, 23″ × 14″, not signed. $4,200

VIRGINIA KEEP (1878–)

The Doll Party, s., live doll series, pencil on board, 12″ × 10¼″. $500

FANTASY ART

by Terry Booth

Terry Booth, whose gallery specializes in fantasy illustrations, defines it as "the realistic portrayal of people in imaginary and generally timeless settings." Illustrator Howard Pyle stated, "American illustrators need not confine themselves to American subjects, but they must treat the subjects in a way that will appeal to Americans." That appeal traces back to Howard Pyle, who gave us images of real people in imaginary settings, from King Arthur to Jules Verne's Captain Nemo.

According to Booth, this qualifies as high fantasy. *Another classification is* heroic fantasy *(swords and sorcery), which portrays real people with superhuman powers. They usually are placed in an imaginary primitive environment with education and a formal judicial system at a minimum or lacking altogether.* Dark fantasy *portrays actual people in supernatural circumstances and contemporary settings. Stephen King's novels are a good example of this category.* Future fantasy *portrays real people in future settings.*

The following Fantasy illustrators, with prices, have been selected as among the most important in the field.

THE BROTHERS HILDEBRANDT (1939–)

The brothers Hildebrandt are identical twins who developed an early mutual fascination with art, their major influences being Walt Disney and N. C. Wyeth. Greg and Tim learned and worked together very closely until the early 1980s, when they parted to pursue separate careers. Except for a brief period at the Meinzinger School of Art, the brothers are essentially self-taught. Their development gained immeasurably from the wide variety of experiences they had, which included five years at the Jam Handy film studios and five years of producing documentary films. In 1969 they began producing watercolor illustrations for children's book publishers and got their big break when Ballantine selected them to do the J. R. R. Tolkien calendar for 1976. It was an immediate hit, and by 1978 their calendar had sold over 1 million copies; the Brothers Hildebrandt were stars. Paperback covers, advertising work, movie posters (including the famous original *Star Wars* poster), other calendars, and their own book (*Urshurak*) followed, each meeting with success.

The brothers separated in 1981 to pursue their own careers. Because

The Brothers Hildebrandt. "Mount Doom." Acrylic on panel. Signed lower right, 1977. J. R. R. Tolkien calendar, 30 × 40 inches, $25,000. PHOTO COURTESY OF BRANDYWINE FANTASY GALLERY.

Tim and Greg individually continue to produce outstanding fantasy art and have gone in somewhat different directions, in all probability there will be little further work produced by the brothers combination that so stirred the public's imagination in the late 1970s.

The Land of Giant Mushrooms, 1981 Atlantic calendar, s. lower right, acrylic on panel, 25″ × 33″. $15,000
Mount Doom, 1977 J. R. R. Tolkien calendar, s. lower right, acrylic on panel. $25,000
The Balrog, 1977 J. R. R. Tolkien calendar, *The Art of the Brothers Hildebrandt*, Ian Summers, Ballantine, 1979; p. 33; s., lower right, acrylic on panel, 48″ × 48″. $32,500

GREG HILDEBRANDT (1939–)

Greg Hildebrandt aggressively pursued his career as an independent artist in 1981, the year in which the ''Brothers Hildebrandt'' separated. Shortly thereafter, the paintings for the first of his annual classics was underway (*A Christmas Carol*), art for a Mary Stewart *Merlin* calendar was being planned, and many other projects were demanding attention. Since then, eleven other classics have each required from 20 to 48 of Greg's paintings (and additional drawings) and have consumed the lion's portion of Greg's time with an occasional poster, book cover, or advertising assignment filling the balance.

Captain Hook Fighting Peter, *Peter Pan*, James Barrie, Unicorn Publishing, 1987, p. 155; s. lower right, acrylic on panel, 20″ × 16″. $16,500

Snowdrop, *Greg Hildebrandt's Favorite Fairy Tales*, Unicorn Publishing, 1984, s. lower right, acrylic on panel, 20″ × 16″. $13,000

TIM HILDEBRANDT (1939–)

Tim Hildebrandt began his independent career in 1981, when he and his twin brother Greg (the Brothers Hildebrandt) separated. While each brother's individual art bears a strong relationship to that of the brothers, significant new delights and combinations emerge. Tim tended to be more responsible for the brothers' wonderfully detailed backgrounds, and he has continued this strength in much of his current work. He has expressed great satisfaction in doing landscape paintings, and anyone who has studied one of Tim's willow or sycamore trees can see why. His fertile imagination does not stop there, however, and has produced equally delightful dragons, wizards, and ogres.

Tim has worked closely with his wife, Rita, in pursuing a wide range of ventures that have included a cookbook, a growing collector plate business, and a recent Famous Romantic Figures series for Hamilton Mint. Tim's fascination with Disney has recently been encouraged as well, with a series of children's books done in the Disney style.

The Great Sycamore, 1985, s. lower right, acrylic on panel, unpublished. $15,000

The Giants Clash, 1984 Realms of Wonder calendar, TSR, centerfold illustration, s. lower right, acrylic on panel, 21½″ × 46½″. $6,500

DON MAITZ (1953–)

Don Maitz was raised in Connecticut and graduated from the Paier School of Art in Hamden, Connecticut. His published work includes over 150 commissions, most of them science fiction or fantasy book covers, with several advertising commissions also (notably the "Captain Morgan" rum ads for Seagram's).

Poker Face, cover illustration, Barrington J. Bayley, *The Grand Wheel*, Daw, 1977, s. lower right, acrylic on panel, 26″ × 15½″. $2,000

Seal Level, Shulamith Oppenheim, *The World Invisible*, Berkley, s. lower left, acrylic on panel, 26″ × 35″. $12,000

ROWENA MORRILL (1944–)

Rowena Morrill is the most successful woman in fantasy art today. She has developed a highly individual style and produces artwork of outstanding color and clarity. Born into a military family and hence used to travel, she had a variety of educational experiences that included studying music, and she did not take up painting until she was twenty-one. Once involved with painting, she became deeply committed and dedicated the next years of her life to becoming an artist. Although she studied at the Tyler School of Art in Philadelphia, she credits her artistic abilities primarily to the four ensuing years in which she taught herself to paint.

Morrill has developed a wide following, in Europe as well as in the United States, and has had articles devoted to her art in such prestigious publications as *Omni*, *Zoom* (French), and *L'Espresso*. Her art has graced the covers of a number of important fantasy books, including Anne McCaffrey's Dragon Hall series, Piers Anthony's Xanth series, and the 1981 J. R. R. Tolkien calendar. Her work is done in thin layers of oil on illustration board (leaving no brush strokes), and the bright and wide range of colors she achieves are ideally suited to her careful design and composition.

The Search for Shelter, Anne McCaffrey, *Dragonsinger*, Bantam Books, s. lower right, oil on illustration board, 21″ × 26½″. $11,500

KEITH PARKINSON (1958–)

Keith Parkinson studied at Michigan State University and Kendall School of Design. Following graduation he worked as a freelance artist and produced artwork for pinball machines. In 1982 he was hired as a staff artist by TSR, creators of the "Dungeons and Dragons" phenomenon. His style is highly realistic and colorful and rises above the "swords and sorcery" limitations of many of his peers. His art has been included in all three Dragonlance calendars produced by TSR, with Keith's 1988 calendar centerfold winning the Dark Fantasy Award at the 1987 World Fantasy Convention. For the last year, Keith has worked as a freelance artist and has produced a significant number of paperback covers during this time.

The Dark Lord's Tower, game module cover, Stephen Bowne, *Saga of the Shadow Lord*, TSR Inc., 1986, s. lower right, acrylic on illustration board, 18″ × 19″. $2,500

BORIS VALLEJO (1948–)

Boris Vallejo emigrated to the United States in 1964, after having studied art for several years at the National School of Fine Arts in Lima, Peru. After two years in New York advertising work and eight years as a free-lance artist (much of it in fashion art), Vallejo began producing covers for a number of heroic fantasy magazines that became extremely popular. A series of twenty-four cover paintings for a new edition of Burroughs's Tarzan books cemented his popularity and led to a successful 1978 calendar (a Boris calendar has appeared every year since).

Fear No Evil, cover illustration, *White Magic*, Ace, New York, 1979; puzzle illustration, *White Magic*, Waddington's Puzzles, 1979; Boris Vallejo, *Fantasy Art Techniques*, Arco, 1985, p. 31; cover illustration, J. Robert and L. Bland; *Wizard's Betrayal*, Mayfair Games, 1987; s. lower right, oil on illustration board, 27″ × 17″. $12,500

MICHAEL WHELAN (1950–)

Michael Whelan is the most highly regarded artist in the science fiction and fantasy field today in the judgment of his peers. He has won the World Science Fiction Convention's coveted annual Hugo Award as best professional artist in eight of the last nine years (he withdrew his name in the other year), and in 1988 he won an unprecedented second Hugo when his *Works of Wonder* was named best nonfiction book. He majored in art at San Jose State University (graduating in 1973 as a President's Scholar) and studied at the Art Center College of Design in Los Angeles. Whelan strives to create a "sense of wonder" in each of his paintings that reflects the magic of his own artistic vision and has developed a wide range of techniques that help him effect that communication.

Whelan has produced work in all areas of fantasy and prefers to continue to do so. His objective is to produce the "definitive cover" for the various novels he is asked to illustrate and has met with substantial fan acclaim for his artwork for Anne McCaffrey's Dragonriders of Pern series, Isaac Asimov's Foundation series, and H. Beam Piper's Fuzzy series.

No Exit, cover illustration, H. Beam Piper, *Fuzzies and Other People*, Ace, 1984, init. lower left, acrylic on watercolor board, 28″ × 34½″. $10,000
Storm Warning, Anne McCaffrey, *Killashandra*, Ballantine, 1985, init. lower left on landsled, acrylic on watercolor board, 32″ × 21″. $9,000

FASHION

by Beverly Sacks

For twenty years, Beverly Sacks has been in the business of buying, selling, and collecting vintage American illustration art, specializing in fashion illustrations. As an active member of the Society of Illustrators, she has been a co-chairman of their scholarship fund and contributes articles for their Illustrators Annual. *She ran the first major auction of American illustration art for Phillips Auction Gallery.*

Collecting original fashion illustrations is a very fascinating category in the general field of illustration. The study of fashion trends is, in effect, a reflection of the times. The hemlines go up and down depending on the state of the nation. Since the latter half of the 20th century, the fashion magazines have relied mostly on the use of photography. We have found that the most available and also the most collectible original works date from the 1920s, 1930s, and early 1940s. It was during those periods that the majority of the major fashion illustrators worked.

Currently, the designers of our contemporary fashion do the sketches for their designs and these are primarily used as working sketches and are not reproduced for the general public in today's fashion periodicals. Sometimes, original fashion drawings are still used when advertising fashions in daily newspapers for department store ads.

The original illustrations that I will concentrate on were those reproduced in early fashion magazines (several still exist today) such as *The Delineator, Harper's Bazaar, Vogue, Ladies' Home Journal*, and similar publications.

Some of the earliest fashion illustrations were the *Godey's Lady's Book* prints, which were accompanied by patterns for the home sewer to copy. As fashion designs became more sophisticated, important fashion illustrators began to emerge and grace the covers of the Parisian and American fashion magazines.

Some of the French publications, such as the 1920s *Bon Ton*, produced stunning pochoir (silk screen) prints in wonderful bold colors. These are also collectible today by print collectors. They are wonderful for those with limited funds because they are priced considerably lower than original works and can still be bought for under $100.

Most of the early fashion illustrators worked in gouache, watercolor,

*George Lepape. "Francois." Vogue magazine cover, 1922. Watercolor,
13¼ × 7 inches, signed. Also reproduced in "The Art of the Vogue
Cover," p. 22, $6,000.* PHOTO COURTESY OF SACKS FINE ART, NEW YORK.
*Vogue copyright © 1926, 1927 (renewed 1954, 1955) by The Condé Nast
Publications Inc.*

and pen and ink on illustration board. Therefore, because of the fragile nature of the board and the materials used, they might not be in the best of condition when found. During the periods that they were reproduced, the importance of the art was in the reproduction. Many of them were neglected and suffered abuses in basements and such, many of them tossed out and destroyed. Chances of finding an original illustration in excellent condition would be greater if purchased from a reputable art dealer who would have had the work carefully restored to its original condition and have framed the work with acid-free materials.

In my opinion, the most desirable works were the highly stylized works of the Art Deco period. It was then that such illustrators as George Lepape, Benito, René Bouche, Christian Beraud, George Wolf Plank, André Marty, Helen Dryden, Pierre Brissaud, and Carl "Eric" Erickson worked. Eric worked for *Vogue* magazine from 1925 until his death in 1958. He was a very important fashion illustrator and was referred to as the American Toulouse-Lautrec. He had a major exhibition of his work at the Brooklyn Museum of Art posthumously in 1959. In 1982, Eric became a member of the elite Hall of Fame of the Society of Illustrators Museum of American Illustration, an honor bestowed on the greats of American illustration.

Several of the artists mentioned here were French. I included them because many works were reproduced in American magazines. Also, just as fashions from Paris were copied in our country, many American illustrators were inspired by their French counterparts.

The prices of original fashion illustrators varies greatly depending on where it is found. Certain illustrators, such as George Wolf Plank, are very rare and would command high prices, probably as high as $10,000. I have never seen an original work by Plank. Works by other artists would range from $1,500 to $10,000 for original cover designs. Works that are not in color or that were reproduced inside the magazine in black and white would be worth considerably less, probably, several hundred to several thousand dollars.

Again, prices depend on where you find the work. Comb antique shops, flea markets, and auctions if you are adventurous. If not, dealers who specialize in this field are always the best source. Even if you pay a premium price, you are assured of getting a work that has a dealer's guarantee behind it.

Beware of fakes! Try to get a money-back guarantee if possible, and take your purchase to an expert for authentication. Do your homework.

Wherever you find your original fashion illustrations, have fun doing it and then enjoy their beauty on your walls.

Earl Cordrey. "Wish You Were Here." Gouache, signed. Reproduced King Features Syndicate. Cover illustration, 21½ × 14¼ inches, $175. PHOTO COURTESY OF GUERNSEY'S.

EARL CORDREY (1902–1977)

California-born, Earl Cordrey moved to New York City, where he studied under Pruett Carter and Harold Von Schmidt. He gained fame for his illustration of beautiful girls; the first ones were for Broadway theatrical posters. From there he took his talent to such magazines as *The Saturday Evening Post, Collier's, American Weekly, Redbook,* and others.

Western Landscape, s., watercolor, 20″ × 28″. $350
The Marrying Kind, *Collier's*, July 13, 1946, s., gouache, 21½″ × 14½″; copy of tearsheet included in lot. $500
Beautiful girl reading note while seated at dressing table, s., gouache, red, black, and white, 17½″ × 13″. $250
Wish You Were Here, reproduced: King Features Syndicate Mat, cover illustration, s., gouache, 21½″ × 14¼. $175
The F. Scott Fitzgerald Story, reproduced: *American Weekly* magazine, s., gouache, 20½″ × 14¼″. $125
Caviar or Cole Slaw, *American Weekly*, March 27, 1948, s., gouache, 18″ × 18″. $150

CARL OSCAR AUGUST ERICKSON (ERIC)
(1891–1958)

Eric

Carl Oscar August Erickson (Eric) had two years of formal art training at the Chicago Academy of Fine Arts. His first career experiences were

Carl "Eric" Erickson. "The Flower Hat." Gouache on board. Signed and dedicated to Peggy, 15 × 12 inches, $4,500. PHOTO COURTESY OF SACKS FINE ART, NEW YORK.

with Marshall Field and Lord & Thomas advertising agencies. In 1914 he moved to New York, where he did his first fashion drawings for the *Dry Goods Economist.* He traveled in 1920 to Paris, where he began illustrating for French publications. In 1923 he became a staff illustrator for *Vogue* magazine. By 1940 he had returned to America, still working for Condé Nast. His experience as a society portrait painter in Paris, combined with his work in fashion, led to a wealth of assignments.
Meeting the Celebrity, s., watercolor, 25.5″ × 18″. $650

HARRISON FISHER (1875–1934)

Like so many illustrators, Harrison Fisher began his career at an early age. In Fisher's case, by the age of sixteen he was drawing for the *San Francisco Call,* followed by the *Examiner.* His early instruction had come from his father, a landscape painter, and from studies at the Mark Hopkins Institute of Art. Shortly after moving to New York, he was hired as a staff artist. His talent for drawing beautiful women, especially "the Fisher Girl," established him as a popular cover artist for magazines like *Cosmopolitan* as well as for book publishers.

Carl "Eric" Erickson. Seated woman. Watercolor. 12 × 15½ inches, $3,000. Note: This was done before "Eric" became a famous illustrator and is signed Erickson. PHOTO COURTESY OF AUTHOR.

Edwin Georgi. "The Negligee." Unsigned. Reproduced in Cosmopolitan *magazine. Opaque watercolor, 17 × 13 inches, $675.* PHOTO COURTESY OF GUERNSEY'S.

The Red Cross, s. Harrison C. Fisher, d. 1918, lower left, pastel on canvas, 44″ × 30″ (111.8 × 76.2cm). $24,200
Couple Riding Bicycles, *Puck*, s., pen and ink on paper, 15″ × 12″. $1,200
Fisher Girl, illustrated for *Saturday Evening Post, Life*, and *Scribner's*, 12″ × 9″, watercolor on paper. $330
A Token of Esteem, s., d. 98, illus. for *Puck*, 1898, 19¾″ × 27″, pen, brush, and black ink on board. $495

EDWIN GEORGI (1896–1964)

Georgi

Edwin Georgi began his career as an advertising illustrator but gained his fame as a magazine illustrator specializing in beautiful women in lavish surroundings. His work appeared in such national magazines as *Redbook, Ladies' Home Journal*, and *The Saturday Evening Post*. Since some of his work isn't signed, collectors should learn to recognize his dramatic use of color. His early advertising illustrations, done for Crane Paper Co., Yardley & Co., and Hartford Fire Insurance, are highly collectible.

Two story illustrations: (a) Rehearsal, "The Opportunity" by John Cheever, *Cosmopolitan*, Dec. 1949, s. lower right, trans. and opaque watercolor, 18″ × 26.25″, (b) Administering Smelling Salts, "Cafe Perli," *Saturday Evening Post*, ink and yellow watercolor, 16″ × 16.5″, not signed. $600
The Key, reproduced *Woman's Home Companion*, Jan. 1947, s., gouache, 21″ × 16″, tearsheet included in lot. $1,400
The Negligee, reproduced *Cosmopolitan*, opaque watercolor, 17″ × 13″, unsigned. $675
Clinch under the Blossoms, preliminary sketch, gouache, 25″ × 16″, not signed. $450
Emergency Wife, by May Edginton, black and white watercolor, 9″ × 22″, not signed. $450
Thought-reading machine, "The Prying Professor," *Saturday Evening Post*, s., gouache, 9.5″ × 25″. $1,600

JOHN HOLMGREN (1897–1963)

HOLM
GREN

Keeping up with the fashions of the time, beginning in the 1920s, was John Holmgren's approach to illustration. From the flappers he drew in his first cover illustrations in the 1920s to the fashions of the 1940s, his heroines were as contemporary as his use of color. He also did advertising illustrations for Ford, Alcoa, White Rock, Cunard Lines, and others.

Girl with Two Soldiers, "There'll Come a Day," *Collier's*, s., gouache, 12″ × 14″. $450
Fainted Woman, magazine illus., s., gouache, 16.25″ × 15″. $550
Widow's Weeds, 200 Years of American Illustrators, The Illustrator in America 1880–1980, American Illustrators 1900–1960, Albany, GA, Nov. 1985, s., watercolor, 18″ × 14½″. $1,100

JOHN LaGATTA (1894–1971)

John LaGatta was born in Naples, Italy, and educated in America, where he studied at the New York School of Fine and Applied Art. He began his career in advertising. By the 1930s his illustrations of curvaceous women in clothes that accentuated their sexuality were in demand by *The Saturday Evening Post, Ladies' Home Journal, American*, and other magazines. Advertising clients were equally enthusiastic.

Relaxation and Conversation, s., d. Nov 1935, 28¼″ × 36¼″, gouache and charcoal on board. $3,850
By the Fire, sight size 22″ × 32″, watercolor and gouache on board. $66
White Slip, s., oil on canvas, 21¾″ × 25¾″. $1,600

COLES PHILLIPS (1880–1927)

COLES PHILLIPS

Coles Phillips was an Ohioan who attended Kenyon College. While there, his first pictures were reproduced in the student magazine. After graduation he moved to New York, where he eventually sold his first illustration—a double-page spread—to the old *Life* magazine. It was there he developed "The Fadeaway Girl" that launched his career. He used a fashionable and beautiful young woman who appeared to fade away when the colors of her costume and background merged as one. The total effect was poster-like.

Phillips found a ready audience for his illustrations among such advertising clients as Holeproof Hosiery, Oneida Ltd., Silversmiths, and among book publishers.

Bag and Baggage, *Life*, Dec. 15, 1921, watercolor, 17.25″ × 19.5″, not signed; this painting consists of the upper half of the original; the lower portion was destroyed many years ago. $9,500

R. John Holmgren. *"Widows Weeds."* Watercolor, signed, 18 × 14¼ inches, $1,100. PHOTO COURTESY OF GUERNSEY'S.

John LaGatta. *"Beach Couple."* Watercolor, signed, $1,100. PHOTO COURTESY OF GUERNSEY'S.

Henry Patrick Raleigh. The artist has freely used colored inks, colored pencils, Wolff pencil and opaque watercolor. "They bought all the flowers and dropped them one by one below." Signed, $7,500.

HENRY PATRICK RALEIGH (1880–1944)

Henry Patrick Raleigh was one of the most prolific and popular illustrators in the 1920s and 1930s as a chronicler of the fashionables and high society. He began his illustrious career at nineteen as a newspaper illustrator for the *San Francisco Examiner*. He next moved to the *New York Journal* and then to the *New York World*. His depictions of romantic scenes and glamorous women found their way to most of the leading fiction magazines. *The Saturday Evening Post, Vanity Fair, Good Housekeeping*, and *Woman's Home Companion* used his work into the early 1940s. Book illustrations were done for such authors as F. Scott Fitzgerald, Booth Tarkington, Sinclair Lewis, and William Faulkner.

"He's Just Scalped His Self!" story illustration, "Kamp Kosy," *Saturday Evening Post*, 1924, s., d.'24, Wolff pencil, red and black watercolor, 12.75" × 19.5". $400

Young Couple and Baby, story illustration, 1927, s., d., dry brush and wash, 17.5" × 15.5". $750

Seated Couple, story illustration, "Here was love knocking at the door . . . and she must give no sign," *Cosmopolitan*, s., brush and brown ink, 13.25" × 20.75". $2,200

Couple in Love, s., d.'32, brown ink and yellow wash, 11.5" × 8.5". ..$450

Man Fixing Wagon Wheel, story illustration, s., Wolff pencil and wash, 10″ × 11.5″. $200

Young Woman and Older Man Seated on a Patio, story illustration, s., brown ink on paper, 12.75″ × 19.5″. $2,400

Two Girls at Fence, brown ink on paper, 18½″ × 15½″, unsigned. $475

Watercolor, *Saturday Evening Post*, Jan. 10, 1931, s., 14¾″ × 11¾″, copy of tearsheet included in lot. $175

All the Kings Horses #5, *Good Housekeeping*, Apr. 28, 1930, watercolor, 20½″ × 18¼″, unsigned, copy of tearsheet included in lot. $300

Girl and Dog by Fence, brown ink on paper, 17″ × 14½″, unsigned. ...$150

Couple with Son and His Toys, story illustration, "This is quite possibly the last nice present you'll ever have." "Diagnosis" by F. Scott Fitzgerald, *Saturday Evening Post*, Feb. 20, 1932, s., brown ink and watercolor, 12.5″ × 17″. $1,800

Man and Woman at Wooden Gate, story illustration, "Because I'm in love with you, Jon," s., brown ink and yellow wash, 13.25″ × 17.75″. $2,200

Reclining Figure, story illustration, "Her hand was cold. I thought that I'd murdered her," "Hide in the Dark," *McCall's*, s., d.'29, dry brush and watercolor, 16.5″ × 16.75″. $2,300

Altercation in the Rain, story illustration, "I'd hate to shoot you," "The Duchess," *Woman's Home Companion*, s., dry brush and blue wash, 16.75″ × 14.75″. $700

Woman Held Prisoner, story illustration, "Fifteen minutes. That's all the time the arrow poison takes!" "The House of the Arrow," *Cosmopolitan*, s., d., dry brush and watercolor, 13.25″ × 24″. $1,450

Fight Aboard Ship, story illustration, "Kick," May 1924, s., d.'24, dry brush and watercolor washes, 14.5″ × 16.5″. $850

Group Looking Toward the Sea, story illustration, s., d., watercolor, 15.25″ × 13.75″. $2,500

Henry Patrick Raleigh. "Adagio Dancers. Cafe Paris." Wolff pencil, 13 × 10 inches, signed lower right, $3,000. PHOTO COURTESY OF AUTHOR.

Woman and Holdup Man, story illustration, "And there framed in the aperture appeared the pretty blonde of the casino," s., d.'32, dry brush and wash, 19″ × 21.5″. $1,900

Woman Tossing Petals over Balcony, story illustration, "They bought all the flowers and dropped them one by one below," s., watercolor, colored pencil and ink, 19″ × 15″. $7,500

A Couple Camping, story illustration, "I'll make a dandy husband. I'll bait your hook and gig your flounder," "The Duchess" by Nick Boddie Williams, *Woman's Home Companion*, s., sepia and yellow ink, 11″ × 18″. $1,800

Man Seized by Overhead Machine, story illustration, "Who could cut off this devil's power?" *Saturday Evening Post*, s., d. '24, Wolff pencil and wash, 20.5″ × 14″. $650

Looking for Her Pearls on the Dance Floor, story illustration, "Pearls Bring Tears," *Delineator*, Dec. 2, 1927, s., d.'27, dry brush and watercolor, 18″ × 14.5″. $2,000

Ventriloquist Blowing Smoke Rings, story illustration, "How Pinto . . . managed to throw so natural a voice into the mouth of that quaint little thing was really remarkable," "Forlorn Hope" by Cosmo Hamilton, *Ladies' Home Journal*, Nov. 1929, s., Wolff pencil and watercolor, 15″ × 17″. $850

The Proposal, story illustration, " 'Antoinette!' he cried, flinging himself at her feet," *Cosmopolitan*, s., d.'26, brown ink, 18.75″ × 14.75″. $1,800

HISTORY AND
HISTORICAL THEMES

by Benjamin Eisenstat and Jane Sperry Eisenstat

Benjamin Eisenstat

Benjamin Eisenstat and Jane Sperry Eisenstat are a multitalented husband and wife who have received numerous awards as artists and illustrators. He has had thirty-two one-man shows, as well as group shows, at the Metropolitan Museum, and other places. As an illustrator, he has had clients such as The New York Times Book Review, Hearst Publications, and others. A busy lecturer and teacher, he also collaborates with his wife, Jane Sperry, on travel and historical articles. She has exhibited oil and water color paintings at the Museum of Modern Art and the Art Institute of Chicago. She has illustrated and authored a juvenile novel, The Challenge of AAb and others. The Eisenstats reside in Palo Alto, California, and collect American illustrator art.

In the 1870s the nation's publishers went through a period of intense expansion, responding to improved printing techniques and the demands of a burgeoning population that took great pride in their comparatively new nation and were anxious to learn as much as possible about its history. As a result, writers and illustrators were often commissioned topics of historic interest.

Foremost among the earlier artists was Felix Octavius Darley (1822–1888), the first American illustrator to see his name listed on the title page. Previously, artwork was considered unimportant. Books were simply listed as "illustrated" or containing "numerous illustrations." In fact, many publishers plagiarized reproductions from already published works, generally of British origin. Beside illustrating most of Washington Irving, James Fenimore Cooper, and Charles Dickens, much of Darley's subject matter pictured conflict with Indians and highlights of the Revolutionary War, often featuring George Washington mounted on a prancing white steed.

In the latter part of the 19th century, a good deal of reading matter focused on the reconciliation between North and South. The Civil War was reevaluated and agonized over for many years in publications such as *Harper's*, *Scribner's*, *McClure's*, and the like. Illustration was used to re-create battles and depict scenes of the homefront.

Edwin Austin Abbey (1852–1911), famed for his pen-and-ink technique, became an internationally acclaimed painter. He started his career doing historical illustrations of Revolutionary times for *Harper's* magazine in New York. With success came the freedon to paint large studio pictures, such as *Columbus in the New World*. He had moved to England and shared the largest studio in the country with John Singer Sargent. Although Abbey concentrated on British history at this time and became the most noted graphic interpreter of Shakespeare, his career ended as it began, with American history. The murals *Penn's Treaty with the Indians*, and *The American Army at Valley Forge*, in the state Capitol in Harrisburg, Pennsylvania, were among his final works.

While Abbey was famous in international circles, the greatest influence on American artists was his close friend, Howard Pyle (mentioned elsewhere in this book). Pyle illustrated three books on George Washington for Woodrow Wilson: *The Works of Francis Parkman*, *Hugh Wynne—Free Quaker*, by S. Weir Mitchel, and *The Story of the American Revolution*, by Henry Cabot Lodge. He painted the murals *The Landing of Carteret* and *The Battle of Nashville*, to name a few.

Of all the Pyle students, Stanley M. Arthurs (1877–1950) was the most devoted to history and spent his entire life painting and researching the American past. He illustrated fifteen volumes of *Pagent of America*, James

Benjamin Eisenstat. "Elfreth's Alley" (oldest continuously lived-in street in America). Gouache, 16 × 20 inches. Done for Ford Motor Co. Signed lower right, $2,500. PHOTO COURTESY OF BENJAMIN EISENSTAT.

Truslow Adams's *History of the United States*, and *The American Historical Scene*, published by the University of Pennsylvania, with sixty pages in full color depicting U.S. history from early explorers to World War I.

N. C. Wyeth (mentioned elsewhere in this book) is the most famous Pyle student. Wyeth's repertoire includes Washington as a farmer at Mt. Vernon, as a military commander, and a president; Lincoln as a young boy and as the beleaguered president. He painted a Pilgrims' feast of Thanksgiving, the Civil War from both viewpoints, Custer's last stand, Ben Franklin at Independence Hall, Paul Revere's ride, and many other historical subjects.

Some Pyle students specialized in one particular aspect of history. John Wolcott Adams and Clyde Deland were mainly involved with the American Revolution; William J. Aylward, Clifford Ashley, Anton Otto Fisher, and Edward A. Wilson, with naval history. Frank Schoonover and W. H. D. Koerner concentrated on the Old West; and while Harvey Dunn's reputation came from similar subject matter, he was also the foremost illustrator of World War I.

The American West held a fascination for other artists, unconnected to Pyle. High on any list of excellence would be Harold Von Schmidt, outstanding draftsman and inventive composer; the brothers Benton and Matt Clark, Donald Teague, and Tom Lovell, all of whom were greatly influenced by Charles Russell and Frederic Remington.

Two pen-and-ink experts in the field of historical illustration were Norman C. Price and Henry Pitz. Price came from Canada and studied in Europe; Pitz was a product of The Philadelphia College of Art. Both men combined action with authenticity, and although they were noted for working in black and white, they were equally skilled when using full color.

Notable work in the field of historical illustration was never exclusively confined to specialists. Maurice Bower, Dean Cornwell, Thomas Fogarty, Jules Gotlieb, Frederic R. Gruger, Frank Reilly, Mead Schaeffer, William A. Smith, and Robert Thon all made outstanding contributions. Current history can bring out greatness in an artist. During World War II, three combat artists, Howard Brodie, Kerr Eby, and Albert Gold, were so moved by their experience they transformed mere reportage into something special and inspiring.

Today, when events are immediately recorded on film, there remains a need for individual interpretation beyond the reach of a photograph. Among contemporary illustrators working in this direction are Paul Calle, Alan Cober, Ben Eisenstat, Bernie Fuchs, David Grove, Tom Hall, Mort Kunstler, James McMullen, Fred Otnes, Jerry Pinkney, and Robert Weaver.

Over the years certain illustrators have created images that came to symbolize our national character. James Montgomery Flagg was famous for "pretty girls." But his "I Want You" poster made history. J. C. Leyendecker, who invented the "Arrow Collar Man" and the "Happy New Year" cherubs, did a *Saturday Evening Post* cover of George Washington praying at Valley Forge that became an American icon. Folksy Norman Rockwell painted *The Four Freedoms*, a dramatic poster of a machine gunner, a magazine cover of a returned soldier in the back yard on his way home, and a gripping illustration of federal marshals escorting a little black girl to school, all instances of illustration becoming history.

For the collector looking for investment, historical subjects have a built-in value. Whether current event or the captured spirit of other times, it gives added dimension. Beyond the merit of the work or reputation of the artist will be the significant theme.

EDWIN AUSTIN ABBEY (1852–1911)

E A Abbey

Abbey began his career doing black-and-white illustrations for the old *Harper's* magazine. His work is notable for its authenticity. He is best known for his historical subjects and his illustrations done for the plays of Shakespeare in pen and ink. Long considered a fine artist and illustrator, his later illustrations were done in water color or in oils.

Note: Works by Abbey are scarce, as the majority of them are in the collection at Yale University.

Beatrice Dancing by Courtiers, "A Measure," *Much Ado About Nothing*, 1904, s., d., oil on canvas, 83.75″ × 54.5″. $125,000
Woman and Friar, story illustration, "A Castle in Spain," *Harper's Monthly*, May 1883, s., d. 1879, gouache en grisaille, 9.5″ × 7.5″. $4,400
A Medieval Lady Wearing a Wimple, s. E. A. Abbey, d. 1895, 19″ × 27″, pastel on paper. $3,300
A Lady, s., d. Mar. x 1905, i., prov., illus. for *All Sorts of People* by Gladys Storem, 1929, 3⅝″ × 3⅛″. $99
Greeting at the Door, s. EA Abbey, d. 1883, 10½″ × 13½″, watercolor and gouache on paper. $660
Gentleman Gardener, drawing, s. and d. EA Abbey 1882, ex-coll., subject is the father of the English painter Alfred Parsons, 19¾″ × 15¾″, pencil on paper. $800

STANLEY MASSEY ARTHURS (1877–1950)

S. M. Arthurs

Deeply influenced as a student and friend of Howard Pyle, Arthurs specialized in American historical subjects, among them a series of episodes from early colonial days through the Civil War era. Like Pyle, he researched every detail for his illustrations, including trying to capture the mood and character of his subjects. His paintings are distinguished by their bold use of color. He illustrated many history books and painted several murals that can be seen at Delaware College, the state Capitol, Dover, Delaware, and elsewhere. His work rarely comes to auction. Collectors today seek out Arthurs's paintings, his stagecoach and colonial American scenes especially prized. An Arthurs oil will generally range from $2,000 to $7,500, and a particularly desirable historical or Western scene can bring more.

Playing Checkers by the Fire, s., charcoal, 15″ × 15″. $1,250

WILLIAM JAMES AYLWARD (1875–1956)

w. J· Aylward—

Nautical subjects and the sea were favored by William James Aylward. Many of his historical adventure illustrations show the influence of his teacher, Howard Pyle, in his use of color and dramatic impact.

Aylward wrote as well as illustrated articles on early seafaring. Among the books he illustrated were Jules Verne's *Twenty Thousand Leagues under the Sea* and Jack London's *Sea Wolf*. During World War I he was an official artist with the A.E.F.

Four Willing Hands Helped Him into the Cross Trees, s., "Norman's Woe," oil en grisaille on canvas, 16″ × 24″, exhib. New York Historical Soc. "200 Years of American Illustration" (1976). $3,600
Fish Market, "Les Sables d'Olonne," s., oil on canvas, 24″ × 30″. .$3,000
A Halt For Repairs Was Necessary, "The Sea Voyage of a Dry Dock," *Scribner's* magazine, May 1907, s., black-and-white gouache, 9.5″ × 15.75″, one of 11 pieces comprising all the illustrations for the story, sold as a group only.
....$7,500

BENTON CLARK (1895–1965)

Benton Clark—

Benton Clark, like his brother Matt, illustrated Western themes. Influenced by other Western painters, such as Frederic Remington, Harvey Dunn, and Frank Hoffman, he developed his own style to depict the history of the West.

He studied at both the Art Institute of Chicago and the art school of the National Academy of Design in New York. He began in the art department for MGM in Culver City, California, and also worked at art studios in Chicago.

Liberty magazine was his first magazine assignment, in 1927. It was followed by other important magazines such as *Cosmopolitan*, *Good Housekeeping*, *McCall's*, and *The Saturday Evening Post*.

The Steamboat Race, s., d., oil on canvas, 34″ × 24½″. $1,400
Renegades, reproduced: *American Weekly* magazine, s., oil on canvas, 26″ × 22″. $750
The King's Son, *Cosmopolitan*, 1935, s., d., oil on canvas, 22″ × 28″.
....$1,700

Alice Bolam Preston. "I Am an American." Watercolor, gouache, and pencil, 16⅛″ × 10⅜″, $3,500–$12,000. PHOTO COURTESY OF CHILDREN'S ILLUSTRATIONS, NEW YORK.

Haddon Sunblom. "Santa Claus." Painted for Coca-Cola, watercolor, signed, 11½″ × 14″, $3,250. PHOTO COURTESY OF MORT AND CATHY WALKER.

Harvey Dunn. "Water, Water." Reproduced "Off the Trail" by George Patullo in McClures *magazine. Oil on canvas, signed and dated (1910) on lower left, $75,000.* PHOTO COURTESY OF LES MANSFIELD FINE AMERICAN ILLUSTRATIVE ART, LAKEWOOD, OHIO.

Charles M. Russell. "In the Enemy's Country." Oil on canvas, signed on lower left, dated 1921, 24" × 36". Large major Russell paintings such as this can command prices exceeding $1,000,000. PHOTO COURTESY OF J. N. BARTFIELD GALLERIES.

N. C. Wyeth. *"John Oxenham." Reproduced Charles Kingsley, Westward Ho, 1920. Oil on canvas, signed on upper left, 40" × 30", $85,000.* PHOTO COURTESY OF BRANDYWINE FANTASY GALLERY, CHICAGO.

Robert Benney. *"Vietnam Episode, I Corps Area, 1968–1969." "In a quiet dugout, the night silence is broken by a signal—a mountain village is under attack by the VC and is in flames." A dramatic example of combat illustration. Oil on canvas, 30" × 44", $10,000.* PHOTO COURTESY OF ROBERT BENNEY. COLLECTION OF THE U.S. MARINE CORPS–COMBAT ART BRANCH DIVISION OF INFORMATION.

Philip R. Goodwin (1882–1935). "An Early Morning Thrill." Reproduced Outdoor Life *cover, August 1931. Oil on canvas, 30" × 22", signed on lower left, $18,000.* PHOTO COURTESY OF LES MANSFIELD, FINE AMERICAN ILLUSTRATIVE ART, LAKEWOOD, OHIO.

Harold Von Schmidt. "Something to Brag About." Reproduced The Saturday Evening Post, *January 26, 1946. Oil on canvas, signed and dated on lower left (1946), © 1991, $25,000.* PHOTO COURTESY OF LES MANSFIELD, FINE AMERICAN ILLUSTRATIVE ART, LAKEWOOD, OHIO.

John Held Jr. Watercolor,
signed on lower left,
$8,500. PHOTO
COURTESY OF
ILLUSTRATION HOUSE,
INC., NEW YORK.

Dean Cornwell. "The Slave Market." Story illustration for The Robe,
Life, 1942. Oil on canvas, 34″ × 45″, signed, $30,000. PHOTO
COURTESY OF ILLUSTRATION HOUSE, INC., NEW YORK.

Joseph C. Leyendecker. Magazine cover, Collier's, January 6, 1917, "Automobile Number." Oil on canvas, mounted, 28″ × 19¼″, signed on lower right, $25,000. PHOTO COURTESY OF ILLUSTRATION HOUSE, INC., NEW YORK.

Eduardo Benito. "Under the Palms." Vogue magazine cover, January 1927. Gouache on board, signed, 11½″ × 11½″, $3,000. PHOTO COURTESY OF SACKS FINE ART, INC., NEW YORK.

Paul Branson. Cover illustration for The Saturday Evening Post, *February 7, 1931. Signed on lower right,* © CPC 1991, $8,000. PHOTO COURTESY OF ILLUSTRATION HOUSE, INC., NEW YORK.

Henry Patrick Raleigh. Magazine illustration. Couple in the tropics, pen and ink with color wash, signed on lower right, 14″ × 21½″, $3,000. PHOTO COURTESY OF PRIVATE COLLECTOR.

Stevan Dohanos. Little girl praying at bedside. Oil on canvas, vignette, signed on lower right, 26″ × 21½″, $4,000, magazine illustration. PHOTO COURTESY OF PRIVATE COLLECTOR.

Benjamin West Clinedinst, NA. Lilien Diemarty, an artist, walking in snow. Watercolor, signed on lower right, magazine illustration, 14½″ × 11¾″, $291. PHOTO COURTESY OF PRIVATE COLLECTOR.

Henry Hutt (1875–1950). Group of fashionable ladies, turn-of-century. Magazine illustration, gouache, signed on lower left, 27½″ × 21½″, $2,500. PHOTO COURTESY OF PRIVATE COLLECTOR.

*Jules Gotlieb.
"Puritan Girl
Teaching Indians."
Watercolor.
28½ × 21¼
inches. Signed,
dated '46.
Reproduced in*
American Weekly
magazine, $100. PHOTO
COURTESY
OF GUERNSEY'S.

JULES GOTLIEB (1897–?)

GOTLIEB

Jules Gotlieb traveled in many out-of-the-way parts of the world, from North Africa to the jungles of Dutch Guiana, collecting background material for his illustrations. He also accumulated a library of over 2,000 volumes for reference in doing historical illustrations for nearly every national magazine, including *Collier's, Cosmopolitan, Redbook, American, Woman's Home Companion, Liberty, This Week, Ladies' Home Journal,* and for several books.

A native New Yorker, Gotlieb studied at the National Academy School of Fine Arts, the Pennsylvania Academy at Chester Springs, and the Art Students League. Among his teachers were George Bridgman and Harvey Dunn. He later taught at the League himself from 1932 to 1934.

The Globe, reproduced, *American Weekly* magazine, Sept. 9, 1951, watercolor, 27½" × 11¼", unsigned. $50
Cave Dwellers, reproduced, *American Weekly* magazine, gouache, 21¼" × 37½", unsigned. $325
Puritan Girl Teaching Indians, reproduced, *American Weekly* magazine, s., d. 46, watercolor, 28½" × 21½". $100

WILLIAM H. D. KOERNER (1878–1938)

W. H. D
Koerner

W. H. D. Koerner became best known for his paintings of the American West, but he did a variety of rural and domestic scenes as well. The majority of Koerner's work was done for *The Saturday Evening Post*. Both Koerner and Frederic Remington have their studios preserved in the Buffalo Bill Museum in Cody, Wyoming. Koerner's work is generally oil on canvas or oil on board. Like El Greco's figures, Koerner's often look a little taller than life. As he got older, he used a somewhat impressionistic style of painting and mixed a wide range of colors into his paintings to achieve the desired effects. While most of his work ended up being reproduced in black and white, this never stopped Koerner from making good use of his great sense of color. A good portion of his paintings were done as vignettes (some edges and corners of the work not being painted). Vignettes may range from $3,000 to $10,000 in price; full oils may range from $5,000 to $15,000 and over. Koerner's good Western paintings may bring double these estimates.

Jubilo's Return, story illustration, *Saturday Evening Post*, July 5, 1919, s., oil on canvas, 26″ × 36″. $8,000
Couple by the Shore, s., oil on canvas, 35.25″ × 29.25″. $6,800
Man in Wheel Chair, appeared in *Seventeen* magazine or *Charm* magazine, s., watercolor, 19½″ × 15″. $125
Illustration for White Men, s., d. 1918 on the stretcher, prov., exhib., 28″ × 36″. $7,425
Herding Across the River, s. W.H.D. Koerner, d. 1923, 24″ × 36″. $11,000
Summer Days, s. W.H.D. Koerner, d. 1916, bears estate stamp verso, prov., possibly an illus. for "Robert" by Alice Cowdrey, Feb. 1917, *Harper's Monthly*, 36″ × 26″. $7,150
Hurry Up, Bob, s. and d. whd/Koerner/ 1924 recto, i. verso, 36½″ × 30″. $4,400
Benevolent Exploitation, benefiting the Edna Gladney Center, 12″ × 36″. $5,000
Self Portrait, s. W.H.D. Koerner, d. 1922, prov., 30″ × 36¼″. $1,320

NORMAN M. PRICE (1877–1951)

Norman Price

Known as an illustrator's illustrator for his dedication and attention to detail in the historical subjects he painted, Norman Price worked in both the magazine and book field. His pen-and-ink drawings depicting historical themes are considered among the finest examples of the media. *Cosmopolitan* magazine and *Woman's Home Companion* are two of the many magazines he did illustrations for. He also did illustrations for a series of historical novels by Robert W. Chambers.

Woman serving soldiers, advertisement, "La Belle Chocolatiere," *Bakers Chocolate*, c. 1917, s., watercolor, 21.5″ × 14.5″. $1,600
War, Paint and Rouge, *American* magazine, 1931, ink on paper, 8″ × 6″.
.... $200
The Schooner Hannah Returning to Port with Her Prize, Sept. 1775, s. Norman Price, identified and i. verso, sight size 10⅝″ × 13⅛″, watercolor with gouache on paper. $275
A Scene from Treasure Island, s., 11″ × 20″, pen and black ink on paper.
.... $385
Embargo, The Happy Part, s., 20″ × 30″, gouache pen and black ink on board. $1,210
Redcoat Flees Couple in Bedroom, watercolor, 12.75″ × 25″. $5,000

HAROLD VON SCHMIDT (1893–1982)

**HAROLD
VON
SCHMIDT**

Early training with Harvey Dunn was the major influence on the style of Harold von Schmidt. Another influence was the history of the West and the works of Remington and Russell. Twelve of his paintings of pioneers and the events of the westward movement and the gold rush of 1849 hang in the governor's office in Sacramento, California. Five Civil War paintings are in the permanent collection of the U.S. Military Academy at West Point.

He also did posters for the U.S. Navy during World War I and was an invited artist-correspondent for the U.S. Air Force, European Theatre of Operations; in addition he was artist-correspondent for King Features Syndicate in the Pacific Theatre of Operations.

Collectors can recognize his style by its sweeping, epic panoramas.

When the Pace Was Slow, "A Man of Plots," Ben Ames Williams, *Saturday Evening Post*, Oct. 17, 1925, init. WHDK lower right, oil on canvas, 28″ × 40″. $12,500
Let's Bring Him Home Quicker, s., d. 1944, appeared in *Collier's* Apr. 15, 1944, for the John B. Stetson Co., 37″ × 35″. $3,080
Two unpublished drawings for von Schmidt's 1928 masterpiece, *Death Comes for the Archbishop* by Willa Cather: "Fording a Stream," heading, Book 1, Chap. 1, black-and-white watercolor, 11″ × 26″, not signed. $1,800
Monk Fleeing at Night, heading, Book 5, Chap. 2, black-and-white watercolor, 10.25″ × 26″, not signed. $850
Stagecoach, s. von, gouache, 5″ × 7″. $500

Harold Von Schmidt. "The Shootout." Oil on canvas. Signed, dated 1956. Reproduced in October 1956 True *magazine, 21 × 48 inches, $33,000.*
PHOTO COURTESY OF CHRISTIE'S, NEW YORK.

Man carrying girl in flood, story illustration, *Woman's Home Companion*, 1940, s., d., gouache, 24″ × 38″. $800
Shepherd of Guadaloupe, s., d. 1928, i. "I feel immensely flattered/ that you'd like to see me the/ wife of a crook," 33¾″ × 30¼″. $3,300
Tugboat Annie lounging in chair, story illustration, "Tugboat Annie Refuses to Budge," *Saturday Evening Post*, oil on canvas, 21″ × 28″, not signed.
.... $1,000
Departure of the Stage, "The Man from Texas," *Saturday Evening Post*, 1950, s., blue and black, oil on canvas, 30″ × 40″. $21,000
Knife Fight, black-and-white watercolor, 10″ × 12″, not signed. $420
Lifeboat in Alaska, "Forlorn Island," Mar. 1932, s., monochrome green gouache, 20″ × 18″. $1,500

ROMANCE

Long before the "soaps" conveyed romance to the masses, the illustrations in magazines and books captured the essence of love. Whether it was the bittersweet partings of a Civil War soldier and his sweetheart or the World War II farewells, the illustrator brought it home in advertisements and magazine illustrations. Magazine serials, some lasting years, made their illustrators celebrities—and wealthy. Pruett Carter's romantic illustrations were so popular they were often reproduced as prints. For the most part, the magazine reproductions were clipped and framed by millions of young women. Although Mike Ludlow was among the most popular romance illustrators of the 1950s, few of his works have come up for sale. On the other hand, Jon Whitcomb, Alfred Parker, and Coby Whitmore, equally (if not more) popular, are more readily available to collectors.

With the growth of photography and the demise of many magazines, combined with television serials, fewer illustrators were used to depict romantic situations. However, one new channel opened up during the 1970s and continues—the return of the romantic novel in paperback.

M. Coburn Whitmore. "The Lover's Rendezvous." Signed upper right. Oil on canvasboard, 15½ × 24 inches, $2,200. PHOTO COURTESY OF SKINNER GALLERIES.

Record album covers are another source. Romantic illustrations are alive and doing well. Would you expect it to be otherwise?

WALTER BIGGS (1886–1968)

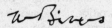

When it came to capturing the feeling of romance, especially scenes of the South, Walter Biggs was at his best. Born in Elliston, Virginia, he came to New York to study art at the Chase School, later renamed the New York School of Art. Among his teachers were Edward Penfield and Robert Henri. His illustrations in watercolor and oil appeared in the *Ladies' Home Journal*, *Woman's Home Companion*, *Good Housekeeping*, and others.

Women climbing steps, autos in background, advertisement, International Silver, 1925; oil on canvas, 32″ × 32″, not signed; reproduced, *Advertising Art Annual* award, 1925. ....$11,000
The Hunting Year, indistinctly s., 28″ × 40″. $3,000
Wedding Anniversary, s., t. and d. verso, 22″ × 40″. $2,860
Horse in the Woods, s., d., 18½″ × 11″. $230

PRUETT CARTER (1891–1955)

For nearly forty years Pruett Carter's attention to fine detail made him a favored illustrator of romantic themes. He approached his assignments as if he were directing a motion picture, paying attention to the roles of his characters as well as the costumes and scenery. His use of color was influenced by his former teacher, Walter Biggs. Magazines like *McCall's* and *Ladies' Home Journal* were among the many who appreciated his sensitive portrayals of women.

Sweet Child, reproduced, *McCall's*, Sept. 1955, s., watercolor and pencil, 17¼″ × 20¾″. $175
Woman Reading at Table, story illustration, s., oil on canvas en grisaille, 33″ × 26″. $1,200
Cowboy and Woman in Clinch, ''The Long Goodbye,'' s., d.'38, oil on canvas, 39.5″ × 18″. $2,200
Officer and Girl at Soda Fountain, preliminary sketch for *Cosmopolitan*, oil on paper, 21″ × 25.5″, not signed. $380

ELBERT McGRAN JACKSON (1896–1962)

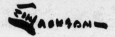

Although Elbert Jackson usually illustrated stories of romance and high society, he was equally at home with mystery and masculine adventure as well. His early training as an architect came in handy doing the backgrounds for beautiful-woman subjects. His illustrations appeared in *Good Housekeeping*, *Collier's*, and others. He also did covers for *The Saturday Evening Post*, *Collier's*, and *Ladies' Home Journal*.

Scared by His Own Shadow, *Saturday Evening Post*, Oct. 30, 1926, s., oil on canvas, 22.5″ × 17″. $4,800
Japanese Lanterns, *Collier's*, s., oil on canvas, 25.5″ × 19.5″. $6,600
Stealing the Funnies, s., oil on canvas, 28″ × 20″. $4,500
She Loves Me, She Loves Me Not, s., oil on canvas, 25″ × 18″. $7,500
Caddy with hands over ears, magazine cover, "Husband and Wife Golf Tournament," s., oil on canvas, 25″ × 20″. $2,300
Wedding Couple, s., oil on canvas, 28″ × 21″. $4,800
Custom Inspector, s., oil on canvas, 22.5″ × 17″. $4,200
Christmas Boy, *Ladies' Home Journal*, Dec. 1930, s., oil on canvas, 26″ × 19.75″. $8,000
Blue Marigolds, *Good Housekeeping*, June 1934, s., oil on canvas, 30″ × 30″. $675

TOM LOVELL (1909–)

Though Tom Lovell's illustration subjects have ranged from adventure to nature, military, and Western, many of his works coming to auction are in the romance or family category. He used a documentary approach with a backup of research. His first illustrations were done for pulp magazines while he was still in college. As a professional illustrator, his work has appeared in most of the important national magazines. During World War II he was a staff sergeant in the U.S. Marine Corps Reserve and did paintings of Corps history, now in the permanent collection of the Marine Corps. His paintings of Western subjects, done in the 1970s, were awarded medals from the National Cowboy Hall of Fame and the Prix de West, awarded by the National Academy of Western Art.

Common Ground, *Good Housekeeping*, June 1940, s., oil on canvas, 34″ × 25¾″. $550

*Tom Lovell. "Common Ground."
Oil on canvas.* Good
Housekeeping *magazine, June
1940. Signed, 34 × 25³/₄ inches,
$550.* PHOTO COURTESY OF
GUERNSEY'S.

The Triangle, *Collier's*, March 1941, tearsheet included in lot. The Illustrator in America 1900–1960, Albany, GA, Nov. 1985, oil on canvas, 30½" × 38". $3,000
Couple in Chemistry Lab, init., gouache and pencil, 11" × 8". $750
The Rescue, s., oil on board, 20" × 16". $1,400
Discovering the Bloodstain, s., d. 41, illus. for *Saratoga Trunk, Saturday Evening Post*, 1941, 31" × 22". $1,650
Couple in clinch, story illustration, s. lower left, oil on canvas, 32" × 23". $2,200
News from Quinto, two studies, *Good Housekeeping*, Nov. 1943: (1) Man's head, s., gouache, 9¼" × 4¼", (2) Lady's head, gouache, 9¼" × 4¼", unsigned; lot is accompanied by the magazine reproduction and a letter from Tom Lovell to the gentleman he gave the paintings to. $200
Family Talk, s., oil on canvas, 21" × 40". $3,500
Young Couple Quarrelling, s., oil on illus. board, 15¾" × 16". $1,500
Until She Met the Sailor, *American* magazine, s., blue and black, oil on board, 18" × 24". $850
Colonist with Redcoats, inits., sight size 12" × 8½", watercolor, gouache, pen and black ink on paper laid down on board. $440

MIKE LUDLOW (1921–)

Mike Ludlow

Mike Ludlow's first illustrations were done for the Sunday supplement of the *Journal American* in 1948. His beautiful girls in romantic situations brought him assignments from such magazines as *Good Housekeeping*, *Family Circle*, *Today's Woman*, *The Saturday Evening Post*, and others. He also painted a variety of luscious females for *Esquire* magazine. Other assignments were for national advertisers.

Young couple at table having a drink, s., gouache, 14½″ × 23″. $100

ALFRED PARKER (1906–1985)

a parker

Versatility describes the illustrations of Alfred Parker. From the mid-1930s till his death in 1985, Parker was one of the most popular magazine illustrators, so much so that he was widely imitated. One of his covers for the *Ladies' Home Journal* in 1939—a mother and daughter—not only led to a series of fifty but sparked the demand for the new style of matching mother-daughter fashions. The final series was in 1951.

Alfred Parker. Girl on the beach. Signed lower left, $2,500.
PHOTO COURTESY OF ILLUSTRATION HOUSE, INC.

Parker continually experimented with his style and even illustrated an entire issue of *Cosmopolitan* magazine, using a different style and name for each story. Collectors can expect to find his work in every media and combinations of media. Some of his work has turned up unsigned.

Two Renaissance Men, "Then and Now" by W. Somerset Maugham, *Cosmopolitan*, May 1946, s., gouache, 16″ × 20″. $550
Girl Sewing, gouache, 20½″ × 15″, unsigned. $150
Watching from the Stone Gate, *Saturday Evening Post*, s., gouache, 15″ × 12″. $950
Roman Romance, *Saturday Evening Post*, 1950, s., gouache on masonite, 20″ × 18″. $1,000
A Covetous Machiavelli, "Then and Now" by W. Somerset Maugham, *Cosmopolitan*, May 1946, gouache, 20½″ × 15″, not signed. $1,200

MARTHA SAWYERS (1902–)

You could say it was fate that was responsible for Martha Sawyers becoming an illustrator. William Chessman, art editor of *Collier's*, saw Sawyers's drawings and paintings of China and Indonesia in an exhibit.

Martha Sawyers. "Thanksgiving." Collier's magazine cover, November 29, 1947. Signed backwards. Oil on board, 28 × 23 inches, $900. PHOTO COURTESY OF GUERNSEY'S.

He gave her her first illustration assignment, a story with an Oriental setting. *Collier's* sent her to the China–Burma–India area during World War II as an artist-correspondent. She also illustrated for authors Pearl S. Buck and Mona Gardner as well as doing many covers for *Collier's* and illustrations for their stories. Until the Wale auction of illustrator art in 1988 at Guernsey's in New York, few examples of her work had reached the marketplace.

Man crouching before another man, story illustration, "Hassah Hangat," *Collier's*, Sept. 17, 1940, oil on board, 29″ × 11.5″. $300
China Gold, reproduced *Collier's*, oil on canvas, hung on board, 14½″ × 29″. $1,600
Poster, reproduced *Collier's* "China Sky," by Pearl S. Buck, Mar. 1, 1941, s., canvas hung on board, 27½″ × 15¾″. $500
Roots, *Collier's*, s., pastel, 20½″ × 23½″. $600
Pastel, reproduced *Collier's* cover, Oct. 5, 1940, 29″ × 24″. $4,500
Thanksgiving, *Collier's* cover, Nov. 29, 1947, s. backwards, oil on board, 28″ × 23″, copy of cover included in lot. $900

JON WHITCOMB (1906–1988)

jon whitcomb

Romance, young love, and glamorous women were the themes of Jon Whitcomb's most popular illustrations. After graduating from Ohio State, where he had done pictures for the school publications, he got jobs in a variety of studios. There he did travel and theater posters along with general advertising illustrations. When he moved to New York in 1934, his first magazine illustrations were for *Collier's* and *Good House-keeping*.

Whitcomb's pretty-girl illustrations brought him acclaim. During World War II, his series of advertising illustrations on the theme "Back Home for Keeps" was a popular pin-up fad for the women back on the home front. In the 1950s he did a monthly series of sketches and articles about movie stars for *Cosmopolitan* titled "On Location with Jon Whitcomb." He also wrote and illustrated several short stories and two children's books about poodles.

Clinch, "One Night in Cincinnati," *Cosmopolitan*, June 1948, s., green and black gouache, 16″ × 12″. $425
Egyptian Chorus Girls, *Cosmopolitan*, Feb. 1952, s., gouache, 16″ × 24″. $1,200
Ingrid Bergman, *Cosmopolitan* cover, s., oil and tempera on canvasboard, 16″ × 20″. $1,500

Jon Whitcomb. *Couple dancing on a rooftop,* $1,600.
PHOTO COURTESY OF
ILLUSTRATION HOUSE, INC.

The Cosmopolitan Girl, *Cosmopolitan*, Feb. 1946, s., gouache, 17″ × 12″;
several of America's top illustrators who were noted for their ability to portray
the beautiful girl were commissioned by *Cosmopolitan* to paint their version of
the "Cosmopolitan Girl"—this was Jon Whitcomb's rendering; a Xerox copy
of the magazine reproduction is included in the lot. $650
Gouache, *Ladies' Home Journal*, May 1941, s., 15½″ × 13½″, magazine tearsheet included in lot. $200
Bobby Soxer, story illustration, s., ink and gouache, 13.25″ × 19″. ..$1,300
WW II factory workers greeting sailor, advertisement, s., gouache, 19″ ×
27″. $1,300
Girl Holding Poodle, alternate drawing for *Pom Pom's Christmas*, s., gouache,
13″ × 14″. $400
Portrait of Brigitte Bardot, *Cosmopolitan*, Nov. 1958, s., gouache, 13″ × 9″.
....$1,800
Portrait of Van Johnson, *Cosmopolitan*, s., carbon pencil, 8″ × 6″. $250
Couple embracing, *Pamela*, Bantam, 1982, s., acrylic on canvas, 24″ × 24″.
.... $800
Portrait of Jeannete Elphick, a.k.a. Victoria Shaw, s., mixed media, 11″ ×
9″. $700
Portraits of Hermione Gingold and Richard Boone, two drawings, both s.;
first, 10″ × 8″; second, 6″ × 10½″; first, pencil, marker, Chinese white on
paper; second, crayon on paper. $66
Day Dreaming and The Texas Lady and the Singing Cowboy, two, both s.;
second, illus. for "The Most Beautiful Girl in Texas" by Shirley Shapiro Pugh,
Cosmopolitan, Jan. 1951; first, 15″ × 18″; second, 19¾″ × 27″, gouache, pen
and black ink on board. $330

SATIRE AND HUMOR

by Rick Marschall

When it comes to the field of humor—from the subject of humor in illustrations to cartoons and comics—Richard Marschall has just about covered it all. Beginning in 1972 as a political cartoonist for the Connecticut Herald, *he went on to a variety of jobs as editor, comics writer, author, professor, and lecturer on his favorite subject. Among his many honors, he was the recipient of the Yellow Kid Award at the 14th International Salon of Comics, Illustration and Animation in Lucca, Italy, 1980. He has organized important exhibits for major museums, such as the Whitney Museum of American Art. He is on the board of directors for the Museum of Cartoon Art, Rye Brook, New York, and the San Francisco Academy of Comic Art. He has authored* America's Great Comic-Strip Artists *and* The History of Television.

IT IS TO LAUGH

Illustration is pretty serious stuff these days, especially since the Establishment is starting to listen to some of our broken records about art forms and painterly techniques and reflections of societal mores. After all, Michelangelo himself did work to his clients' orders. The Society of Illustrators is now referred to more as a museum than as a clubhouse, and it's been years since those raucous Illustrators' Balls were held. Important colleges conduct classes on the history of illustration.

If you'll take a peek, however, the understated opprobrium formerly reserved for illustration in general is now accorded to a certain category of illustration, namely, humorous illustration. This surely does not result from an organized conspiracy of critics, museums, or galleries (indeed, certain galleries have specialized in humorous illustrators), but generally, the texts and histories, the shows and retrospectives, have given token credit to the humorists among the Abbeys, Pyles, Cornwells, Fuchses, and Peaks—the Valleys being implicitly reserved for the funnymen.

Frost and Sullivant seem to be regarded as odd ducks for their specialities. Charles Dana Gibson, although a founder of the Society, rankled at being called an illustrator or caricaturist; he was a cartoonist who valued the niche he had carved out for himself within the rich tradition of humorous illustration. It seems that the slights uniformly dealt Norman Rockwell throughout his career were due more to his light themes than to his manner of representation or his technique.

We should be careful in going that route; it is when we praise illustration primarily for its similarity to fine art, so called, that we deny exactly what makes illustration different and unique—a proud discipline to be warmly defended and maintained for its own qualities, not those that resemble others. Illustration didn't evolve through 200 years in America, defining its role and essence, attracting some of the most astounding of creative artists, innovating and experimenting, only to be compared to gallery art.

It is open to debate whether humorous illustration is the purest form of illustration, so we'll remove one chip from our shoulder in this little combative and self-assertive (or -defensive) corner, but we can make one irrefutable claim: all of American illustration has its origins in the humorous illustration. In the earliest days, before we were yet a nation, much of the illustration was political and propagandistic, and it did not always aim for belly laughs but sometimes employed satire, ridicule, and parody; but humorous it was.

Flowing from that source have been four distinct streams, forming not only a neat metaphor but distinct categories within humorous illustration: editorial graphic humor (including book and magazine work and advertising art), cartoons (both social and political), caricature, and comic strips (sequential narration, not always employing classical illustration techniques but often utilizing a set of visual shorthand devices). Their histories and achievments combine to make humorous illustration a remarkably inventive tradition.

Although pictorial representation was problematic in the primitive printing shops of colonial America, illustrations appeared with hopeful frequency in almanacs, broadsides, books, pamphlets, and eventually newspapers. Even the purely moralistic and political drawings were cartoons and ultimately were termed so. In crude woodcuts and painfully executed engravings, which were less crude for all of the handiwork, these illustrations appeared to serve a public that was not only dispersed over a vast new land but was also to a large extent illiterate. Hence, the humorous illustration in its various forms was usually not a diversion but rather a vital means of communication and persuasion.

Benjamin Franklin, the father of so many things mechanical and human, was also the father of the humorous illustration in America. In his *Plain Truth* pamphlet of 1747, he drew and engraved the political allegory ''Heaven Helps Those Who Help Themselves''; seven years later he created the classic icon entitled ''Join or Die''—a snake chopped into sections, each labeled as a separate colony. It was a pictorial representation of his famous admonition to fellow patriots: "If we do not hang together, surely we shall all hang separately."

James Akin produced caricatures both humorous and political, and after independence, Elkanak Tinsdale designed the mythical beast, the Gerrymander, after the rough silhouette of an electoral district torturously structured to favor Elbridge Gerry in Massachusetts. (For years the illustration was attributed to painter Gilbert Stuart.) Similarly, Alexander Anderson created the snapping-turtle icon named the Ograbme— "embargo" spelled backwards—to illustrate a political position before the War of 1812.

William Charles was the first cartoonist whose work amused the broad public and was not produced on behalf of a specific party or interest; born in Scotland, he was a stylistic disciple of Gillray and Rowlandson. He led the way for a new phase of humorous illustration, as, after the War of 1812, the field concerned itself less with politics and national affairs and more with social themes (the humorous illustrations and series of another Briton, William Hogarth, were also influential among American artists). David Claypool Johnston was called "the American Cruikshank"; he published an annual collection called *Scraps*, with humorous illustrations and cartoons in engravings and lithographs. Edward Williams Clay and Napoleon Sarony were also prominent in the new field of social humor and caricature.

After 1831, the comic almanac became a fixture on the American scene—a way-station between the traditional almanacs with information and maxims, such as *Poor Richard's* (Franklin's), and the humor magazines of the next generations. Much of the text humor was crude, simplistic, or bawdy, and in reality the illustrative "accompaniments" were actually their high points. Some titles can suggest the comic almanacs' general tone: *The Rip Snorter*, *The Devil's Comical Texas Oldmanick*, *Whim Whams*, and *Elton's Comic All-My-Neck*. Tall tales and primitive graphics filled *Davy Crockett's Almanac of Wild Sports of the West and Life in the Backwoods*, edited by the legendary frontiersman, congressman, and Alamo defender and continued almost twenty years after his death.

Due to advances in technology—and perhaps spurred by the popularity of lithographed illustrations, sold as prints—newspapers began with some regularity using illustrations after 1839, although the woodcuts were very crude and usually anonymously produced (probably to the ultimate relief of the original illustrators, whose works were transferred to wood by middlemen). Breaking out of anonymity and standing as America's first professional, full-time illustrator was the humorous artist Felix Octavius Carr Darley, mentioned elsewhere in this book.

It was the advent of the humor magazine like *The Lantern*—sixteen pages of text and illustrations, topical social and political humor, poems and stories—that provided the next step toward the establishment of a regular profession known as humorous illustrating, heretofore usually a sideline. Following in Darley's footsteps were a corps of artists who likewise graced magazines, books, penny prints, and other outlets. Perhaps the most prominent was Frank Henry Temple Bellew; in spite of rivaling Darley's laundry list of first names, he signed his illustrations and cartoons with a simple triangle, and "Triangle" he was professionally called. He drew for the *Lantern* and many other humor magazines, and he was a major contributor to *Harper's Weekly*. And although he executed political cartoons, he was as well known for his social cartoons and "series," depictions of everyday farces that presaged strips. His son, Frank P. W. Bellew, was also a cartoonist. Little boy Bellew signed his work Chip (presumably being off the old block). Tragically, he died in his early thirties in 1894, only six years after Triangle, whose career began in the early 1850s.

Bellew was one of several artists whose careers spanned not only several decades but several periods of journalism and stages of technology, for the evolution from the engraving to the woodcut to the lithographic stone to the photoengraving (allowing artists to see their pen-and-ink work reproduced directly to paper for the first time) resulted in greater freedom of expression, ease of application, and expansion of the ranks. Thomas Worth, for instance, was one of Currier & Ives's most prolific printmakers of humorous subjects (particularly racetrack and black themes) starting in the 1860s, but he continued as a busy cartoonist through the decades, drawing for *Judge* magazine and contributing some of the first colored newspaper cartoons to the New York *Herald*.

Frank Beard also drew for Currier & Ives and later for *Judge* before he became America's most notable cartooning advocate of Prohibition. Michael Angelo Woolf began his career as a humorous illustrator in the 1850s, and when he died in the 1890s, he was the most prominent cartoonist of social realism themes of urban life. Other humorous artists included E. Jump, Augustus Hoppin, and Ben Day, the cartoonist and engraver who was the son of the New York *Sun*'s founder and inventor of the reproduction-and-shading process that bears his name.

The Civil War again brought politics and national affairs to the fore. Currier & Ives found themselves producing large numbers of partisan prints, but the purely humorous series were a permanent fixture in America; after Worth, their most popular humorous illustrator was Sol Eytinge. Among the propagandists, the rebellion's most notable illustrator was Adalbert J. Volck, who signed his classic *Twenty-Nine Confederate*

War Etchings V. Blada. In the North, the most popular humorous illustrator was Thomas Nast.

During the war, *Harper's Weekly*, *Leslie's Weekly*, and their imitators were established as fully illustrated newspapers, using copious amounts of woodcuts—news scenes, portraits, fine art reproductions, and many humorous illustrations and cartoons. Soon thereafter, the "literary monthlies" like *Harper's*, *Century*, *Scribner's*, and even the children's magazine *St. Nicholas* used humorous illustrations, cartoons, series, and decorated light verse in great numbers.

The rise of these outlets reflected a change in American society in the postwar years. There were signs of a growing prosperity and middle class that could indulge itself in the luxury of laughter. America was becoming more literate and certainly more cosmopolitan, and the remaining Puritan tendencies of confusing pleasure and vice had finally disappeared. These new developments, plus the explosion of outlets, allowed illustrators who had begun in humorous fields to descend into serious picture-making; two such artists were named Winslow Homer and Edwin Austin Abbey.

Nevertheless, humor asserted itself with a lighthearted vengeance in the 1870s and 1880s. Scores of humorous papers and magazines were inaugurated at the time, and the chief architect was Henry Carter, who called himself Frank Leslie and started many short-lived humor magazines, including *Budget of Fun*, *Phunny Phellow*, *The Jolly Joker*, and *The Comic Monthly*.

The first American humor magazine had been *Salmagundi* (founded by Washington Irving in 1807), but the graveyard of later efforts included such titles as *American Punch*, *Boomerang*, *Chic*, *Phunniest of Awl*, *Punchinello*, *Texas Siftings*, *Tid-Bits*, *Time*, *Truth*, *The Wasp*, and *Wild Oats*, all from the '70s and '80s. For all the failures, this movement provided a major impetus to the cause of American graphic humor: themes were defined, techniques were refined, the public's appetite was regularly being whetted, and artists throughout America and Europe were being attracted to the field of humorous illustration. It was at this time that American humor became an industry.

The "industry" flowered in large part because of the perfectly symbiotic relationship between illustrators and text humorists. For all of the fame of Darley and Bellew and Currier & Ives's humorous prints, it was an emerging crop of humorous authors, newspaper columnists, comic lecturers, and local colorists who were the first superstars of American humor, and they all brought illustrators in tow.

Through the end of the 19th century, a group of talented humorous illustrators serviced the needs of best-selling funny authors and no doubt helped sales and reception of their work. H. L. Stephens was Artemus

Ward's chief illustrator. True Williams illustrated *Tom Sawyer*, *Peck's Bad Boy*, and the "Samantha" stories of Marietta Holley. Livingston Hopkins illustrated the funny stories of Josh Billings and Bill Nye. F. Opper illustrated Bill Nye's *Comic History of the United States* (and individual Nye stories), as did Zim and Walt McDougall and Samantha at Saratoga.

Opper also decorated the works of Mr. Dooley and Eugene Field; E. W. Kemble illustrated Mark Twain (including *Huckleberry Finn*), Mr. Dooley, and many others; and A. B. Frost contributed legendary illustrations to the works of Max Adeler and Joel Chandler Harris (*Uncle Remus*). C. Frink illustrated other *Peck's Bad Boy* farcical sagas, and Dan Beard (founder of the Boy Scouts of America) drew for Mark Twain (*A Connecticut Yankee in King Arthur's Court*). John T. McCutcheon illustrated for George Ade, Mr. Dooley, and Irvin S. Cobb.

The major seedbeds of American humorous illustration and cartoons at this time, however, were the three major humor weeklies, *Puck*, *Judge*, and *Life*. *Puck*, founded by Joseph Keppler, succeeded where the others had failed; it was a lively sixteen-page magazine with text and cartoons featuring three full-color lithographed drawings each issue. Keppler was its chief artist, followed by F. Opper (who was regarded as the dean of American cartoonists during his career, which spanned the 1870s to the 1930s), F. Graetz, C. J. Taylor, Syd B. Griffin, F. M. Howarth, J. S. Pughe, L. M. Glackens, Will Crawford, W. F. Hill, A. Z. Baker, and finally, Keppler, Jr., who succeeded his father. *Puck* was born in 1877 and died in 1918.

Judge was a carbon copy founded by former *Puck* artist James Albert Wales (Keppler evidently tired of the prints of Wales) in 1881; three years later it was underwritten secretly by the Republican party and enriched by the presence of two more Puck renegades, the talented Eugene Zimmerman (Zim) and Bernhard Gillam. *Judge* was consciously more raucous in its approach than *Puck* and provided an outlet for some remarkable graphic experimentation (including exaggerated anatomy and animation) by its artists, who included Grant Hamilton, J. H. Smith, F. Victor, T. S. Sullivant, Art Young, Albert Levering, Gus Dirks, C. W. Kahles, James Montgomery Flagg, Emil Flohri, Penrhyn Stanlaws, Ralph Barton, L. Fellows, Johnny Gruelle, Percy Crosby, R. B. Fuller, S. J. Perelman, and Dr. Seuss (yes, as illustrators and cartoonists), Gardner Rea, Bill Holman, and Ted Key. It died in the 1940s.

Life, however, was a different story. Founded in 1883 by John Ames Mitchell and E. S. Martin (a founder of the *Harvard Lampoon* humor magazine), this was the *Life* magazine that was intentionally funny; after its death in 1936 Henry Luce resurrected it as a newsweekly. The original *Life* was smaller in size and all black and white. It had a more sophisticated editorial policy in text and art, being more genteel and society-oriented than its two colored neighbors. Three years after its founding, Charles Dana Gibson sold his first drawing to *Life*, and it was he—whose Gibson Girl and dashing man defined the fashions of a generation and the style of a generation of illustrators—who embodied *Life*'s tone.

Of the three magazines, *Life* certainly had the most notable humorous illustrators in its pages, including C. G. Bush, E. W. Kemble, A. B. Frost, Albert Wenzel, Oliver Herford, Albert Sterner, Hy Mayer, Orson Lowell, Walt Kuhn, Anton Otto Fischer, Angus MacDonall, Gluyas Williams, Rollin Kirby, John Held, Jr., Norman Rockwell, Maxfield Parrish, the Leyendecker brothers, Russell Patterson, Rube Goldberg, Milt Gross, Edwina, Don Herold, and Perry Barlow. When Gibson was offered $100,000 in 1904 to draw exclusively for *Collier's*, he accepted, with the proviso that he also could contribute to *Life*; and by 1920 he had purchased controlling interest in the publication that had discovered him and showcased his work through the years.

Among other publications had been the New York *Daily Graphic*, founded in the 1870s as the first fully illustrated daily in America; although it used woodcuts, it was able to perform its seemingly arduous task by utilizing the new technology of photoengraving and employing dozens of illustrators. *Harper's Weekly* elevated Thomas Nast to almost legendary status as a cartoonist and illustrator in the 1870s, when he began his campaign against the corrupt Democratic machine in New York City; his success versus Tammany Hall's "Tweed Ring" was almost single-handed and immensely raised the visibility and respectability of the humorous illustrator.

In the wake of the period of great humor magazines was *The New Yorker*, founded in 1925 by Harold Ross. Ross had been an associate editor of *Judge*, but he patterned his new cosmopolitan weekly humor journal after *Life*, which *The New Yorker* resembled during its first decade. The list of its cartoonists through the years reads like a Hall of Fame of graphic humor, as much for their approach to sophisticated humor as their artistic excellence. It includes Peter Arno, Charles Addams, Rea Irvin, Garrett Price, George Price, Mary Petty, Cobean, Alain, Whitney Darrow, Jr., Steig, Helen Hokinson, James Thurber, Alajalov, Al Frueh, Reginald Marsh, Carl Rose, Otto Soglow, Charles Saxon, Saul Steinberg, Robert Kraus, George Booth, and Lee Lorenz.

Through this period a crop of illustrators arose who worked independently for book publishers or for weekly general-interest magazines whose stories were often collected in book form (as in the case of *The Saturday Evening Post*). Among these are the pioneer women illustrators Rose O'Neill and Grace Drayton, as well as Strothman, Peter Newell, Clare Victor Dwiggins, Groesbeck, Gelett Burgess, and Reginald Birch. Up through the 1920s, the humorous illustrator clearly reflected the change in American humor and American life. The cracker-barrel dialecticians surrendered their place to suburbanites and a new middle class, and their drawings reflected the shift.

An offshoot of humorous illustration at the turn of the century was the manifestation of nothing more momentous than the culmination of civilized man's 6,000-year groping for an ideal form of communication. This was, of course, the comic strip.

The 1920s has been called the Time of Laughter. New illustrators, cartoonists, writers, and comedians emerged during the Roaring Twenties, roaring with a new kind of laughter. Illustrating the "little man" school of humor led by Robert Benchley was Gluyas Williams, decorating the sauciness of Anita Loos was Ralph Barton, and Miguel Covarrubias contributed caricatures to the parody and interview books of John Riddell (Corey Ford). Many of these illustrators—along with William Gropper, Dr. Seuss, and others—were regular contributors to the elegant but irreverent *Vanity Fair* of the day, a magazine that is very dead and very long gone.

Caricature came into its own as another subgroup of humorous illustration in the 1920s. Barton and Covarrubias were the first prominent caricaturists. Others were Al Hirschfeld, Irma Selz, Al Frueh, Peggy Bacon, Sam Norkin, and Bruce Stark. David Levine reigns as the most influential of contemporary caricaturists.

In the popular magazines, fewer illustrators served as exclusively comic artists; many, such as Wallace Morgan with Wodehouse's "Jeeves" stories and Anton Otto Fischer with the "Glencannon" and "Tugboat Annie" stories, merely displayed their versatility by handling humorous assignments along with their other work. In the several decades after the 1920s, however, there were some specialists in humorous illustrations in books and magazines. These included Albert Dorne, Tony Sarg, Raeburn Van Buren, Harry Beckhoff, Floyd Davis, and others.

Compared to most periods of illustration history, the mid-1950s through the late 1970s was relatively bereft of humor in the traditional modes of book and magazine illustration. Many humorous illustrators moved into the field of children's books, where humor virtually choked out traditional themes of adventure and daring. Dr. Seuss (Theodor Seuss Geisel) is only first among many; some of the many include Jack Kent, P. D. Eastman, Eric Gurney, Hardie Gramatky, Roy McKie, and of course, Maurice Sendak. Jack Davis used the springboard of the irreverent *Mad* magazine—the breeding ground for many inspired illustrator/cartoonists, including Harvey Kurtzman and John Severin—to become a major presence in advertising, magazine covers, and record jackets.

Appropriately, the renaissance in humorous illustration in America came from the political realm, and it has brought the field full circle. Social and political ferment in the '60s and '70s was translated by a rising generation of cartoonists and humorous illustrators into vital, clever graphic humor.

Humorous illustration has rebounded with vigor in advertising and editorial assignments. Three of the most prominent schools are represented by the purely humorous (as opposed to political) artists Robert Weber, chronicler of suburbanites; Elwood H. Smith, who has revived the feel of 1930s strips and animated figures; and Arnold Roth, whose humorous flights can soar into the surreal. David Levine has made the pen line respectable again and, with his literary and current-affairs caricatures has spawned a generation of imitators.

Much of the work of the so-called New Illustrators—irreverent, iconoclastic in the true sense, inspired by bubble-gum machine trinkets and neon art—is humorous in theme or intent. Among these illustrators are Gary Panter, Mick Haggerty, Lou Brooks, and Robert Risko.

Whether conventional or avant-garde, humorous illustration abounds today in newspapers, magazines, advertising, books, record jackets, apparel, movie credits, animation, comic strips, greeting cards, and probably, if we look hard enough, in the designs made by cheese melting on the surface of Sicilian pizzas. Does America need to laugh any more today than in the recent past, when the pendulum swung in the other direction? Probably not: every generation has its ideals, its apocalypses, its happy middle grounds. The many humorous illustrators working today—established artists and aspiring funny folks alike—are part of a tradition, and it is a proud, rich tradition, insufficiently appreciated and chronicled but basic to the very function of illustration arts.

To consider the two extremities of our time-line, it might seem tenuous to relate Benjamin Franklin and the New Illustrators; after all, he did not store his pen nibs in various pierced portions of his earlobes, as some New Illustrators are rumored to do. But on the other hand, depicting America as a vivisected snake . . .

This lightning tour has skimmed the surface of history for the best names in humorous illustration, just as this book represents the best of an incredibly active and fertile collecting field. Great names from the past can remind us of illustrations's basic function: to illuminate and accompany. But the function of humorous illustration is more finely tuned: it is to inspire, to anger, to mollify, to teach, to preach, to attack, to tell stories. And it is to laugh.

PUTTING A PRICE ON
HUMOROUS ILLUSTRATIONS

Original art before the age of photoengraving—roughly, the middle 1870s—is very rare because illustrations were previously reproduced by steel engraving, stone lithography, or woodcuts. Original prints by Franklin and Revere can sell for as much as $7,500; Currier & Ives cartoons are worth less (as a rule, some Lincoln images being an exception) than pastoral scenes but can fetch as much as $1,500; and Thomas Nast's famous cartoons of the Tweed Ring can be found for as little as $10 each. His woodcuts were no further removed from "original" status than others' plates or prints, but they suffer from being perceived as magazine tearsheets instead of prints.

Pencil sketches by illustrators of the era before pen and ink are very rare. Darleys can sell for several hundred dollars, Nasts perhaps for a thousand (whereas his later pen-and-inks for reproduction are valued in the $1,500–$4,000 range); and the sky would be the limit for a Franklin rough sketch. Printers' proofs of such work have a special value; recently press proofs of Joseph Keppler's cartoons from *Puck* (c. 1876–1880) were snatched up at auction for roughly $100 apiece.

The humorous magazine illustrators have entered a realm of their own, an echelon with the "upscale" illustrators like Abbey, Pyle, Wyeth, et al. But their craft was no less honored in their day and is scarcely less valued today. A. B. Frost's illustrations are prized; an oil can approach five figures, while pen and inks can be found for as little as $1,000. Many illustrators have particular followings, making their work desirable and more valued: Palmer Cox's Brownie drawings ($300–$2,000), Peter Newell's novelty illustrations ($750–$3,000), Rose O'Neill's Kewpies ($1,250–$3,000 and $750–$2,000 for her adult drawings), and Grace Drayton's kid cartoons (she created the Campbell Soup Kids, originals of which would be worth triple her normal $750–$1,500 range) are examples. Illustrations of famous characters in books and magazines—Huck Finn, Penrod, Little Lord Fauntleroy, Tugboat Annie, Jeeves, et al., down to the present—clearly have special interest.

The single-panel cartoon has served many functions in American history, from inciting political emotions to commenting on social trends. Originals of social cartoons are accessible from the period of *Puck*, *Judge*, and *Life*, the great cartoon weeklies of the last century. Many now-obscure illustrators and cartoonists of the first rank drew for these periodicals, and when originals appear on the market, they are often priced at surprisingly low ranges of $50 to $250; this applies to artists like F. Opper, C. J. Taylor, Zim, and Ehrhart. Only slightly higher

Jessie Willing Gillespie. "Ladies' Larger Lingerie." Crayon on board, 1915, signed lower right, 14½ × 21¼ inches, $750. PHOTO COURTESY OF AUTHOR. *(See Special Notes [26] at back of book.)*

($250–$600) are illustrators like Gluyas Williams and Percy Crosby, who were also book illustrators and comic-section cartoonists. It is when collectors get to the levels of Charles Dana Gibson and John Held, Jr., that classical illustration prices are met: $1,500–$7,000.

Since 1925 the single-panel magazine cartoon has almost been synonymous with *The New Yorker* magazine. Little original art from the magazine has traditionally been available, although the Barbara Nichols Gallery in New York and others have represented individual artists. Prices for popular illustrators like Peter Arno, Charles Addams, George Price, Charles Saxon, and George Booth can start close to $1,000 and, in the case of the late Arno, Addams, and Saxon, be as high as $4,000.

It is rather surprising that there has not been more of a market for the collecting of political cartoon originals. A relatively high number of artists produce them virtually every day of the year, and the form has been a staple of American life for more than a century. While there is not a plethora of political cartoon art available—many originals were routinely destroyed or donated en masse to institutions—collectors can acquire pieces by many famous cartoonists for relatively low prices. Cartoonists like Rollin Kirby and "Ding" Darling, each of whom won multiple Pulitzer Prizes, appear on the market for $150–$400. Recent "stars" in the

Jessie Willing Gillespie. "Feather Brained or the Chicken-Hatchery." Pen and ink. Signed and initialed upper right, 8¾ × 16 inches, $450. PHOTO COURTESY OF AUTHOR.

field, like Pat Oliphant and Jeff MacNelly, often release their originals to galleries and charity auctions, whose prices can reach $1,000; but on the other hand, many other cartoonists will respond to letters addressed to them at their newspapers and sell particular favorites for as low as $100 or a donation to a charity. One exception is the great Herblock: virtually none of his originals is in circulation.

Caricature is a related art, a special form that deals in political and social commentary as well as entertainment and celebrity affairs. Political cartoonists can be caricaturists but not necessarily; their primary

Constantin Alajalov. "Wedding Day." Gouache on illustration board. New Yorker *magazine, May 27, 1933, 14 × 11 inches, $5,000.* PHOTO COURTESY OF AMERICAN ILLUSTRATORS GALLERY/JUDY GOFFMAN FINE ART, NEW YORK.

Pen and ink drawing of Elvis by Al Hirschfeld, 24 × 17 inches. Signed lower right, $7,500 to $8,000 range. PHOTO COURTESY OF THE MARGO FEIDEN GALLERIES. *Note:* An etching of this same piece would sell for $1,400.

aim is the issue, not always the personality, but caricature plays a role in their work. Caricature is practiced by relatively few cartoonists and illustrators, so the availability of American caricature is scant on the collectors' market. Generally, it is books by past masters like Covarrubias or prints by the facile Al Frueh that are more accessible; besides, originals rarely surface on the collectors' market. Originals by these two masters of the '20s and '30s, and by Ralph Barton or Mal Eaton of the same era, would be valued at $1,000 to $1,500. It would seem to some that American caricature began and ended with Al Hirshfeld, so much has he dominated two generations of illustrators. That would not give historical masters like Keppler and Gillam their due, or recent lights like Sam Berman and Mort Drucker, but Hirshfeld's "look" and influence set him apart. For years his originals have been handled by gallery representation, with prices beginning around $1,500.

CONSTANTIN ALAJALOV (1900–1987)

[signature: a lajalov]

Constantine Alajalov sold his first cover to *The New Yorker* in 1926 and has since painted a long and colorful series of satirical vignettes of American life for *The New Yorker* and *The Saturday Evening Post*.

Alajalov was born in the Russian town of Rostov-on-the-Don. The revolution came when he was seventeen and a student at the University of Petrograd. He survived this period by working as a government artist, painting huge propaganda pictures and portraits, and he eventually made his way, in 1921, to Constantinople, which was an international refugee haven.

Although largely self-taught as an artist, Alajalov earned a precarious living by sketching portraits in bars or painting sidewalk advertisements for movie houses. After two years of this, he saved enough to pay his passage to America.

The Dieter, s., tempera, 18″ × 16½″. $1,900

PEGGY BACON (1895–1987)

Both an author and an illustrator, Peggy Bacon studied under John Sloan and George Bellows. Known for her humor, she worked for a variety of magazines such as *The New Yorker*, *Vanity Fair*, and *Town and Country*. She did a series of caricatures of famous artists that was published with the title "Off with Their Heads." Her work was also published by Viking Press, Harcourt, and Macmillan.

In the Forest, s. Peggy Bacon, i. *Black Sabbath*, 13½″ × 11″, pen-and-ink wash on paper. $385
Golden Age, s. Peggy Bacon, d. 1959, 13¾″ × 18″, oil on board. $3,850
The Rabbit, s. Peggy Bacon, matted 3⅛″ × 4½″, pen and ink on paper.
.... $275

RALPH BARTON (1891–1931)

[signature: Ralph Barton]

Born in Kansas City, Missouri, Ralph Barton studied art in Paris, then settled in Manhattan. This artist, cartoonist, and drama critic had a styl-

Ralph Barton. *Woman seated at piano, satirical. Tempera on board, signed upper right, 20 × 14¼ inches, $3,500.* PHOTO COURTESY OF AUTHOR.

Harry Beckhoff. *"John Dingle and the Homing Cats."* Signed upper right, $1,600. PHOTO COURTESY OF ILLUSTRATION HOUSE, INC.

ized, satirical style, drawn in line and flat tone or color. His work appeared in *Judge*, *Puck*, *Vanity Fair*, *Smart Set*, *Cosmopolitan*, and the old *Life* magazine.

He also illustrated such books as *Gentlemen Prefer Blondes*, Balzac's *Droll Stories*, and others.

All Good Jokes Go to Heaven, s., pen and ink, wash, 12″ × 17″. $350

HARRY BECKHOFF (1901–1979)

HARRY
BECKHOFF

Harry Beckhoff studied with Dean Cornwell and Harvey Dunn but said it was the French illustrators, Martin, Brissaud, and Marty, who influenced his style.

His works began with tiny sketches that contained even the smallest detail that would be used in the final composition. He then pantographed the drawing, about five times larger, and inked in the outlines; color areas were painted in with flat washes. While he worked for many major magazines such as *Collier's*, he is probably best known for his portrayals of the characters in Damon Runyon stories.

The Sightseers, s., opaque watercolor, 20″ × 11″. $900
Hillbilly Fight, reproduced *Collier's*, s., watercolor, green, black, and white, 11½″ × 20″. $375
Hoe-Down, story illustration, "Welcome Home, Willy," s., watercolor, 15″ × 14.5″. $375

JAMES MONTGOMERY FLAGG (1877–1960)

JAMES MONTGOMERY FLAGG

For over thirty years James Montgomery Flagg did illustrations, posters, and portraits. One of his early assignments was a cartoon feature entitled "Nervy Nat." He also illustrated the humorous P. G. Wodehouse stories for many years. One of his best-known illustrations was the "I Want You" Uncle Sam recruiting poster. He worked quickly, doing portrait sketches of his friends, including many celebrities, and portraits in oil as well.

Portrait of Young Girl with Oriental Fan, s. J.M.F., 15″ × 24″, watercolor. $1,045
Portrait of a Man Seated in an Interior, s., d. 1905, 39″ × 30″. ... $1,320
Woman frying fish outdoors, s., oil on canvas, 34″ × 25″. $1,600

Indian Couple, story illustration, s., i., lower right, pen and ink, 14.25″ × 20″. $900
Portrait of Walter Trumbull, s., charcoal, 19″ × 14″. $350
The Discussion, 2 illus. (1) 19½″ × 13″, s., (2) 21½″ × 12½″; pen and ink. $850
Fox, Beautiful and Dumb, and Beautiful and Not Dumb, three drawings; first, inits.; second and third, inits. and i. with t.; largest, 14″ × 11″; first, brush and black ink on board; second and third, charcoal on paper. $110
Twin Sisters, s., *Cosmopolitan*, Jan. 1916, 20¼″ × 24¾″, pen, black ink, and pencil on board. $825

ARTHUR BURDETT FROST (1851–1928)

A. B. Frost.

Rural America was the subject matter for many of the illustrations done by Arthur Burdett Frost. It is interesting that Frost was red-green colorblind. He got around the problem by reading the labels on the paint tubes and placing the colors in the correct order on his palette. These days he is best remembered for his illustrations for the Uncle Remus tales by Joel Chandler Harris.

Nearly bus' his brains out, story illustration, "The Trial of Jonathan Goode," *Scribner's*, Dec. 1920, s. lower right, Wolff pencil, 11.75″ × 10.25″. ... $800
Studies of a Gentleman Painting the Dining Room Door, *Harper's Bazaar*, Nov. 1884, s., pen and ink, 9.5″ × 12.5″. $1,800
A boy with his dog, "For Always," s., black-and-white gouache, 17″ × 15″. $1,500
Man in bed, "Out Cold," s., black-and-white gouache, 15″ × 18.5″. $1,500
The Accusation, s. A. B. Frost, 11½″ × 9¾″, pen and ink, ink wash, and Chinese white on paper. $330
Hanging Woodcocks, s., d. 1899, 16½″ × 14″. $3,850
The Inspection, s. A. B. Frost, sight size 16″ × 18½″, watercolor en grisaille. $825
Hello, He Called to the Mayor Cheerily, s., d. 1901, t.; t. verso, prov., 13″ × 8½″, gouache en grisaille on board. $1,045
Duck Hunter in a Blind, s., 13″ × 20″, watercolor. $2,310

JOHN HELD, JR. (1889–1958)

John Held Jr

The highly stylized drawings of John Held, Jr., appropriately defined the free-spirited Roaring Twenties. From the flirty flappers to collegiate mores, Held's light touch said it all. His illustrations appeared not only in *The New Yorker* but *College Humor*, *Cosmopolitan*, *Liberty*, *Judge*, and the old *Life*. By the 1930s, with the changing mood brought on by the Depression, his drawings went out of fashion.

Commuters, advertisement, H.O. Farina, s. lower right, pen and ink, 18″ × 18″. $1,700

Girls Sunbathing, "Sunspots," 1925, s., ink and wash, 13.5″ × 18″. $1,500

Passing Parade, advertisement for the Jos. Horne Co., s., pen and ink, 10″ × 14″. $700

Flappers Having Lunch, "Dumb Bunny" from *The Flesh Is Weak*, 1930, brush, pen and ink, 9½″ × 7″, estate-stamped. $1,250

The Three Christmas Cowboys, s., d. 38, 11¼″ × 19″, watercolor on paper. $990

WALLACE MORGAN (1873–1948)

W. MORGAN —

Trained as a newspaper artist used to doing quick sketches, Wallace Morgan was highly successful as one of the official artists assigned to the A.E.F. during World War I. His ability to quickly capture the humor and mood of his subjects adapted easily to *The Saturday Evening Post* P. G. Wodehouse stories as well as other magazine stories. He was president of the Society of Illustrators from 1929 to 1936. His charcoal and pen-and-ink illustrations are still available for under $1,000.

In the Old Dominion, s., charcoal, 17″ × 21¾″, Wallace Morgan gave this illustration to Woodi Ishmael when Woodi was a student at the Art Students League. $200

Shrimp boats, story illustration, "The Island of Lost Men," Dec. 26, 1931, init., ink and wash, 10.5″ × 10.5″. $100

"Youth and Beauty" by Rita Wieman, s., charcoal and wash, 15″ × 21″. $450

Self-portrait, brush and ink, 13″ × 13″, not signed. $200

The Corsage, s., charcoal, 16″ × 11″. $400

THOMAS NAST (1840–1902)

Th. Nast.

Thomas Nast (mentioned elsewhere in this book) was best known as a political cartoonist and caricaturist. Following the Civil War, Nast used his talents to fight the corrupt Tammany political machine in New York, especially Boss Tweed and his gang. His political illustrations are credited with forcing the machine out of office.

John Held, Jr. Pen and ink, $2,500. PHOTO COURTESY OF ILLUSTRATION HOUSE, INC.

Wallace Morgan. "The Corsage." 16 × 11 inches, charcoal. Signed lower right, $750. PHOTO COURTESY OF ILLUSTRATION HOUSE, INC.

A Portly Gentleman, Luggage in Hand, on a Train Platform, wi
formed Porter on Each Side, drawing, s. Th. Nast, uncaptioned ca
Estelle Doheny Collection, 9¹/₁₆″ × 9½″, pen and black ink on heav
....

Bismark Putting It in His Pipe to Smoke, s. Th. Nast, i. with t. and
inscription, 24⅝″ × 21¼″, pen and black ink and pencil on board. ...

RUSSELL PATTERSON (1896–1977)

Russell Patterson was famous not only for his "flappers" and his interpretation of the Jazz Age but also as a designer of costumes and sets for
the *Ziegfield Follies* of 1922 and other Broadway shows. By the late 1930s
he combined advertising illustrations with Christmas toy windows for
Macy's.

This versatile artist designed the Women's Army Corps uniforms during World War II. He also did a comic strip and designed restaurant
interiors and hotel lobbies.

Note: Patterson's work from the 1920s is extremely scarce, as he destroyed most of it.

Three caricatures of black men, s. and i. lower left, pen, brush, and ink, 7.75″
× 7.75″. $600
Guardian Angel, s., i., watercolor and pencil, 10″ × 8″. $125

SPORTS

One of the truly untapped collecting categories of American illustrator art is sports. Collectors can still select a variety of sports, from boxing to horse racing and baseball, that reflects the growth of American interest in sports. That interest developed in the late 19th century as Americans had more leisure time to participate in tennis, golf, and fishing, as well as yachting and hunting, and to attend sporting events.

In England, sporting art was commissioned and collected at the end of the 18th century by wealthy squires for their country estates. For Americans of the 19th century, magazines like *Harper's* offered illustrations of important sporting events. Many of the illustrators who worked for *Harper's* did sporting art as well as covering other news events. Among them was Winslow Homer. In the late 19th century, Arthur Burdett Frost did a woodcut of quail shooting for *Harper's* that certainly qualifies as a fine example of sporting illustration.

As mentioned elsewhere in this book, Frost, who was a dedicated sports enthusiast, did many illustrations of fishing and golfing subjects. In the early 20th century, famous illustrators such as Francis Xavier Leyendecker included sports subjects in their work. As sports became ever more important to the American public, advertisers hired illustrators to tie in their products and companies with famous sports figures and subjects.

Not until the advent of *Sports Illustrated* magazine in 1954 was there a single publication dealing only with sports, although *Field and Stream*, which dealt mostly with hunting and fishing, had been published since the 1930s. In the 1950s, when other magazines were relying more on photography, *Sports Illustrated* used illustrations. It was said at the time they used more illustrators than any other magazine. Among them were Robert Handville, Robert Riger, and Robert Weaver.

According to Jo Schiano, who was administrative assistant to the design director at *Sports Illustrated* from its beginning till her recent retirement, most of the art was returned to the illustrators. Generally, the magazine kept the cover art. Unclaimed art eventually found its way to the storage room. Some early examples are casually hung around the present offices. Now there's a treasure trove awaiting discovery!

Sports cartoons and caricatures are a specialized field. Usually pen and ink, they were used by newspapers and were especially popular in the 1920s, 1930s, and 1940s. Some of the best-known cartoonists and caricaturists are Amadee and Burris Jenkins, Jr.

COLLECTING SPORTS ILLUSTRATIONS

Collectors had a chance to buy original sports art at the "Sporting Auction" in April 1990 at Guernsey's, as well as the previous August, Guernsey's 1989 auction of Topps Company items and original art of baseball and sporting (as well as nonsporting) trade cards. Founded as a gum company in 1938, in 1947 Topps introduced bubble gum cards with art and photos of American sports heroes as well as other famous personalities. The original art from the 1950s, along with original 1970s football posters, were sold at affordable prices. Prices usually depended on the popularity of the players—just as with baseball cards—as well as rarity.

In 1914 and 1915, the Cracker Jack Company issued baseball cards featuring players from the National and American Leagues, as well as players who had gone to the outlawed Federal League. Although the cards were at the Guernsey's auction, the original art wasn't. If it still exists, it represents money in the bank for the lucky collector who discovers it.

Original art for World Series programs should be included in a sports collection, along with programs from other championship meets—if you can find them. Just consider the many important sporting events over the years; if photography wasn't used, the programs were done by an illustrator.

Some sports illustrators to look for are named here even though there are no prices available for their work.

Paul Brown (1893–1958) specialized in his favorite subject: horses. He drew sporting illustrations for Brooks Brothers as far back as 1920 and also worked for many of the important magazines, including *Collier's*, *Harper's Bazaar*, and *Liberty*.

C. Peter Helck (1893–) is mentioned elsewhere in this book, but sports illustrations should include examples of his auto racing paintings and working drawings.

Robert Thompkins Handville, A.N.A. (1924–) was a contributing, commissioned artist-reporter for *Sports Illustrated* from 1962 to 1977. He is also designer of the Yellowstone National Park commemorative postal stamp and the Alfred Verville commemorative airmail stamp.

Robert Riger (1924–) is a sports authority who turned his interests into some of the finest examples of sports illustrator art as well as fine art, photography, and writing. In his book *The ABC Wide World of Sports*, important sports events he covered are written about and illustrated. Much of his work has appeared in *Sports Illustrated* over the years.

Robert Weaver (1924–), considered an important influence on sports

J. F. Kernan. "Babe Ruth, Sultan of Swat." Oil on canvas, 22 × 28 inches, $9,500. PHOTO COURTESY OF GUERNSEY'S.

Mickey Mantle. Color artwork used for Topps baseball card series, 3¼ × 4½ inches, 1953, $110,000. PHOTO COURTESY OF GUERNSEY'S.

illustration, worked in many categories. Among the magazines that used his work are *Sports Illustrated*, *Look*, *Life*, *Fortune*, and *Esquire*.

Ken Dallison (1933–) made a specialty of auto racing, though he covered dozens of subjects for both advertising clients and publishers. His sports illustrations were used in *Sports Illustrated*, *Esquire*, *Car and Driver*, and *Flying*.

AMADEE

Amadee's sports cartoons hang in every major sports Hall of Fame in America. Not only did his cartooning style earn him national acclaim, but he was also known as a gifted portrait artist, with portraits appearing on the cover of the *Sporting News* for over twenty-five years. He left his mark not only as a sports cartoonist but as a designer and illustrator as well.

In 1968, his cartoons of the Cardinals were credited with inspiring the "El Birdo" craze in St. Louis. Amadee is a fixture in the Busch Stadium press box and has been a member of the Baseball Writer's Association of America for forty years.

Tom Seaver, Cincinnati Reds, s., pencil, 7″ × 9″. $225
Joe DiMaggio, New York Yankees, shows DiMaggio forming from steam coming from Mr. Coffee machine, s., pencil and ink, 11¼″ × 14½″. $150
Days of Dazzled Dodgers, s., pen and colored pencil, 11″ × 14½″, matted.
....$160

Amadee. "Will the Cubs Make It Stick?" P. K. Wrigley blows a bubble, with the caption "First Pennant since 1945?" Pencil and ink, signed, 12 × 12 inches, $60. PHOTO COURTESY OF GUERNSEY'S.

Branch Rickey, Pittsburgh Pirates, 1950, s., shows Rickey in Pirate outfit, in Bum outfit, brush and ink, 15″ × 9″. $100

Coogan's Bluff to Candlestick, Giants, s., brush and ink, 10½″ × 13″.
....$100

George Steinbrenner, Steinbrenner is knocked out of elevator by "Dodgers" arm, charcoal, 8½″ × 14″. $200

Harry Caray, Bill White, two illus., s., charcoal, 5″ × 9½″; 4¾″ × 9¼″.
....$100

John McNamara, Roger Clemens, Dave Henderson, and Rich Gedman, Boston Red Sox, two illus., s., charcoal and charcoal and watercolor, 6″ × 10″; 6″ × 18½″. $100

Royals' Rembrandt, shows George Brett painting portrait of Billy Martin with pine tar, exhibiting episode when Martin claimed that Brett used pine tar on bat, s., brush and ink, 9″ × 15½″. $90

Red Schoendienst, Enos Slaughter, St. Louis Cardinals, two illus., colored pencil, charcoal, 6½″ × 10″, 4″ × 5½″. $60

Ty Cobb and Dizzy Dean, two illus., portrait of Cobb, Dizzy speaking to angel at Heaven's gate, pen and ink and brush and ink, 5″ × 4″, 9″ × 11″.
....$1,000

Two baseball cartoons, "From Bare Hands to Bushel Baskets," tracing the enlargement of the mitt, and "Settle for One Winner, Now?" showing the die-hard Browns fans, s., ink and colored pencil, 11½″ × 11″, 11½″ × 14½″, one illustration cut, one with corrections. $50

Three baseball cartoons, "Bankruptcy of Yankee Stadium," "American and National Football and Baseball Leagues in Traffic Jam," "Owners, Players, and Miller Represented by Lemmings of the Sea," 2 s., charcoal and brush and ink, 12″ × 14″, 11¼″ × 14″, 8″ × 12½″. $100

Louis–Charles Bout, shows skeleton in hospital bed, with Heavyweight Division crown, doctor with hypderdermic needle, "Louis–Charles" bout tries to give skeleton life, s., ink and charcoal, 15¼″ × 15″. $50

Leon Spinks, Michael Spinks, two illus.: "Coming Attraction?" show Leon Spinks riding in limo, in ring within police car; portrait of Michael Spinks, s., brush and ink and charcoal, 14″ × 14½″, 4½″ × 10″. $70

Larry Holmes and Primo Carnera, two illus., s., charcoal and brush and ink, 5½″ × 8″, 5¼″ × 7½″. $50

GERALD GARSTON

Gerald Garston is recognized as one of the foremost sports artists in the country. His work is a featured part of the "Diamonds Are Forever: Artists and Writers on Baseball" three-year traveling exhibition, sponsored by Washington, DC's Smithsonian Institution, and has won great acclaim. He studied with Karl Metzler, Louis Boucher, Harry Steinberg, and Josef Albers. Garston had his first one-man show in the 860 Gallery in Baltimore in 1951 and since then has appeared in many museums and galleries throughout the United States, including nine shows at the Pucker/Safrai Gallery in Boston, the "Sport in Art" exhibition in New

York, the Philadelphia Museum of Art, and the Smithsonian Museum in Washington, DC.

Tradition, oil on canvas, 60″ × 48″. $4,000
All Stars, oil on canvas, 42″ × 48⅛″. $4,000

BURRIS JENKINS, JR. (1896–1966)

Burris Jenkins, Jr., was perhaps the best-known cartoonist in the United States from the Prohibition era through the 1960s. His drawings featuring sports commentary and John Q. Public were syndicated throughout the country, appearing in every Hearst newspaper in America. They reflect the mind, imagination, and mood of America. Everyone will remember Jenkins's vivid portrayals of the rivalry between the Giants and Dodgers, Joe DiMaggio, Sonia Henie, and the champion Yankees. He also rendered the large, colorful illustrations displayed throughout the city announcing the rodeo and circus every year. With unflagging creative powers and super technical skills, he portrayed the leading atheletes and major events in baseball, football, boxing, tennis, and swimming, and was widely recognized as the "king" of sports cartoonists in America in the 1930s.

Jenkins was commissioned to design the monumental mural at the Sports Pavillion at the 1939 World's Fair. In 1957 he won the Banshee Silver Lady Award; in 1958 and again in 1960 he won the coveted Headliner's Award. He was also frequently nominated for the Pulitzer Prize for his reporting and commentary.

Pulling Out All the Stops, highlights of first three games of 1947 Series (Yankees vs. Dodgers), s., charcoal, 18½″ × 12″, matted. $375
Any Day Now, Carl Hubbell, with broken arm, tries to leave hospital room as he hears over the radio that the team is 5 runs behind, s., charcoal, 19½″ × 15″. $400
Out in Front for Tonight, public tiring of 4-minute mile promises, s., charcoal, 16¼″ × 20″, matted. $400
Not Like a Woman, Santa looks down a list of players (with each name crossed out) while tennis hopeful stands atop hill, s., charcoal, 19½″ × 18″, matted. .. $300
National Sportsmen's Show at Grand Central Palace, with images of canoer, fisherman, and wildlife above, s., charcoal, 15″ × 20″, matted. $400
Opportunity Sale—Unfilled Shoes, depiction of lack of young talent in 1939, s., charcoal, 19½″ × 16″, matted. $425
Last Hour Lunacy, history of bicycle racing last-hour finishes from 1914 to 1926, s., charcoal, 19″ × 17″, matted. $325
Yes-Sir, the Circus Is in Town, 1940-labeled Dodger player passes cage of wild cats labeled as "Murderers Row, NY Yankees," s., charcoal, 20″ × 16½″, matted. $600

I Still Don't Believe It, Cub balances bats and baseballs (labeled French, Root, Warneke, Lee (baby Chicago infield)—Can Cubs Beat Tigers in 1935 Series? s., charcoal, 20½ ″ × 17″, matted. $325
His Big Moment, Giants in first place humorously shown after winning opener, s., charcoal, 19½ ″ × 16½ ″, matted. $400
1956–7 World Series, the Statue of Liberty's head spins as the Yanks meet the Dodgers in Ebbets Field, 1956 newspaper ad and various players are shown over the skyline of Manhattan in background, s., charcoal, 17¼ ″ × 5¼ ″, matted. .. $600

SUSAN KURTZ

Susan Kurtz has exhibited her work at shows and galleries throughout the United States and Europe, including the Rockville Center Guild for the Arts in 1988 and Mickey Mantle's restaurant in New York City in 1989. Many of her sports illustrations have appeared as covers as well as features in the *South Shore Guide*. She has created numerous drawings for various sports medicine publications in Los Angeles and has done promotional work for the famous Palladium Club in Manhattan. Susan is a member of the League of Sports Artists and is an extremely active member in the Early Childhood Education of the Arts Program. Examples of her work are on permanent display in the Ben Gurion Museum and the Israel Mizra Gallery.

Campy, original painting, acrylic and pastel, 30″ × 60″. $650

DONALD MOSS

Donald Moss is a fine artist and graphic artist specializing in sports. His work has appeared for over thirty years in *Sports Illustrated*, including more than a dozen covers. In addition, his art has been on the covers of *Time* and *Golf Digest*. Mr. Moss's paintings hang in the Baseball, Basketball, Football, and Tennis Halls of Fame, USGA's Golf House, The National Art Museum of Sport, and the USAF Art Collection and were featured in the Smithsonian's "Champions of American Sport" exhibition. His works are included in *200 Years of Illustration in America, The Best of Sports Illustrated, The Best Eighteen Golf Holes in America*, and *Champions of American Sport*.

The U.S. Sports Academy named Moss "Sports Artist of the Year" in 1985, and he was honored with a one-man sports art exhibition and a commission to paint "Sportsman of the Year" Walter Payton. As president of Design for Sports, Moss designed the 1980 Winter Olympics "raccoon" theme art. He also created the posters for Super Bowl XII.

Moss was also commissioned by the U.S. Postal Service to design twelve stamps, including the 100th anniversary of tennis and four U.S. Olympic Games issues. He is a life member of the Society of Illustrators, chairman of the USAF Art Program's annual exhibition, and a trustee of the National Art Museum of Sport.

Willie Mays, original artwork for *Sports Illustrated*, 18″ × 30″. $1,000
Tom Seaver, original artwork for *Sports Illustrated*, acrylic, 13″ × 15″. $500
Vida Blue, original artwork for *Sports Illustrated*, 24″ × 24″. $475
Pete Rose, original artwork for *Boy's Life*, 15″ × 17″. $650
Boy's Life Basketball Cover, used as a cover for a special *Boy's Life* basketball issue, has an action image of English up against Malone, acrylic, 12″ × 16″. $1,000
Cy Young, original art for a special *Sports Illustrated* article, in style of old tintype photographs, paint on board, 11″ × 13″. $375
Walter Johnson, original art for a special *Sports Illustrated* article, in style of old tintype photographs, paint on board, 11″ × 12″. $750
Christy Mathewson, original art for a special *Sports Illustrated* article, in style of old tintype photographs, paint on board, 12″ × 12″, circular. $800
Grover Cleveland Alexander, original art for a special *Sports Illustrated* article, in style of old tintype photographs, paint on board, 12″ × 14″. $375
Charles Radbourn, original art for a special *Sports Illustrated* article, in style of old tintype photographs, paint on board, 12″ × 14″. $180

ROBERT S. SIMON

Robert S. Simon is regarded as one of America's finest sports and illustrative portraitists. His fine art awards and accomplishments include the James R. Marsh Memorial Award for Portraiture and the New York City Council Award for Portraiture.

Simon was recently nominated by the U.S. Sports Academy as "Sports Artist of the Year" for 1987–88, finishing a proud fifth in a field of over 750 artists. His works can be found in the private collections of such notables as Sylvester Stallone, George Steinbrenner, Mickey Mantle, Joe DiMaggio, and the Eagle Club of Washington, DC. His sports art is exhibited in the Baseball Hall of Fame. In addition to creating covers for several national magazines, Simon also was comissioned by the Downtown Athletic Club in New York to produce the official 1984 Heisman Trophy Winner portrait.

Babe Ruth, NY Yankees, 1984, s., oil, 16″ × 20″. $700

ADDITIONAL SPORTS ILLUSTRATORS

BOB BOWIE

Casey Stengel, *Denver Post*, Casey Stengel holds up sack labeled "Duke Maas, Virgil Trucks, Zack Monroe," caption states that Casey's assets add up to well over a million; s., ink and charcoal, 13¼″ × 16½″. $110

JACK DAVIS (1926–)

Y. A. Tittle on the Phone, s. lower right, pen and ink, 7″ × 8″. $475

MORT DRUCKER

Cover for pamphlet, caricatures of the most successful relief pitchers of 1988, s., d. lower right, ink and dyes, 14″ × 15.25″. $850

BILL FORSYTHE

Willie Mays, NY Giants, oil painting of image from 1953 Topps card, 1974, s., 20″ × 30″, framed. $400

ANDY JURINKO

Memorial Stadium, Baltimore, 1988, charcoal and pastel on paper. $650

JEFF KEATE

Five Baseball Illustrations, from the early '50s to mid-'70s, approx. 7″ × 7″. $100

ALAN MAVER

Ted Williams, s., pen and ink, 7″ × 10½″. **Charlie Gelbert**, "Red Hot Reserve," Jim Berryman illustration, *Washington Post*, s., ink and charcoal, 12¾″ × 15¾″. $100

WILSON McLEAN (1937–)

Beam of light on football field, editorial illustration, *Playboy*'s Pro Football Forecast," *Playboy*, 1988, s. lower right, oil on canvas, 28″ × 38″. ..$1,600

HARRY MORSE MEYERS (1886–1961)

Woman in turban, football player on sidelines, s. lower right, oil on canvas, 30″ × 24″. $1,500

SLANUZ

Ben Chapman, original artwork for *New York World-Telegram*, from the Bill Dickey Collection, s., charcoal and ink, 10½″ × 16″, framed. $100
Bill Dickey, NY Yankees, original artwork from the Bill Dickey Collection, s., charcoal and ink, 14¾″ × 17″, framed. $1,100
Shanty Hogan, Bill Dickey, Dave Bancroft, Art Fletcher, original artwork from the Bill Dickey Collection, s., charcoal and ink, 14″ × 20″, framed.
....$150
Bill Dickey, NY Yankees, original illus., s., charcoal and ink, 16″ × 20″, framed, corner missing. $190

EDGAR FRANKLIN WITTANACK

Tennis Player, oil painting on canvas, c. 1922, s. ....\. $3,500

LEO WHITE

Gene Bearden, *Boston American*, Oct. 9, 1948; Bearden shoots arrow into Brave, player behind rock comments, "If He Was a Book, We Could Get Him Banned." s., pen and ink, 12¼″ × 11¼″. $100
Sonny Liston, shows Liston preparing to fight, referring to Patterson, who wore a disguise after he lost the last fight with Liston, s., ink and colored pencil, 15″ × 12½″. $70

WAR AND THE MILITARY

by Carl Sciortino

A military historian–dealer, Sciortino began collecting American military illustrations in 1962. His first illustrations were bought to "decorate" his martial sword and gun collection, begun in 1946. Until his retirement, he was a biology teacher in a New York City high school. He likes corresponding with fellow collectors to swap information and ideas.

Not till I met illustrator-sculptor Carl Pugliesi did I really appreciate the value of the illustrator. He was a knowledgeable collector, and his enthusiasm was infectious. As there were no dealers as such, I scoured flea markets and secondhand and thrift shops. My early finds included a Frank Hoffman Western, Anton Otto Fischer's *Battleship Squadron*, and George Harding's *Civil War Retreat*. A book dealer was the source of Leroy Baldridge's original sketchbook of World War I, which was incorporated into his book *I Was There*.

The educated collector is better equipped to build a fine collection. A personal reference library is worth its weight in diamonds. I missed an Edward Penfield painting at a flea market because I didn't recognize the monogram. Getting familiar with the style of an illustrator you like can open the door to valuable unsigned pieces. A friend bought an unsigned Remington pen-and-ink for $35. As he later told me, "only one man draws boots like this."

Tip: Track down all possible leads. The Frank Hoffman oil was described as a "textured print." My magnifying glass proved it to be an original oil, at that time worth $250.

Military illustration seems to have started during the Crimean War (1853–1856). The *Illustrated London News* sent Joseph Archer Crowe to "send us letters and sketches." They also sent other staff artists to cover the Franco-Prussian War (1870–1871), the India Mutiny (1859) and the various wars of the Victorian era.

The American Civil War (1861–1865) was reported by artists Alfred and William Waud, Edwin Forbes, and Winslow Homer. Gilbert Gaul (1855–) painted *Chasing the Battery* and *Wounded to the Rear*. Rufus F. Zogbaum (1849–1925) wrote and illustrated *Horse, Foot and Dragoons*. Thomas Nast (1840–1902) was hired at fifteen by Frank Leslie to do wartime sketches.

Edwin Forbes (1839–1895) went on to make a lifetime career as a military artist. His folio of etchings, *Life Studies of the Great Army*, recounted his war experiences.

Winslow Homer (1839–1910) was hired by *Harper's* to sketch the first Lincoln inauguration. He then went on to Yorktown and the Peninsula campaign in 1862. He preferred art to reporting and returned to New York to produce his first serious works based on his field sketches.

The Indian Wars were not as heavily covered. Remington rode with General Nelson Miles on his campaign against the Navajos. In 1867, *Harper's* sent Theodore R. Davis to accompany General Hancock's command during the Kansas and Nebraska campaigns. He worked for *Harper's* till 1884, then became a freelance artist.

The year 1898 saw Frederic Remington, Howard Chandler Christy, Davis and William Glackens on the job. Glackens worked for *McClure's* magazine and went on to become one of the founders of the "Ashcan School." Remington's *Charge of the Rough Riders Up San Jaun Hill* put Theodore Roosevelt in the limelight.

Howard Chandler Christy (1873–1952) represented *Leslie's Weekly*. Two examples of his talent as a military artist are *Wounded Rough Riders at Siboney* and *The Second Infantry Landing at Siboney*, which appeared in *Harper's*.

Harvey Dunn, George Harding, and Albin Henning recorded World War I. Harvey Dunn (1889–1952) was a powerful, imposing figure, and this was reflected in his work *The Machine Gunner*. Commissioned as an official war artist with the rank of captain, he lived in the trenches and fought alongside his men.

George Harding (1882–1959) was one of the eight official A.E.F. artists. He portrayed effects of war rather than the heat of battle. These works are in the Smithsonian's collection.

Albin Henning (1886–1943), a pupil of Harvey Dunn, produced some powerful scenes of World War I action. *Horse Artillery at Night* shows his skill.

A large number of illustrators covered World War II: Mead Schaeffer, Tom Lea, Kerr Eby, Howard Brodie, John McDermott, and Anton Otto Fischer.

Kerr Eby served as a staff sergeant in World War I and used his sketches in his book *War*, published in 1936. He landed with the Marines on Tarawa in World War II and produced some gut-grabbing scenes of conflict. His men are strong, faceless, hunched forward, going toward the enemy. His works are the total opposite of the Hollywood treatment of the time. He depicted horror, fatigue, and death at its meanest.

As a *Life* magazine artist, Tom Lea initially portrayed the war in all-American style, but his depiction changed. After he went into the field, his pictures showed the blood and gore of combat.

Clayton Knight. Illustration for The Next War, Liberty *magazine, 12/5/1931. Charcoal and pastel, 15½ × 29 inches, signed lower right, $800.* PHOTO COURTESY OF THE SOCIETY OF ILLUSTRATORS. (See *Special Notes* [27] at back of book.)

Mead Schaeffer, a pupil of Harvey Dunn, painted a series of *Saturday Evening Post* covers on the various branches of the services. His troops were clean, determined, and a bit too neat for my taste—very different from Eby and Lee.

Harold Von Schmidt, also a Dunn pupil, worked in both the Pacific and European theaters. He was quite versatile in his depiction of the seas, the military, wildlife, and Western subjects. A group of his Civil War–subject paintings can be seen in the West Point Museum.

John R. McDermott joined the Marines at the outbreak of World War II. He served as a combat artist on Guam, Guadalcanal, Okinawa, and the Solomon Islands. Some of his works were shown in *Blue Book* after the war.

Norman Mills Price. "Cavalry Charge at Whistling Cat." Pen and ink. Signed, 12 × 4 inches, $1,200. PHOTO COURTESY OF CARL SCIORTINO.

Anton Otto Fischer produced marine paintings, having spent eight years on sailing ships. In 1942, he was commissioned as lieutenant commander and named Artist Laureate of the Coast Guard. This man knows the sea.

Sergeant Howard Brodie, U.S. Army, produced a number of superb drawings of combat on Guadalcanal and in Europe, particularly of the Battle of the Bulge. He caught the true feel of combat, as did Eby and Lea. I regret I can't locate any biographical material on Brodie.

There were many others. Some careers ended with war's end; others went on in the field and gained some fame.

McCLELLAND BARCLAY (1891–1943)

McClelland Barclay was at his best painting beautiful women for advertising clients or wartime posters and officer portraits. His series for the General Motors campaign with the slogan "Body by Fisher," depicting stylish beauties, was done in the late 1920s and early 1930s. Appointed a lieutenant commander, U.S.N.R., during World War II, Barclay turned his attention to military subjects.

McClelland Barclay. Oil on board. Cover illustration for Wings *magazine, Nov. 1942. Signed lower right, 30 × 23½ inches, $2,000.* PHOTO COURTESY OF GUERNSEY'S.

Dancing girl, painting, *Beaux-Arts Ball*, 1938, s., oil on panel, 76″ × 32″, modelled by Collette Nicks, a model often used by Christy, this was created for the last Beaux Arts Ball (held at the Waldorf-Astoria), which had an oriental theme.
....$5,000
Woman buying scarves, story illustration, s., oil on canvas, 32″ × 32″.
....$2,000
Prizefight, s., oil on canvas, 34″ × 40″. $5,000
Couple in Hawaii, oil on canvas, 40″ × 38″, not signed. $2,500
Torpedo Boat, Firing, s. USNR, oil on canvas, 30″ × 36″. $3,500

ROBERT BENNEY (1904–)

ROBERT BENNEY

In the best tradition of the American field artist, Robert Benney began his career as artist in the World War II combat areas, as well as acting as a war correspondent under the office of the surgeon general. Many of his dramatic depictions of combat are in armed services collections. Continuing his "on the scene" approach after the war, he specialized in artwork for industry and agriculture. Beginning with a rough sketch, he would then submit a comprehensive sketch before final art. Among his commissions were American Sugar Refining Company, Chrysler Corporation, and American Tobacco. He also did covers for the Shubert Theater programs, depicting the leading actors and actresses in their roles. His award-winning paintings and drawings are in many museums and private collections. Since they rarely come to the marketplace, any discoveries would be a collector's coup.

ANTON OTTO FISCHER (1882–1962)

ANTON OTTO FISCHER

Eight years at sea gave Anton Otto Fischer the background that he eventually transferred to canvas as an illustrator of marine military subjects. Born in Munich, Germany, Fischer came to America after his youthful sea experiences. In America, he taught seamanship and worked as a model and handyman for illustrator A. B. Frost. He used his earnings to study for two years at the Academie Julian in Paris.

After returning to America, he made his first illustration sale to *Harper's Weekly*. His illustrations appeared in *Everybody's* magazine as well as *The Saturday Evening Post*.

Alaskan Cafe during the Goldrush, story illustration, s., oil on canvas en grisaille, 30″ × 21″, note the prices on the menu. $1,100
Night Battle, reproduced, *Saturday Evening Post*, Dec. 20, 1941, s., oil on canvas, 28″ × 30″. $2,000
Naval Engagement, *Saturday Evening Post*, oil on canvas, 20″ × 42″. $2,250
Man Overboard, oil on canvas, 22″ × 30″. $1,500
Man in Rigging, oil on canvas, 30″ × 20″. $1,500
Shipwreck and Schooner, painting, reproduced, *The Illustrator in America 1880–1980*, p. 126, s., oil on canvas, 17″ × 40″. $3,600
Midnight Intruder, s. Anton Otto Fischer, d. 1940, 28″ × 22″. $605
Sailing into Sunset, 26″ × 28″. $1,650
Schooner among Icebergs, s., d. 23, prov., 16″ × 30¼″. $660
Steamers on Patrol, s., d. 1930, 26″ × 36½″. $1,980
The Discussion, s. A.O.F., d. 1940, 22½″ × 18″. $660
Trimasted Sailing Ship, s., 24½″ × 34½″. $1,980
Confrontation, inits. A.O.F., d. 1933, 22″ × 26″. $715
The Fight, s. A.O.F., d. 1930, 22″ × 22″. $935
Consolation, inits. A.O.F., d. 33; 20″ × 22″. $770
The March of American Privateersmen to Dartmoor Prison, s. Anton Otto Fischer, d. 1930, illus. for "The Lively Lady," *Saturday Evening Post*, Apr. 4, 1931, 24″ × 36″. $2,640
Six Men Leaving Ship, s. and d. Anton Otto Fischer 1934, prov., 24″ × 36″. $1,980
The Standoff, s., d. '32; 22″ × 36″. $1,650
Ships Passing in the Moonlight, s., exhib. label verso, 24″ × 34″. .. $2,090
Clipper Ship on the High Seas, s., 24¼″ × 34¼″. $1,650

GEORGE MATTHEWS HARDING (1882–1959)

George Harding

George Matthews Harding began his studies with Howard Pyle. This was followed by several months among Newfoundland fishing families, where he sketched their daily lives. His first commission was with *The Saturday Evening Post*, followed by other magazines. However, as one of eight official artists for the A.E.F. during World War I, he developed the interest in military subjects for which he is best known. As a world traveler, he also illustrated a series with writer Norman Duncan, who accompanied him.

Zanzibar: Unloading Cargo, "Black Man without a Country," *Harper's Monthly*, June 1920, s., charcoal, 24″ × 36″. $1,600
Turkish Soldiers on Camelback, cover painting for *Collier's*, s., gouache on illustration board, 19″ × 13″. $2,300
Seated Captain and Arabs, story illustration, "New Geography in Trade Routes," s., charcoal on paper, 21.5″ × 25.5″. $750

George Matthews Harding. War scene with lookout. Charcoal and pencil,
22 × 18 inches. Signed lower center, $1,500. PHOTO COURTESY OF CARL
SCIORTINO.

HENRY REUTERDAHL (1871–1925)

Henry Reuterdahl was an artist-correspondent during the Spanish-
American War. Other military-related experiences included going with
the American fleet on several voyages and serving as an artistic adviser
to the U.S. Navy Recruiting Bureaus while a lieutenant commander in
World War I. During this time he did paintings for navy posters. His
early paintings of marine subjects are known for their factual accuracy;
his later paintings have impressionistic influences. Among the magazines
he worked for was *Scribner's Monthly.*

Air Show in Staten Island, 1910s, s., gouache on board, 23″ × 30″.
.... $1,400
Pilot at Staten Island Air Show, s., gouache on board, 23″ × 30″. ...$1,800

HERBERT MORTON STOOPS (1888–1948)

Like so many illustrators, Herbert Morton Stoops worked first as a staff
artist for newspapers in San Francisco and Chicago. After World

Herbert Morton Stoops. Advertisement. Railroad Engineer Rounding Bend. Graybar Electric Co., c. 1926, oil on canvas, 40 × 28 inches, signed, $2,000. PHOTO COURTESY OF ILLUSTRATION HOUSE, INC.

War I ended, his first illustrations were bought by *Blue Book* and *Collier's*, followed by *This Week* and *Cosmopolitan*. Since *Blue Book* published a great deal of adventure fiction, his work was not only of the Old West but also military subjects. He painted *Blue Book*'s cover illustrations for over thirteen years. (See *Special Notes* [28] at back of book.)

Railroad Engineer Rounding Bend, advertisement, *Graybar Electric Co.*, c. 1926, reproduced, *Sixth Annual of Advertising Art*, 1927, p. 34, s., oil on canvas, 40″ × 28″. $2,000
The Posse, 26″ × 36″. $880
Captain John Smith and Pocahontas, s., illus. for ''The Iron Captain'' by George Creel, July 30, 1932, 35½″ × 39¾″. $2,640

FREDERICK COFFAY YOHN (1875–1933)

F. C. YOHN

Historical and military subjects were the specialty of Frederick Coffay Yohn. He was an artist-correspondent during the Spanish-American War. His first illustrations were done for *Harper's* periodicals, and during his career he worked for most of the major magazines and book publishers. He got his training at the Indianapolis Art School and the Art Students League in New York.

Black man dancing, story illustration, s. lower right, oil on canvas, 36″ × 24″. $3,600

"You Are a Scoundrel, Sir!", book illus., *Lewis Raub*, 1915, full-color gouache, 19″ × 12″. $1,800

Frederick Coffay Yohn. "General George Washington Greeting the Troops." Pen and ink, 15 × 12 inches, $1,210. PHOTO COURTESY OF MORTON GOLDBERG GALLERIES, NEW ORLEANS.

RUFUS FAIRCHILD ZOGBAUM (1849–1925)

R.F. Zogbaum

Rufus Zogbaum was a specialist in American war illustrations. He made a lifetime study of depictions of battle scenes. Technically correct, with an attention to detail, his illustrations of battles with Indians, the Civil War, and the Spanish-American War are among his finest works. A writer as well as artist, he did articles for *Scribner's* and wrote and illustrated a book titled *Horse, Foot and Dragoons*.

Hail and Farewell, study for a panel in the Woolworth building, s. R.F. Zogbaum, t. on exhibition label verso, 14^{15}/16″ × 9^{7}/8″. $605
Headquarters in the Battlefield, i. with various notations, 9½″ × 15¼″, pen and ink on paper. $1,760

THE WEST AND WILDLIFE

by Michael Frost

Michael Frost, who is in charge of the J. N. Bartfield Galleries, a premiere New York gallery dealing in Western art and sculpture, began in high school to work part-time for his uncle, Jack Bartfield. "I continued working in the gallery through my college years," he notes, "and had many wonderful opportunities to view other galleries, museums, and auction houses; meet some great collectors and important dealers; and also to see hundreds of great paintings pass through my hands in the gallery every year.

"My love and appreciation for art steadily increased. In fact, so deeply that it caused me to change my major from math and science to art history.

"After graduation from college, I pursued a career in photography, but this didn't last long, for I was drawn back to the gallery. That was over twenty-five years ago. Looking back, art has been one of my greatest pleasures and has opened up doors of knowledge I never dreamed existed."

I use the word *classic*, meaning important in subject. Using Frederic Remington as an example (since he is familiar to most and also the highest-priced Western artist in general), a classic subject would be cowboys or Indians. Should one purchase a European subject, it would be a fraction of the price. Remington was an illustrator for such magazines as *Harper's Weekly, Century, Outing, Collier's, Cosmopolitan*, and others from the 1880s till his death in 1909. There are many other factors in determining the value of artwork. The following should be kept in mind, and you should not hesitate to ask if you are considering making a purchase.

1. What is the most desirable subject for the artist?
2. Which medium was the artist most comfortable working with?
3. What is the best period?
4. What is the condition of the artwork?
5. Is a signed painting always authentic?
6. What is the price range?

To exemplify some of the above, I will again use Remington.

1. I quoted the example of American versus European subjects. Remington painted the cavalry often. The Ninth U.S. Cavalry in Florida

might be painted beautifully but would be worth less money than a similar scene of the Tenth U.S. Cavalry in Arizona.

2. Remington worked well in both watercolor and oil. Some artists, like Edward Borein, who was a wonderful watercolorist, had difficulty in mastering oils. Borein's watercolors generally bring more than his oils.

3. Remington's late-period scenes are the most desirable. After 1905, he took on a very impressionistic style. Besides the fact they are the most sought after, they are also the most expensive. In 1989, a 30-by-45-inch painting was sold at auction for $4,700,000.

4. The condition of the artwork is very important. Most paintings that have aged have some minor restoration that does not really affect the value. If the restoration is severe, such as major tears in figures, the value is drastically reduced. You will have to have confidence in the people you are dealing with because most restoration cannot be seen with the naked or untrained eye.

5. Just because a painting is signed doesn't mean it is by the artist. The majority of fakes have signatures. In Remingtons alone, I must see at least 100 fakes a year. Know whom you're buying from and what kind of guarantee you will get. Unsigned authentic artwork is better than a signed copy.

6. All artists vary in price, as noted above. It is difficult to pinpoint the exact value of any item. Remington really runs the gamut from under $1,000 for an unsigned drawing to about $5 million for the elite examples. Not to say they won't bring more. For the past several years, Western art prices have been showing a moderate and steady gain. In the December 1989 auctions, Western art was healthier than ever, achieving new record highs.

As in the various schools of American art, many of the great Western and sporting illustrators developed their craft while illustrating books and magazine articles. Included in this area are Frederic Remington, Charles M. Russell, Herbert Dunton, Phillip R. Goodwin, and Nick Eggenhofer. Their illustrations were so elaborately executed that they are now collected as fine art paintings.

During the past twenty years, the price of Western art, like other types of art, has fluctuated greatly. Some of these fluctuations are directly related to the following aspects: (a) change in interest rates, (b) stock market, (c) oil prices. The strongest change in the market was during the oil boom in the late '70s and early '80s. Prices of art were soaring, and nobody thought they would stop. When the oil boom came to a sudden halt, so did a great number of Western painting sales. Most affected were the relatively unknown contemporaries, artists sold by a gallery to a strictly local clientele.

John Ford Clymer. Oil on illustration board. "What Makes A Great Day's Fishing." Reproduced in True magazine, April 1952. Signed lower left, 24 × 18 inches. PHOTO COURTESY OF DU MOUCHELLES ART GALLERIES.

These artists did not have a reputation outside their hometown, nor have they ever sold in a major auction where prices could be established by the public. Unaffected by the crash were classic examples by Frederic Remington, Charles M. Russell, Charles Schreyvogel, W. R. Leigh, and the early explorer artists, such as Alfred Jacob Miller, George Catlin, Seth Eastman, and others.

PAUL BRANSOM (1885–1979)

Paul Bransom

Paul Bransom turned his love of animals into a lifelong career as a painter and illustrator of animals. Born in Washington, DC, he left school at thirteen to become an apprentice draftsman, assisting with mechanical drawings for patents. In his spare time he sketched the animals at the National Zoo in great detail. He later moved to New York, where he did a comic strip, "The Latest News from Bugville," for the *New York Evening Journal.* He was influenced by Walt Kuhn; T. S. Sullivant, who did animal cartoon subjects at that time; and Charles Livingston Bull. During this time he drew and painted the animals at the Bronx Zoo. When he showed his work to the editor of *The Saturday Evening Post,* the editor bought four pictures for covers and several smaller drawings.

During his long career he illustrated nearly fifty books on wildlife subjects, among them Jack London's *Call of the Wild*. He continued to do illustrations for most of the major magazines as well as story illustrations.

Greyhounds, s., 27″ × 24″, pastel. $495

Tiger and Python, preliminary sketch, s., pastel on vellum, 10.5″ × 9.5″.
....$350

Collie Destroying Interior, story illustration, "His jaws rent them to rags," "The Tartar Catcher" by A. P. Terhune, *Ladies' Home Journal*, June 1926, s., charcoal and watercolor, 22.5″ × 16.5″. $950

The Hunt, reproduced, *American Weekly* magazine, Mar. 16, 1947, "Americans 30,000 Years Ago," cave dwellers hunting a mammoth, s., pastel, 19½″ × 17½″. $175

Staghorn Deer, init. L.R., pastel on paper, 10″ circle. $175

Deer Family, Mid-Winter, *Saturday Evening Post*, Feb. 7, 1931, s., gouache, 23″ × 17″. $8,000

Rhinoceros Wading, s., watercolor, charcoal, metallic ink, 16″ × 13″.
....$3,000

Mountain Lion Chasing Ibises, magazine cover design, pastel, 23″ × 18″, not signed. $5,000

Terrier Bothering Elephants, s., charcoal and ink, 15.5″ × 21″. $1,500

Protecting Her Young, s., advertisement for General Motors, Aug. 28, 1953, 16″ × 15″, watercolor, charcoal, pen and black ink, and gouache on board.
....$462

CHARLES LIVINGSTON BULL (1874–1932)

CHARLES Livingston Bull

One of our foremost animal illustrators, Charles Livingston Bull, was an expert taxidermist who was knowledgeable about the anatomy of birds and animals. For many years he lived directly opposite the Bronx Zoo in New York, which enabled him to sketch from living models. During his many trips into Mexico and Central and South America, he studied the wildlife in its natural habitat. His book *Under the Roof of the Jungle* is a collection of illustrations of animal life in the Guiana wilds based on his explorations there. To arouse public interest in the plight of American birds, including the American eagle, and their preservation, he made drawings and posters for publicity purposes for the U.S. Biological Survey.

Moosehead, reproduced for Savage Arms Co. ad, s., charcoal drawing, 9″ × 7½″. $225

The Guardian, reproduced, *Country Gentleman* cover, s., gouache, 17¼″ × 16″. $850

Lioness with Cubs, s., 20″ × 18″, watercolor with pen and ink on paper.
.... $605

Fawn in Pond, s., 20″ × 18″, watercolor with pen and ink on paper. ...$688
The Predator, Bald Eagle in Flight, s., sight size 24″ × 20″, gouache, watercolor, and pencil on paper. $1,760
A Bat and a Raccoon and The Hungry Kitten: two drawings, both s.; the second was the cover for *The Saturday Evening Post*; first, 21⅝″ × 15¼″; second, 26″ × 12″; first, charcoal pen and black ink on paper; second, white chalk. $352
Family of Mountain Goats, s., sight size 20½″ × 18″, ink and watercolor on paper. $600
Bear with Cubs, s., 20″ × 18″, watercolor with pen and ink on paper. $605
Rams in Moonlight, s., 20″ × 18″, watercolor with pen and ink on paper.
.... $605

MATT CLARK (1903–1972)

MATT CLARK

Although Matt Clark is known for his masterful depictions of the Old West, he also did hundreds of illustrations on everything from the farm to city life. His first work appeared in *College Humor* in 1929. He used dry brush, often combined with watercolor.

Family in Garden Setting, reproduced, *American Weekly* (twice), 1935, Oct. 3, 1948, dry brush and watercolor, 20¾″ × 24½″. $175
Whipping the Editor, story illustration, *American Weekly*, s., dry brush and watercolor, 23″ × 21″. $400
Vignette, reproduced, *American Weekly*, Feb. 15, 1948, s., dry brush and watercolor, 13¾″ × 23¾″. $125
Renegade Attack, reproduced, *American Weekly* magazine, 1948, s., oil on board, 21½″ × 16½″. $200
Three Boys in Front of Open Safe, reproduced, *American Weekly*, 1945, s., d. 45, dry brush and watercolor, 15¼″ × 21¾″. $125
Poker Shoot Out, reproduced, *American Weekly* magazine, s., dry brush and watercolor, 19″ × 22″. $300

NICK EGGENHOFER (1897-1985)

N. EGGENHOFER

Nick Eggenhofer came to the United States at sixteen with plans to paint his heroes of the Old West. He had become acquainted with the works of Frederic Remington and Charles Russell, which were reproduced in German publications. At night he studied at Cooper Union. In his spare time he made scale models of stagecoaches, wagons, and other Western items.

Pulp magazines such as *Western Story* used his drawings for many

Nick Eggenhofer. "Attack on the Stage." Illustration for Argosy *magazine,* $8,500. PHOTO COURTESY OF ILLUSTRATION HOUSE, INC.

Nick Eggenhofer. "Herding." Illustration for his book, Wagons, Mules and Men. *Gouache and pencil on board. Signed N. Eggenhofer, lower right,* $9,350. PHOTO COURTESY OF CHRISTIE'S, NEW YORK.

years. He wrote and illustrated *Wagons, Mules and Men*, published by Hastings House in 1961. In 1981, his autobiography, *Horses, Horses, Always Horses*, was printed by Sage Publishing Company. He primarily used a dry-brush technique.

Stick-Up at a Card Game, pulp illustration, s., i., dry brush, 11.25" × 13.5", exhib.: Middlesex County Museum, 1987. ....$2,000
Buffalo on Prairie, painting, 1964, s., gouache, 8.5" × 11.5". $3,200
Moving Camp, s. N. Eggenhofer, lower right, tempera on board, 21" × 31". $19,000
Herding, s. N.Eggenhoffer, lower right, gouache and pencil on board, 15⅜" × 20⅛" (39 × 51cm), prov. by descent in the artist's family to the present owner, literature: N. Eggenhoffer, *Wagons, Mules and Men*, New York, 1961, pp. 138–139, illus.; the artist used this gouache in his book. $9,350
Pontiac War, s. Eggenhoffer, lower left, gouache and pencil on board, 16" × 22¾" (40.7 × 57.6cm). $5,280
Lewis and Clark on the Yellowstone, s. N. Eggenhoffer, sight size 14½" × 24½", gouache on paper. $22,000

LYNN BOGUE HUNT (1878–1960)

LYNN
BOGUE
HUNT

Known for his realistic illustrations of wildlife, Lynn Bogue Hunt was the ideal artist for advertisements requiring fish, birds, and animals. Most of his advertising illustrations were for arms and ammunition manufacturers. Some of his first magazine illustrations were done for the old *Outing* magazine, later for *Field and Stream*. The realism and attention to detail were the result of early studies of anatomy of wildlife, even to learning taxidermy. Collectors should look for the few examples using human figures.

Real Sports, s. Lynn Bogue Hunt, 19" × 13½", gouache on paper. ... $1,155
Hunter with Mallards and Pintails, cover illus. for *Field and Stream*, 1932 issue, sight size 21½" × 17½", gouache on paper. $5,500
Rainbow Trout, s. Lynn Bogue Hunt, 8½" × 7", oil on board. $1,980
Upland Game Shooting, Ring-Necked Pheasant, s.,t., frontispiece for *Upland Game Shooting* by H. L. Betten, 16" × 12". $9,500
Ducks Coming In, s., 24½" × 20½". $1,925
Geese Coming into a Rig of Stick-Up Decoys, s. in pencil, presentation, *Field and Stream* cover, 1924 issue, 23" × 18⅞", gouache on paper. $10,500
Ducks on Wing, s. Lynn Bogue Hunt, study for cover illustration, *Field and Stream*, Dec. 1932, 14" × 10", oil on board. $1,320
Upland Game Shooting, Ring-Necked Pheasant, color plate in *Upland Game Shooting* by H. L. Betten, 1944, 15" × 12". $2,530
Ducks Landing on Pond, 13" × 10½", tempera on paper. $1,073

Lynn Bogue Hunt. "The Duck Hunt." Oil on board, 9 × 9 inches, signed lower left. An advertisement for Savage Arms Company, $950.
PHOTO COURTESY OF GUERNSEY'S.

Blue Green Comes into a Field, s., 22¼″ × 16¼″. $4,500
Large Mouth Bass and Rainbow Trout, a pair, both s. Lynn Bogue Hunt, each 7¾″ × 5″, oil on board. $2,475
Bluebills in Flight, s., 32½″ × 24½″. $5,000

FREDERIC REMINGTON (1861–1909)

Frederic Remington—

After studying art for a short time at Yale university, Frederic Remington headed to the West of the 1880s. His early works were somewhat crude and had to be redrawn for use by a staff artist for *Harper's* magazine. However, as his technical ability improved, he was made a reporter-artist by the magazine, not only in the West but around the world. Some of his finest drawings and paintings were made as a war correspondent during the Spanish-American War.

His love of horses led to the publication in 1889 of an illustrated article, titled "Horses of the Plain," in *Century* magazine. Today some of his finest paintings and bronzes are in the Remington Memorial Museum in his hometown, Ogdensburg, New York. His Indian collection can be seen in the Whitney Gallery of Western Art in Cody, Wyoming.

Cow Pony, s. Remington, upper right, oil on canvas, 20″ × 24″ (50.8 × 60.9cm). $68,750
A Sabre Charge (Custer's Last Stand), s. Frederic Remington, lower center, oil on canvas en grisaille, 25″ × 35″ (63.5 by 88.9cm). $275,000
The Loggers, 9″ × 7″, dry brush. $800

Indian Scout, s., watercolor. $1,100
Longhorns, 8″ × 11″, pen and ink. $1,100
Mexican Gendarmes Asking the Way, s. Frederic Remington, d. 90; 14″ × 23¼″, pen and brush and black ink on paper laid down on board. $22,000
General George Crook on the Trail, s. Frederic Remington, lower right, i. "The Grey Fox"/Gen Geo. Crooke—on campaign—Capt. Bourke article, lower left; also i. Gen. Geo Crook on the Trail in another hand, annotated and stamped Art Department/The Century Co.,/Union Square/New York City on the reverse; India ink on paperboard, 17″ × 16″ (43.2 × 40.6cm). $27,500
The Canadian Mounted Police on a Musical Ride 'Charge!' s. Remington, lit., 15¼″ × 23½″, oil on board, en grisaille. $60,500
A Scout and Two Troopers, drawing, 14″ × 16″, pen, ink, and wash. ....
.... $29,000
A Manchurian Bandit, s. Frederic Remington, from the estate of Katherine Matthies, 30″ × 20⅛″, oil en grisaille on board. $37,400
Miners Prospecting for Gold, s. Remington; stamped and i. with t. verso, p. 1887, prov., 18″ × 24″, oil en grisaille on board. $38,500
Mexican Pony, Piedras Neagras, s. Frederic Remington, i. Piedras Neagras, d. Mexico-Mch-1891, prov., exhib., sight size 10¼″ × 14″, watercolor, ink wash, gouache and pencil on paper. $41,250
Out of Grub and the Promised Land in Sight, s. Frederic Remington, t. verso, prov., 18″ × 25″, gouache on paper mounted on board, en grisaille. $60,500
A Tumble from the Trail, s. Frederic Remington, prov., lit., 28″ × 18″, oil en grisaille on canvas. $66,000

Frederic Remington. "Major Wallace F. Randolph, 3rd artillery." Black and white wash. Published Harper's Weekly, July 28, 1894, 12¼ × 18½ inches. Signed lower left, $75,000. PHOTO COURTESY OF J. N. BARTFIELD GALLERIES, NEW YORK.

A Vacquero, s. Frederic Remington, prov., 28″ × 18″, oil on panel............
.... $99,000
Indian Scouts Watching Custer's Advance, s. Frederic Remington, prov., lit.,
22″ × 34″. $170,500
Waneepah, s. Remington, i. Waneepah, originally used as illus. for F. Janvin's
story "Waneepah" in *The Youth Companion*, Mar. 22, 1888, lit., 15¼″, gouache
en grisaille on paper. $9,900
Which Is the Bad Man? drawing, s and d. Remington/88, i. with t. in pencil
on back, 14″ × 10″, pen and ink. $12,000
Candido Ramos, the Wolf of the West, s., executed for an illus. in *Everybody's
Magazine*, Aug. 1903, sight size 15½″ × 8½″, India ink and ink wash on paper.
....$15,400
Mounted Hussar, s. Frederic Remington, prov., from the estate of Charles Mad-
ison, New York, 18″ × 16½″, watercolor on paper laid down on board.
....$15,400

KENNETH RILEY (1919–)

Ken Riley, born in Missouri, began his studies under Thomas Hart Benton, at the Kansas City Art Institute. He also later studied under Harvey
Dunn at the Grand Central School in New York. In his use of color and
capturing the "mood" of his subjects, Riley is considered a master.
Although he has painted hundreds of subjects, today he is considered
one of the most important painters of the American West. He is a charter
member of the National Academy of Western Art and is a member of
the Cowboy Artists of America.

His work has appeared in such publications as *Reader's Digest, The
Saturday Evening Post*, and *Life*. Considered some of his best works were
those he painted to illustrate the historical Captain Hornblower stories
by C. S. Forester in *The Saturday Evening Post*.

Rescue Attempt, "Lonely Mrs. Mingo," *Saturday Evening Post*, s., oil on board,
10″ × 20″. $475
Two Couples at Table, story illustration, "Television #1," *Saturday Evening
Post*, s. lower right, acrylic on board, 21″ × 16.″ $700
Red Flannel, s., ©, d. CA '85, oil on board, 30″ × 48″. $29,700

CHARLES M. RUSSELL (1864–1926)

Like Frederic Remington, Charles Marion Russell spent his early years
in the frontier life of the West and was self-taught. Also, they both

recorded the vanishing life-style of that time in paintings, drawings, and sculpture. During his early years he made drawings strictly for himself or to give to friends. Only when the financial responsibilities of marriage became too great did he begin to market his works. His illustrations were quickly snapped up by such magazines as *Outing* and *Country Life*. He signed his works in a variety of ways: a steer skull, a monogram (CMR), and in script.

Return of the War Party, s. C.M. Russell, with skull, d. 1914, i. ©, lower left, oil on canvas, 24¼″ × 36¼″ (61.6 × 92.1 cm). $1,100,000

Pointing Out the Trail, s. C.M. Russell, with skull, d. 1905, lower left, gouache and watercolor on paper, 13″ × 10¾″ (33 × 27.3 cm). $143,000

Cree War Party, s. C. M. Russell, with skull, lower left, watercolor and gouache on paper, sight size 10¼″ × 16¼″ (26 × 41.3 cm). $71,500

Here's to the Days of the Open Range, drawing, together with a letter; drawing s. and mono., 2″ × 2½″; letter 6″ × 5¼″, ink on paper. $1,430

Blackfoot Scout, inits. CMR, with skull, prov., sight size 5½″ × 4½″, watercolor and pencil on paper. $19,800

Indian Rider, s. CM Russell, with skull, d.'94, exhib., sight size 17″ × 22″, watercolor on paper. $19,800

A Strenuous Matinee, 9½″ × 12½″, watercolor en grisaille. $25,000

Pigeon Hunting Party, s. C M Russell, with skull twice, d. 94, prov., sight size 16″ × 19½″, watercolor on paper. $66,000

Point Out the Trail, s. C M Russell, with skull, prov., lit., 20″ × 27″, watercolor on paper. $99,000

New Year's Greeting, s. with init. and skull, d. 1923, i., 3⅞″ × 12″, India ink, watercolor, and gouache on paper. $17,600

Pack Train, inits. CMR, with artist's device, prov., exhib., lit., 13″ × 21″, ink and wash on paper. $14,300

OTHER COLLECTIBLE
ILLUSTRATORS

Whereas some of these illustrators are listed in detail in books like *The Illustrator in America* by Walt and Roger Reed; *Two Hundred Years of American Illustration*, pubished by the Society of Illustrators and Random House; and various reference books such as *Who Was Who in Art*, there is little information, if any, on others. That isn't to say you should pass up an opportunity to buy their works if you like them. As you will notice, prices range from a high of $7,000 for an *Everybody's* magazine cover by Charles MacLellan to a low of $50 for a paperback cover by Sylvia Bokor. Perhaps they both represent extremes in auction bidding. If several people were fighting it out on the auction floor for the Mac-Lellan, the price could be unrealistic. Or perhaps the price was influenced by the subject, a pretty girl, and the date, 1925. The paperback cover was relatively recent and done in acrylic by an unfamiliar illustrator, which contributed to a low auction price. But this may end up being a sleeper in the coming years.

Browsing in stores dealing in old books can count as research. An especially fine period in book illustration was the 1920s and 1930s. N. C. Wyeth and Howard Pyle are familiar names, but what about James Daugherty? I found a book richly illustrated with his art: *Daniel Boone, Wilderness Scout* by Stewart Edward White, 1922. He isn't listed in books about illustrators. I next looked through *Leonard's Annual Price Index of Art Auctions*, 1987–88 season, and I found him. He was an American, born 1886, died 1974. An oil on canvas board with his signature went for $660. Somebody got a sleeper.

JOHN WOLCOTT ADAMS (1874–1925)

John Adams studied at the Art Museum in Boston, at the Art Students League in New York, and with Howard Pyle. He is known for his pen-and-ink drawings. His work was in *Scribner's*, *Harper's*, *Century*, and *The Delineator*.

Men in Conference, story illustration, "Senator in Defeat," s. lower right, charcoal pencil, 14½″ × 8¾″. $450
The Christmas Coach, s., pen and ink, 6¼″ × 8¾″. $1,350

HAROLD N. ANDERSON (1894–1973)

Harold Anderson (signature)

Harold Anderson's first illustrations appeared in 1919 in *Boy's Life*. After that, he worked both in advertising and for such major magazines as *The Saturday Evening Post*.

Homecoming Soldier, s., oil on canvas, 29″ × 37″. $1,700
Couple by the Fence, watercolor, red, black, and white, s., dated, 15¾″ × 18½″. $775
The Sleeping Farmer, gouache, s., 19½″ × 23½.″ $475

BORIS ARTZYBASHEFF (1899–1965)

Artzybasheff (signature)

Boris Artzybasheff, born in Russia, arrived in America in 1919. His first jobs were in an engraving shop, doing ornamental details, borders, and lettering. He began his illustration career as an artist for over 40 books. After that he did advertising and cover art. In 24 years he painted over 200 covers for *Time* magazine.

Magician and Aladdin, book illustration, *Arabian Nights*, brush and ink, 10″ × 6½″, not signed. $700

JAMES AVATI (B. 1912)

While James Avati worked in a variety of advertising agencies during the Depression, his first break came after World War II. He was hired by the New American Library to paint a cover for William Gardner Smith's *The Last of the Conquerers* in 1948. However, he is best appreciated for his paperback illustrations. His realistic style was ideal for the contemporary writers of the day such as Erskine Caldwell and Irwin Shaw.

All of the following are oil on board. No sizes given.

The Good Earth, Pearl S. Buck (Signet). $9,000
Tobacco Road, Erskine Caldwell (Signet). $6,000
No Star is Lost, James T. Farrell. $6,000
The Seven Story Mountain, Thomas Merton (Signet). $5,000
Lie Down in Darkness (#2), William Styron, (New American Library). ... $1,800

ISA BARNETT (1924–)

Isa Barnett studied at the Philadelphia School of Industrial Art and the Barnes Foundation. His teachers were Robert Riggs, Henry Pitz, and Robert Fawcett. After serving in World War II he sold his first illustration to *Argosy* magazine. Over the years he worked for *Life, The Saturday Evening Post, This Week,* and *Cosmopolitan.*

Suffragette Picket Wilson, oil on board, 20″ × 22″, s. Reproduced in *Life* magazine. $725
Bedowins, gouache, gold, black, and white, s., 14″ × 30″. $325
No. 1, watercolor, 9¼″ × 15¾″, s., downed AF pilot; **No. 2**, watercolor, 15″ × 17″, s., soldiers at tavern. $325
Indian Medicine Man doing Ritual, oil on board, 19½″ × 14″, s. $100

WARREN BAUMGARTNER (1894–1963) N.A.

Warren Baumgartner grew up in the Ozarks. He studied at the Art Institute of Chicago and at the Grand Central School with illustrator-teachers Pruett Carter and Walter Biggs. He is known for his watercolors.

Flamingos, watercolor, 17½″ × 16¾″, s... $400
Lady with Hollyhocks, watercolor on paper, 22″ × 24¾″. $300

CECIL CALVERT BEALL (1892–1967)

Cecil Calvert Beall studied at the Art Students League under George Bridgman and at the Pratt Institute. He did work for *Collier's.* Early examples were done in a bold poster style in watercolors.

Opaque Watercolor, 21½″ × 13″, s. Reproduced in *Collier's* magazine. $150
Police Raid on Casino, story illustration, watercolor, 19″ × 21″, s. $550
Portrait of Abraham Lincoln, s. C. C. Beall, 20″ × 16″, oil on board. $200
The Bathers, s. C. C. Beall, 18″ × 22″, oil on Masonite. $700

LONIE BEE (B. 1902–)

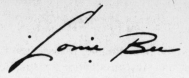

Born in California, Lonie Bee has remained there to become an award-winning "West Coast Artist." As magazine illustrator and cover artist, he worked for *Collier's, Cosmopolitan, Woman's Home Companion, The Saturday Evening Post*, and others. His advertising illustrations and posters were done in mostly watercolors and oils.

Uncle Sam Enjoying a Glass of Beer, advertisement, "America's First Choice," oil on canvas, 21″ × 45″. $1,900

GEOFFREY BIGGS (1908–)

GEOFFREY BIGGS

Geoffrey Biggs studied at the Grand Central School of Art with Harvey Dunn and others. His illustrations first were bought by *Collier's*. During his career he has worked for *The Saturday Evening Post, Woman's Home Companion*, and *Good Housekeeping*, as well as many major advertising agencies in New York. His work is highly detailed and realistic.

The Expedition, gouache, 17¼″ × 22″, s. twice. Reproduced in *American Weekly* magazine. People from safari looking at ancient drawings on side of cliff. $125

JAMES R. BINGHAM (1917–1971)

Bingham

James Bingham grew up in Pennsylvania and studied at the Carnegie Institute of Technology. During World War II he did some animating for Army Air Force films. He began his illustrating career with pictures for the Erle Stanley Gardner "Perry Mason" serials for the *Saturday Evening Post*, as well as for the "Tugboat Annie" series. Among his many advertising assignments were Gulf Oil Corporation and the Caterpillar Tractor Company.

Comprehensive Study for Reader's Digest Cover, gouache on board, 7½″ × 6½″, s. $50

HAROLD BRETT (1880–1955)

Harold Matthews Brett

After spending his youth in Brookline, Massachusetts, Harold Brett studied at the School of the Museum of Fine Arts in Boston. After moving to New York he studied at the Art Students League with such teachers as Walter Appleton Clark. He later studied with Howard Pyle in 1906. His first assignments were with *Harper's Weekly*. He eventually did illustrations for most of the national magazines.

Lathe Operator, illustration, oil on canvas, 39″ × 30″, s. $450
An Old Melody, oil on canvas, 36″ × 25″, s. $1,650

AUSTIN BRIGGS (1909–1973)

A native of Detroit, Michigan, Austin Briggs first studied at the Wicker Art School. His interest in illustration led to a beginning job as assistant to an automobile illustrator. He made some sample drawings for the *Dearborn Independent*. Taking these to New York, he got his first assignments from *Collier's, McClure's*, and *Pictorial Review*. Over the years, his work was purchased by a variety of magazines including *The Saturday Evening Post, Cosmopolitan*, and *Redbook*.

Don't Give Up, gouache, 17″ × 16½″, s. Reproduced in American Airlines ad. *Saturday Evening Post*, 12–10–49. Tearsheet from magazine included in lot. $850
Couple on the Beach, marker on gesso board, 10½″ × 14″, s. $100
Flash Escapes! Flash Gordon Sunday page, 9/14/47, brush and ink, 15″ × 22″, s. Before becoming the great illustrator, Briggs "ghosted" this excellent adventure strip for Alex Raymond during the years of WW II. A letter from Brigg accompanies the drawing. $550
Girl Meeting Boy under Arbor, story illustration, oil on panel, s. $400
In the Whitehall Club–Chicago, advertisement, *TV Guide*, litho pencil on paper, mounted, 16¾″ × 14½″, i. The series of ads Briggs did for *TV Guide* was widely admired when they appeared in the early 1960s for their reportorial authenticity and spontaneity. $600

E. MELBOURNE BRINDLE (1906–)

Melbourne Brindle

Even without formal art training, E. Melbourne Brindle worked his way up to doing art for a San Francisco advertising agency. His career as a magazine illustrator began in 1940 with *Woman's Home Companion*.

Peace, oil on board, 25″ × 20″, s. Reproduced in *Saturday Evening Post* cover, 4/20/1946. ....$4,000

ARTHUR WILLIAM BROWN (1881–1966)

Canadian-born, Arthur William Brown began his long career as a chalk-plate artist on the Hamilton, Ontario, *Spectator*, while only fifteen. In four years, he had saved enough money to move to New York and study with Walter Appleton Clark, at the Art Student League.

When a friend did a circus article for *The Saturday Evening Post*, Brown submitted drawings. They were accepted and from then on, he did illustrations in magazines and books.

The Channey Syndicate, charcoal, 15″ × 19″, s. Reproduced in *Saturday Evening Post*, 5-16-25. Tearsheet included in lot. $325
Shipdeck Fight, 1912, Wolff pencil, ink wash, white highlights, 12″ × 13½″, s. lower right. $225

Arthur William Brown. "The Channey Syndicate." Reproduced in Saturday Evening Post. *Charcoal, signed, 15 × 19 inches, $325.* PHOTO COURTESY OF GUERNSEY'S.

Arthur William Brown. "Seven to Go." Reproduced in Ladies' Home Journal, March 1943. Signed, black and white, watercolor, 13 × 27½ inches, $425. PHOTO COURTESY OF GUERNSEY'S.

CHARLES E. CHAMBERS (1883–1941)

Charles Chambers was adept at both advertising and editorial illustrations. For Steinway & Sons he did a series of musician portraits. Other advertising assignments were for Chesterfield and Palmolive Soap. Among his magazine clients were *Redbook*, *Harper's*, and *Cosmopolitan*. He also did illustrations for such authors as Louis Bromfield, Pearl Buck, and W. Somerset Maugham.

Visting the Office, oil en grisaille on canvas, 25″ × 30″, s. $950
As She Entered, He Let the Notes Drop into the Battered Grate, oil on canvas, 30″ × 25″, s. $1,450
Librarian, oil en grisaille on canvas, 30″ × 25″, s. $800
Girl in Bathing Suit, cover painting for *Redbook*, oil on canvas, 24″ × 18″ s. $2,100
The Kimono, *Redbook*, October 1930s, oil on canvas, 24″ × 18″, s. . $2,800
Renting a Room, oil en grisaille on canvas, 30″ × 25″, s. $800
Man Writing at Desk, story illustration, "The Price of Love," *Harper's*, 1914, oil on canvas, 30″ × 20″, s. $1,800
The Shoot Out, s. C. E. Chambers, 30″ × 30″, oil en grisaille, heightened with gouache on canvas. $2,420
The Price of Love, s. C. E. Chambers, t. verso, 30″ × 20″. $660
The Disappointment, s. C. E. Chambers, 36″ × 26¾″. $660
Dinner Time, s. C. E. Chambers, 36″ × 26¾″. $1,540
The Tennis Player, s., 33″ × 24″. $1,100
A Local Hide-A-Way, s. C. E. Chambers, 23¾″ × 33″. $1,650

DAN CONTENT (B. 1902)

[signature: Dan Content]

High adventure is the theme for most of Dan Content's illustrations for such magazines as *Good Housekeeping, Liberty, Cosmopolitan, The Ladies' Home Journal, Collier's*, and *The Woman's Home Companion*. Many of his works show the influence of his teacher, Dean Cornwell.

Cosssack and Woman under a Tree, story illustration, oil on canvas, 45″ × 34″, i. lower right. $2,200

BRADSHAW CRANDELL (1896–1966)

[signature: Bradshaw Crandell]

Bradshaw Crandell studied at the Art Institute of Chicago. In 1921 his career as an illustrator was launched when he sold his first cover to *Judge* magazine. During the 1930s and 1940s, he did beautiful-girl covers for *Cosmopolitan*. His work appeared over the years in *Redbook, Collier's, The Saturday Evening Post*, and *The Ladies' Home Journal*.

New Year's Cover, pastel, 27″ × 21½″, s. Reproduced. Cover illustration for the *Ladies' Home Journal*. $1,000
Portrait, Rita Hayworth, charcoal, 20″ × 15″, s., dated. $300
Seated Nude, figure study, conté pencil and pastel, 13″ × 11¾″, not signed. $225
The Football Star, pastel, 21½″ × 20″, s. Reproduced: *Cosmopolitan* cover illustration. Exhibited: The Illustrator in America, 1900–1965. .... $1,000
Lady on the Staircase, charcoal, 26¼″ × 18″, s. $500
Pastel, 21″ × 19½″, s. Reproduced: *Cosmopolitan* magazine cover. Cover included in lot. $800

BERNARD D'ANDREA (B. 1923)

[signature: D'Andrea]

Bernard D'Andrea was born in Buffalo, New York. He began working as an illustrator in 1950 as a U.S. Army artist. He continued as an illustrator through the 1980s for magazines and publishers. Noteworthy was the series of paintings he did for the National Georgraphic Society of Washington, D.C. for a major atlas, *People and Places of the Past*.

Couple and Jealous Woman on Phone, story illustration, gouache, 15″ × 23″, s. lower right. $650
The Fall Guy, gouache, 7″ × 7″, s. Reproduced: *Saturday Evening Post*, 9-29-51. Copy of tearsheet included in lot. $100

CHARLES BUCKLES FALLS (1874–1960)

Falls

During a long career, Charles Buckles Falls did illustrations for magazines (including covers), advertising art, and books. Early in his career, in 1918, he designed a "Books Wanted" poster for the armed forces. He has also done woodcuts and murals.

Immigrants on Passage Boat, story illustration, dry brush, 10¾″ × 11″, s. $500

MAUD TOUSEY FANGEL

Maud Tousey Fangel

Maud Tousey Fangel attended the Massachusetts Normal Art School, Cooper Union, and the Art Students League in New York. She is known for her special flair of illustrating babies. Many of her illustrations were done in pastels. Her work has been in *Woman's Home Companion, The Ladies' Home Journal*, and others. She also was an illustrator for such advertising clients as Squibbs Cod Liver Oil and other baby products.

Baby on Stomach on Blanket, preliminary for advertisement, conté pencil, 12″ × 15″, s. lower right. $850

ERNEST FUHR (1874–1933)

E. Fuhr

Fuhr's works often reflect the influence of Frederic R. Gruger, especially those done in black and white. After studying with artist William Chase in Paris, he became a newspaper artist for the *New York Herald* and the *New York World*. He illustrated stories for *The Saturday Evening Post*, various juvenile magazines, and others.

Three illustrations for aviation stories: a) W. W. I Biplane Dogfight, **Wild Man Flint**, charcoal and watercolor, 14¼″ × 18½″, s. upper right; b) Man crawling out of cockpit of Biplane, **Head Work–Zero**, charcoal and watercolor, 10½″ × 15″, s. lower right; c) Parachutist shooting signal flare, **Head Work–Zero**, charcoal and watercolor, 14″ × 19″, s. lower right. $700

JOHN F. GOULD (1906–)

John F. Gould did thousands of detective story and adventure illustrations before selling to *The Saturday Evening Post*. He went on to work for *Redbook* and *Collier's* as well as many advertising clients.

The Monitor and the Merrimac, gouache on ill. board, 17¾″ × 33″, s. Reproduced: *Argosy* magazine, April 1957. .... $1,700

HARDIE GRAMATKY (1907–1979) N.A.

Before he was an illustrator, Hardie Gramatky was a "ghost" comic strip artist for the Ella Cinders comic. Studies at the Chouinard Art Institute in Los Angeles led to a job as animator in the Walt Disney studio for six years.

He moved to New York in 1936 and sold some of his freelance work to *Fortune* magazine. After that he successfully worked for magazines, fiction, and advertisers.

Small Town Christmas, *Good Housekeeping*, watercolor and gouache, 13″ × 15″ s. $900

GORDON HOPE GRANT (1875–1962)

Gordon Hope Grant began his art career as a war correspondent during the Spanish-American War. His illustrations were used in newspapers in New York and San Francisco. While his early work was on many subjects, he eventually specialized in nautical subjects. Among his most important works is his painting of the *Constitution*, used by the Navy Department to raise funds to preserve "Old Ironsides." He also illustrated many books, some of which he authored.

Yesterday and Today, *Puck*, Dec. 2, 1912, pen, brush, and ink, 14¾″ × 21″, s., dated. $350

H. TOM HALL (B. 1932)

H. Tom Hall studied at the Tyler School of Fine Art and the Philadelphia College of Art. Among his teachers were Benjamin Eisenstat and Henry Pitz.

He began illustrating a children's book, which he wrote while stationed in Japan in the U.S. Army. The book was published by Knopf after his return to the States. He worked successfully as a children's book illustrator for twelve years. In 1970 he began doing illustrations for adult magazines and books. *The Saturday Evening Post*, Bantam Books, and other paperback publishers used his work.

Montage and Lipstick, paperback book cover, gouache on masonite, 24″ × 36″, s. $450
The Harder They Fall, gouache, 17″ × 13¾″, s., *Woman's Home Companion*, Aug. 1947. Woman and movie studio. $100

W. E. HEITLAND (1893–1969) N.A.

Wilmot Emerton Heitland is known for his watercolors. He studied at the Pennsylvania Academy of the Fine Arts, the Colarossi School in Paris, and the Art Students League in New York. Among his teachers were Harvey Dunn and Walter Biggs.

His career began in 1922 with his first sale to *Collier's Weekly*. After this, he did illustrations for *McCall's, Cosmopolitan*, and others.

Road to the Valley, watercolor, 20½″ × 22¾″, s. $750
Figure in Victorian Parlor, watercolor, 26″ × 21½″, s., *Woman's Home Companion*, dated 1930. .... $1,000
The City Side Street, s. W. Emerton Heitland, N.A. and i. w/t., 26¼″ × 19½″, watercolor and pencil on board. $880
Indian Market, s. Wilmot Heitland and d. 1921, i. verso, 20½″ × 25½″, watercolor and pencil on paper. $1,210
Venetian Brooklyn, s. Heitland and d. 1922, 21½″ × 23½″, watercolor and pencil on paper. $1,320
A Spanish Beauty, s., also bears t. and annotations verso, 38″ × 35″. $1,320

GEORGE HUGHES (1907–)

Hughes —

After studying in New York at the Art Students League and at the National Academy of Design, George Hughes worked as both a fashion illustrator and special designer in the automobile industry in Detroit. In the following years he did many covers for *The Saturday Evening Post*. His editorial illustrations have appeared in the *Post* as well as *American, Woman's Day*, and *Cosmopolitan*.

Grandfather and the Black Widow, gouache, red, black, and white, 12½″ × 15¼″, s., *Saturday Evening Post*, July 14, 1945. ....$125

FRANCES TIPTON HUNTER (1896–1957)

Frances Tipton Hunter —

Children were the specialty of Frances Tipton Hunter. She graduated from the Philadelphia Museum of Industrial Arts and continued her stud-

Frances Tipton Hunter. "Not His Favorite Pastime." Watercolor, signed, 25 × 15 inches, $1,100.
PHOTO COURTESY OF GUERNSEY'S.

ies at the Philadelphia Academy of the Fine Arts and the Fleisher Art Memorial. Her first illustrations appeared in the *Woman's Home Companion* and *Collier's* as well as *Good Housekeeping* and *Liberty*. She did many covers for *The Saturday Evening Post*. Over a period of eleven years, she did a series of popular calendar paintings. Her advertising assignments included Occident Flour and Listerine.

Beautiful Girl Leaning against Tree, Young Boy Admires her from Distance, pencil, 11¾″ × 9¼″, s. Comprehensive study for *Saturday Evening Post* cover.
....$150

WOODI ISHMAEL (1914–)

Woodi Ishmael painted illustrations and covers in all mediums from the late 1930s until 1961. Over fifty of his covers were done for the *Elks* magazine. Other magazines he worked for included *The Saturday Evening Post* and *Woman's Home Companion*. He also illustrated over thirty-five books. In 1961 he began writing and illustrating a syndicated column for the Associated Press titled "Power of Faith." Collectors look for these graphite illustrations.

Bayview Station, gouache, 21″ × 15½″, s. Woodi. *Elks* magazine cover.
....$950
Comprehensive study for the Mack Truck Co. (almost identical to the finished painting), watercolor, 12″ × 19½″, s., Woodi. **Artist proof for another Mack Truck ad**, 12½″ × 17″, framed, tearsheet for #1 (*Saturday Evening Post*), Oct. 27, 1956. ....$175
Colonial Man and Little Boy, horse-drawn plow, two men at fence, pen and ink, 10″ × 7″, s.; **Indian Sneaking Up on Settler**, pen and ink, 10″ × 7″, s., book illustrations. $50
The Slick Newsboy, oil on board, 21″ × 21½″, s. Woodi. *Elks* magazine cover illustration. American Illustrators, 1900–1960, Albany, GA. November 1985.
....$1,500
Scratchboard, two illustrations. **The Midas Touch**, 4″ × 7″, monogrammed; **The Tugboat**, 4″ × 6½″, monogrammed. $80

VICTOR KALIN (B. 1919)

Victor Kalin (signature)

Victor Kalin's first illustration assignments were for *American Weekly* magazine. However, in recent years he has been associated with paperback covers, record album covers, advertising, and hardcover publishers including Holt, Reader's Digest Books, and Rinehart and Winston.

Blonde and Castle on Island, gothic paperback cover, acrylic on board, 20″ × 14″, s. $300

MORGAN KANE (1916–)

MORGAN KANE

Born in Wilmington, Delaware, Morgan Kane won a scholarship to the Cleveland Art Institute. After serving in World War II, he began his art career doing illustrations for Chicago advertising agencies. Over the years he did illustrations for many of the major magazines. During the early 1960s he dropped out of the illustration field and became a full-time photographer. By the 1970s he had returned to illustrating paperbacks and movie posters for Universal Studios, United Artists, and Warner Brothers, along with advertising illustrations.

The Bath, opaque watercolor, 24″ × 15″, s. $1,100
Gouache, 20¼″ × 15¾″, s., *American Weekly* cover, May 16, 1954. ....$100

ARTHUR IGNATIUS KELLER (1866–1924)

Arthur Keller received his art training at the National Academy of Design and with Loeffz in Munich. His work appeared in *The Ladies' Home Journal*, *The Century* magazine, and others. Beginning with his preliminary studies through the finished art, he shows his skilled drawing techniques, often crowding the canvas with many figures.

Shipboard scene, story illustration, gouache en grisaille, 13½″ × 20½″, s., reproduced: *200 Years of American Illustration*, p. 151. .... $1,900
Indians, 19″ × 11″, pen and ink wash heightened with gouache on board. $440
Running the Rapids, 16½″ × 21⅛″, s., gouache on artist board. $467

MORT KÜNSTLER (1931–)

Mort Künstler is a native New Yorker who got his art training at Pratt Institute studying illustration. He began his career in a variety of the men's magazines. After that he sold to *The Saturday Evening Post*, *Reader's Digest*, and *Newsweek*. Much of his work is done for advertising clients such as Texaco, Exxon, General Electric, and U.S. Steel.

Arena Angel, illustration in *Saga* magazine, Dec. 1955, gouache on board.
....$770
The Snow Herder, s., exec. c. 1966, reproduced as cover illustration for *Blizzard Range* by Todhunter Ballard, 23¾″ × 19″, oil on masonite. $2,090

ROBERT LAMBDIN (1886–1981)

Robert Lambdin received his training in the newspaper art department, after a year of study at the Read Art School in Denver. His career began with the *Rocky Mountain News* and eventually he became an illustrator of feature stories for the *Kansas City Star*. Moving to New York in 1917, he sold his first assignment from *Greenbook* magazine. Over the years he worked for nearly all of the important magazines, as well as doing illustrations for books and advertising clients. Collectors can recognize his early work done in pen and ink. Later, he worked in oils and halftone washes.

Girl Holding Black Mask, pen and ink, 16″ × 21″, s., *Collier's* story illustration, July 21, 1928, *Emperor of America Returns* by Sax Rohmer. $350

ORSON LOWELL (1871–1956)

Orson Lowell's father, a landscape painter, encouraged his art endeavors. Lowell studied at the Art Institute of Chicago, where he also became an instructor. In 1893 he moved to New York to become an illustrator. He sold his work from the beginning to such major magazines as *The Century, Scribner's, McClure's, Collier's*, and others. He also did illustrations for many books. In 1907 he joined *Life* magazine, where he did illustrations for many years.

Scoutmaster Santa, *Judge*, c. 1915, oil on canvas, mounted, 23½″ × 20½″, s.
....$2,800
Woman's Portrait, pen and ink, 15″ × 10″, s. $550
Some Prefer Wild Flowers, pen and ink, 21″ × 32½″, s. $1,100
Leslies, oil on canvas, 33″ × 28½″, s., *Leslies* magazine cover. $2,000
The Recital, s., exec. c. 1920, 24″ × 21¼″, pen and black ink, and Chinese white on paper. $1,045
The Happy Medium, illustrated in *Judge* magazine, Nov. 6, 1920, illus. on catalog cover, 22″ × 20″, s., pen and black ink, Chinese white, and pencil on paper. $1,045

Neysa McMein. "Cover Girl."
Pastel, 19 × 13 inches, $550.
PHOTO COURTESY OF GUERNSEY'S.

NEYSA MORAN McMEIN (1890–1949)

Neysa Moran McMein studied at the Art Institute of Chicago. Her first cover was painted for *McCall's* magazine in 1923. Her specialty was pastel portraits of attractive and important young women. Her covers were also popular with *The Saturday Evening Post* and *Woman's Home Companion*.

Cover Girl, pastel, 19″ × 13″, s. Of the hundreds of cover girls that Neysa McMein painted, none of them were ever depicted smiling. $550

CHARLES DAVIS MITCHELL (1887–1940)

Charles Davis Mitchell specialized in attractive and fashionable young women. His work was used in *Redbook, McCall's, Cosmopolitan, Good Housekeeping, The Ladies' Home Journal*, and others.

Come to My House, Wolff pencil, 18″ × 14½″, s. Reproduced: *Liberty* magazine, 1920. .... $400
The Rivals, charcoal, 15¼″ × 14½″, s. $350

THORNTON OAKLEY (1881–1953)

T Oakley -

Thornton Oakley studied architecture at the University of Pennsylvania and illustration with Howard Pyle. Many of his subjects were men at work, using heavy equipment and other industrial subjects. He often wrote and illustrated for such magazines as *Scribner's*, *Collier's*, *Century*, and *Harper's Monthly*. During World War II, he painted a series of forty-eight paintings of "American Industries Geared for War," and similar subjects for *National Geographic*, published in 1942, 1943, and 1945.

Oil on canvas, s. Thornton Oakley and inscribed 10 S. 18 St. Philadelphia on the reverse, 27⅛″ × 18⅛″ (68.9 × 45.9 cm.) *Literature*: E. Hungerford, "The Weaving of the Bridge," *Harper's Monthy* magazine, July 1909, p. 223, illus.
.... $9,900
The Castle of the Good King René, from *The Heart of Provence*, pen and ink, 9½″ × 6″, not signed. $250
Purdah Cart, Udaipur, India, cover painting for *Century* magazine, August 1912, gouache, 24¾″ × 17¾″, s. $3,800
Simple Simon, gouache and charcoal, 9¾″ × 7½″ s. and inscribed. $100
Isle of Robinson Crusoe, 21¾″ × 29″, s., watercolor on paper. $550
Roping a Pig, mat 4½″ × 8″, pen and ink on paper. $55

ROBERT PATTERSON (1898–1981)

Robert Patterson

Chicago-born Robert Patterson studied at the Chicago Art Institute. Among his later teachers were Harvey Dunn, Ralph Barton, and Walt Louderback. He began doing fashion illustrations in New York in 1922, after sharing the Patterson studios in Chicago with his brother Loran. Among the major magazines he worked for were *Judge*, *McCall's*, *The Ladies' Home Journal*, *Good Housekeeping*, and *Redbook*.

Couple Under Umbrellas, story illustration, gouache, 15″ × 21″, initialed.
.... $200
Couple in the Garden, gouache, 13″ × 12″, s. $70

HERBERT PAUS (1880–1946)

P A U S

Herbert Paus began his career as a cartoonist for the *St. Paul Pioneer Press*. He also studied at the city's Fine Arts School before moving to

Herbert Paus.
"The Wingwalker."
Popular Science *cover.*
Opaque watercolor,
21 × 15 inches,
signed, $850.
PHOTO COURTESY
OF GUERNSEY'S.

Chicago and finding work in a local art studio. After next settling in New York, he illustrated posters during World War I. This "poster" style was used in his illustrations for magazines and covers. He also did covers for many years for *Popular Science Monthly*.

Never Too Late to Learn, pen and ink and watercolor, 4″ × 9½″, s. ... $175
The Wingwalker, opaque watercolor, 21″ × 15″, s., *Popular Science* cover. Copy of cover included in lot. $850

HENRY JARVIS PECK (1880–unknown)

Henry J Peck

Henry Jarvis Peck studied at both the Rhode Island School of Design and the Eric Pape Art School in Boston. He studied with Howard Pyle in Wilmington for three years. His special expertise was New England marine subjects and country. His illustrations were used by *Harper's Weekly, The Century, Outing, The Saturday Evening Post*, and others.

HERMAN PFEIFFER (1874–1931)

Herman Pfeiffer did both magazine and advertising illustrations. He studied with Howard Pyle in 1903 and 1904. His work appeared in most major magazines such as *The Ladies' Home Journal, Woman's Home Companion, Associated Sunday Magazine,* and *Scribner's Monthly.* His advertising clients included Procter and Gamble's Ivory Soap.

Three Men at Table, Regarding Door, story illustration, *McClure's,* charcoal, 14″ × 22″, monogrammed. $300

HENRY CLARENCE PITZ (1895–1976) A.N.A.

Henry C. Pitz

Early in his life, Henry Pitz showed a talent for drawing. He was an admirer of Howard Pyle's work, and after graduating from West Philadelphia High School, was awarded a scholarship to the Philadelphia Museum School of Industrial Art, where he was able to study with former Pyle students. Talented in many mediums, he is known for his line drawings and book illustrations. Over the years, following World War I, he wrote and illustrated many books, both for the general public and art students. Beginning in 1934, he also taught at the museum school. Among his students were Edward Smith and Isa Barnett. His illustrations also appeared in such magazines as *The Saturday Evening Post* and *St. Nicholas.* He exhibited nationally and internationally. His work is in the Library of Congress in Washington, D.C. and the Philadelphia Museum of Art, as well as many public collections.

WILLY POGANY (1882–1955)

Willy Pogány

Hungarian-born William Andrew Pogany began his career in caricaturing in first London, then America. Much of his work was book illustration. He was influenced by illuminated books and Oriental artists. He also did illustrations for most of the important magazines.

The Dead Men Stood Together, *Rime of the Ancient Mariner,* book illustration, watercolor and gouache, 1910, 11¼″ × 7¼″, s. $5,000

Witchcraft, s., 21¾″ × 14¾″, pen, black ink, ink wash, watercolor, and Chinese white on board. $550

GARRETT PRICE (1896–1979)

Garrett Price

Garrett Price was best known for his humorous illustrations that appeared in *The New Yorker*. He attended both the University of Wyoming and the Chicago Art Institute. His first illustrations were sketches for *Chicago Tribune* news stories in 1916. Several years later he illustrated not only his *New Yorker* covers, but illustrations for the old *Life, College Humor, Scribner's,* and *Collier's.*

End of the Season, *The New Yorker*, 1950s, watercolor, 11½″ × 8¼″, s.
....$750

WILLIAM REUSSWIG (1902–1978)

Reusswig

Reusswig, born in New Jersey, studied at Amherst College and the Art Students League in New York. His first illustrations were sold to *Collier's*

William Reusswig. "Strike 3." Comprehensive study for True *magazine cover. Gouache, signed, 11½ × 8¼ inches, $225.* PHOTO COURTESY OF GUERNSEY'S.

magazine when he was just twenty-three. Masculine subjects, sports, and adventure were his specialties. Married to illustrator Martha Sawyers, they had the best of both worlds—working together and traveling the world.

Saracen Horsemen, dry brush on illustration board, 10″ × 25″, s. $600
Indians and Cavalry, s., d. Reusswig '73, 24″ × 36″, oil on board. . $1,760

MORTON ROBERTS (1927–1964)

Morton Roberts

Morton Roberts, born in Massachusetts, graduated from the Yale School of Fine Arts. In his short career he did some of his finest works for *Life* magazine, among them a series on the "Story of Jazz." His illustrations also appeared in *True, Reader's Digest, Collier's*, Bantam Books, and *Redbook*.

Autumnal Still-Life, *Reader's Digest*, Oct. 1957, watercolor, 16½″ × 15″, not signed. $2,500

RUTH EASTMAN RODGERS

A sportswoman and artist, Ruth Eastman Rodgers put her favorite pastimes together and became among the most successful of women illustrators. Many of her illustrations glorified the American girl. She studied art in London and at the Art Students League in New York City. Her work included covers appearing in such magazines as *Harper's Weekly, The People's Home Journal, Collier's*, and *Judge*. She designed posters for the Red Cross and Women's Suffrage.

A Real Christmas, gouache, brown and white, 27″ × 20″, s. $325
Golfing Couple, gouache on board, 28″ × 22″, s. Reproduced: *Judge* magazine cover illustration. $1,200
A Good Match, opaque watercolor on board, 21½″ × 17½″, s. Reproduced: *Judge* magazine cover. Magazine cover included in lot. $1,400

ALEX ROSS (1909–)

Alex Ross

Alex Ross, though basically self-taught, began his career in several art studios, ending up in New York. Two years after his arrival he sold his first cover design to *Good Housekeeping*. From then on he did illustrations for *The Saturday Evening Post*, *Collier's*, *The Ladies' Home Journal*, and *Cosmopolitan*. He also did book illustrations.

Gouache, 16″ × 9″, s., *Saturday Evening Post*, November 27, 1943. Tearsheet included in lot. $150

How About Tonight?, 1951, story illustration, clinch, gouache, 12¾″ × 17¾″, s. $300

Ruth Eastman Rodgers. "Golfing Couple." Reproduced: Judge *magazine cover illustration. Gouache on board, signed, 28 × 22 inches, $1,200.* PHOTO COURTESY OF GUERNSEY'S.

MAURICE SENDAK (1928–)

In 1962, Maurice Sendak changed the concept of children's book illustration with *Where the Wild Things Are*. Born in Brooklyn, he attended the Art Students League. His illustrations were first used in 1948, with a title for McGraw Hill. He has devoted more time recently to set designing for opera productions. Among his illustrated books, which he also wrote, are *In the Night Kitchen* and *The Juniper Tree—Tales from Grimm*.

Seven Monsters, sight size 5½″ × 4¼″, gouache painted celluloid. $286
Seven Monsters, sight size 2½″ × 5″, celluloid. $341
Where the Wild Things Are, one of the earliest studies by Sendak for his book of the same t., c. 1962, sight size 5″ × 6¼″, s., watercolor and ink on paper. $8,800
Gockel, Hinkel and Gackeliah, drawing, used in book by Clemens Bremtano, 1961, of same t., sight size 8″ × 6″, s., ink and wash on paper. $3,300
Gockel, Hinkel and Gackeliah, a study for a book illus., s., i. never used in final publication, 13″ × 19″, ink wash and blue pencil on paper. $990
Visually Handicapped, three drawings, s. on finished drawing, framed in common mount, commissioned by Hunter College Special Education Program for Teachers, sight size 3¾″ × 8¾″, and similar, two pencil on paper, other ink on paper. $1,650
Literary Feast, s., d. April '83, similar character used in a Reading Is Fundamental Campaign, catalog cover illus., sight size 7″ × 5″, ink and watercolor on paper. $8,800
Mentally Retarded, three drawings, s. on finished drawing and d. on first drawing June 7, 1969, framed in common mount, work commissioned by the Hunter College Special Education Program for Teachers, largest, sight size 3¾″ × 8¾″, one pencil on paper, two ink on paper. $1,430

WILLIAM T. SMEDLEY (1858–1920) N.A.

William Thomas Smedley was born in Pennsylvania and educated at the Pennsylvania Academy of the Fine Arts in Philadelphia. His career began at Harper and Brothers, first as a pen and ink artist. Later he worked in opaque water and color.

Landlord of Zion's Head, part 11, black watercolor, 10¼″ × 13¼″, s., dated 1890. ....$750

BENJAMIN ALBERT STAHL (1910–1987)

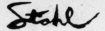

Benjamin Albert Stahl began as an errand boy and apprentice for a Chicago art studio. Within five years he was an artist for one of the city's top studios. He began his career as a magazine illustrator for *The Saturday Evening Post* in 1937, with an assignment to illustrate a sea story. He has illustrated for most of the magazines as well as for numerous advertising campaigns. Other examples of his work include illustrations for the Bible and a book he wrote and illustrated, *Blackbeard's Ghost*. He designed the Museum of the Cross in Sarasota, Florida, and painted mural-size Stations of the Cross for the interior walls. The entire collection of paintings was stolen and never retrieved.

French Revolution scene, story illustration, "Jack of Swords," *Saturday Evening Post*, 1940s, s., casein on board, 9″ × 14″. $300
No Love in Her Heart, *Saturday Evening Post*, Feb. 23, 1952, s., oil on canvas, 29½″ × 29½″, copy of tearsheet included in lot. $900
Butch at the Outdoor Concert, *American Weekly* cover, Aug. 25, 1957, s., watercolor, 20″ × 17¾″. Copy of cover included in lot. $1,700

HADDON SUNDBLOM (1899–1976)

For nearly forty years, Sundblom influenced advertising art, winning medals and citations. Among the advertisers he worked for were Coca-Cola, Maxwell House Coffee, Procter and Gamble, and Palmolive, Peet & Company. To collectors, the Santa Claus he painted for Coca-Cola is most familiar. For over twenty years it was a well-recognized feature appearing on the back cover of national magazines. What collectors may not be aware of is that Sundblom modeled for the Coca-Cola Santa in his later years.

His influence was extended when, as a magazine illustrator in his own Chicago studio, he trained a group of young artists who followed his style. They later went on to become famous illustrators; among them were Matt Clark, Coby Whitmore, and Edwin Henry. Sundblom was a dominant force in the Chicago art field that developed in the 1920s.

Friends from Across the Lake, oil on board, 17¼″ × 15″, unsigned, comprehensive study for the U.S. Brewers Foundation Series "Homelife in America"; finished painting was #110 in the series; obtained from the estate of Donald R. Blomquist, art director for the J. Walter Thompson Agency. $325

HARRY LAVERNE TIMMINS (1887–1963)

Timmins

Harry Timmins was born in Nebraska and studied at the Art Institute of Chicago. He was co-founder of the Academy of Art in Chicago and worked in all forms of media. He did illustrations for numerous advertising clients as well as for such magazines as *This Week, Collier's, Cosmopolitan,* and *Woman's Home Companion.*

The Speakeasy, s., watercolor on board, 22½″ × 13½″. $375

FREDERIC VARADY (1908–)

Varady

Frederic Varady left his native Hungary for the United States in 1927. Before that he had attended the Royal Hungarian Academy of Art. After graduating, he began working on theater set designs, fashion drawings, and movie posters and worked as a fashion artist in Paris and Berlin. In 1939, he did his first illustration for an American magazine, followed by work for important magazines such as *Good Housekeeping, The Saturday Evening Post,* and others.

Couple in Coach, watercolor, 13″ × 12″, unsigned. $50
Magician at a Party, story illustration, "The Payoff," Apr. 1950, s., gouache on board, 17″ × 25″. $1,400

Frederic Varady. "Say Yes Dear." Redbook, June 1954. Gouache on illustration board, signed lower left, 18 × 18 inches, $600. PHOTO COURTESY OF ILLUSTRATION HOUSE, INC.

JOHN L. SCOTT WILLIAMS (1877–1976) N.A.

·J· Scott Williams·

Born in England, John Scott Williams began his studies at the Art Institute of Chicago. Early illustrations appeared in 1905 in *The Saturday Evening Post*. In the following years he did illustrations for other leading magazines of the day, including covers for the magazine section of the *New York Herald Tribune*.

Couple in Arbor, "Pieces of Eight," s., charcoal, 20″ × 19″. $650
The Queen of Hearts, s. lower left, d. 1921, oil on canvas mounted on board, 29½″ × 57½″. $12,500

MORTIMER WILSON, JR. (1906–)

Mortimer Wilson jr

Nebraskan Mortimer Wilson, Jr., studied painting at the Art Students League in New York. He also worked in summer theater as a director and taught painting on the side. He began doing illustrations for *American* magazine, *Woman's Home Companion*, and *The Saturday Evening Post* to add to his income. His advertising clients included Woodbury Facial Soap and Maxwell House Coffee.

Soldier and Woman on Red Couch by Hearth, story illustration, "The Swan at Dawn," *American*, c. 1942, oil on canvas, 31″ × 34.5″, not signed.
.... $5,200
Couple Embracing on Terrace, story illustration, "Friends of Mr. Morison's," oil on canvas, 35″ × 26″, not signed. $3,200

BEN WOHLBERG (1927–)

Ben D. Wohlberg

Ben Wohlberg studied at the Chicago Academy of Fine Art and the Art Center School in Los Angeles. He did his first illustrations in 1960 for *Redbook*. However, his work has also been used by the *Ladies' Home Journal*, *Woman's Day*, *Good Housekeeping*, *McCall's*, and *Guideposts*. His illustrations have been in hardcover books published by *Reader's Digest*, and paperback covers were done for Ballantine, Dell, and others.

Couple by Rectory, paperback book cover, acrylic and pencil, s., 12.5″ × 12.5″. $75

GEORGE HAND WRIGHT (1873-1951) N.A.

J. Wright

George Hand Wright studied at the Spring Garden Institute and the Academy of Fine Art in Philadelphia. His interest in rustic subjects and the common man were doubtless influenced by his own humble birth as the son of a blacksmith. He made his finished art from the sketches and drawings, sometimes at the scene. His work is known for its detail.

Fox Hunting by Haystacks, s., pastel, 16.25″ × 20.5″. $4,000
Alma's Room, s., watercolor, 8½″ × 10″. $300
Country Auction, story illustration, s., watercolor and charcoal, 21″ × 15″. $600
Holding On, s., sight size 14″ × 11″, pencil on paper. $33
The Confrontation, s. G. Wright, i. verso, 15″ × 19½″, pencil, charcoal, and watercolor on paper. $55
Village Scene, s., sight size 18″ × 21″, pastel on paper. $1,760
Tenant Farm, drawing, s., 13″ × 16″, charcoal. $247

ADDITIONAL ILLUSTRATORS

ELENORE PLAISTED ABBOTT (1875-1935)

Knight and Lady Fair, s., oil en grisaille on canvasboard, 23″ × 16.5″ $1,150

CLARK AGNEW (1905-1959)

Pin-Up in Blue, s., oil on canvas, 30″ × 24″. $850

HARRY ANDERSON (1906-) A.N.A.

Young Woman in Arbor, s., gouache, 23″ × 17″. $800

PETER ARNO (1904-1968)

The Circus, *The New Yorker*, Apr. 4, 1964, s., watercolor, 13.5″ × 10″. $3,800

RALPH AVERY (1906-1976) A.N.A.

Red and White Roses, *Reader's Digest* cover painting, s., watercolor, 15½″ × 19½″. $800

JOHN D. BATTEN (1860-1932)

Man blowing seashell horn, book illustration, ''The Farmer and the Money-lender,'' *Indian Fairy Tales*, pen and ink, 6.25″ × 3″, not signed. $200

ROBERT BAXTER

Nude with clock, dreaming, magazine cover, "Sleep," *Medical Times,* s., oil on canvas, 36″ × 36″. $1,200

GERRIT BÉNEKER (1882–1934)

Knight and Lady on a White Horse, 1905, s., d., oil on canvas, 23″ × 16″. $900

HARRY BENNETT (1925–)

Horace the Falcon, the Egyptian Sky God, illustration, s., acrylic on masonite, 16.75″ × 21″. $400

THOMAS BJAMORN

Priest and Rainstorm, story illustration for "Father Duddleswell's Silver Lining," *Reader's Digest,* Sept. 1978, s., gouache, 17″ × 21″. $400

MAHLON BLAINE

Girl's Head, reproduced in *The Art of Mahlon Blaine,* c. 1925, s. with emblem LR, pen and ink, 18″ × 16″. $300

SYLVIA BOKOR

Woman and Mannikins, paperback cover, *The Red Carnelian,* s., acrylic on board, 16″ × 14″. $50

STAN BORACK (1927–)

Ambush, reproduced, cover for *Saga* magazine, s., oil on board, 13½″ × 14½″, copy of cover included in lot. $400
Boot Hill, reproduced, book cover illus., Bantam Books, s., oil on board, 20¼″ × 12¼″. $250
The Sky and the Forest, reproduced cover illus. for book by C. S. Forester, Pyramid Books, s., watercolor, brown and white, 16″ × 11½″. $350
Custer's Last Stand, reproduced *Saga* magazine cover, s., tempera, 16¾″ × 13¼″ $850

JAMES BOREN

Morning in Montana, c. 1973, s., watercolor on paper, 21″ × 29″. ...$1,200

M. LEONE BRACKER

Two charcoal drawings, s., (1) "Young Couple," 25¼″ × 23″, (2) "Three Men Talking," d. 1922, 27″ × 20¾″. $125

Worth Brehm (1883–1928).
"Some Beau." Signed.
Charcoal, 25½ × 16¾
inches, $475. PHOTO
COURTESY OF GUERNSEY'S.

NELL BRINKLEY (?–1944)

Little Man, Big Man, *N. Y. Journal*, 1935, s., d., pen and ink, 8″ × 10″.
....$450

UMBERTO BRUNELLESCHI (1879–)

Courtly Love, s. in plate, pochoir print, 9.25″ × 15.5″. $300

F. SANDS BRUNNER (1886–1954)

Sabbath Candles, *This Week*, s., oil on canvas, 26″ × 20″. $4,800
Calling Everyone, pretty girl "calling everyone" through megaphone, s., oil on
canvas, 28″ × 15¾″. $500

CHARLES JAY BUDD (1859–1926)

Courtier, s., d. 1877, watercolor, 6.75″ × 4.25″. $150
Monk, s., d. 1877, watercolor, 6.75″ × 4.25″. $150

CARL BURGER

Mary Pickford, reproduced *American Weekly* magazine, cover, Jan. 22, 1950,
s., gouache, 21″ × 15″. $300

PAUL C. BURNS

Boy and Girl with Toys, illus., s. lower right, gouache and charcoal pencil,
13.5″ × 10.25″. $350

C. Broughton (unknown).
"He refused to be entangled
in the concerns of Fairyland."
Pen and ink, 15⅝ × 13¼
inches, $7,500. PHOTO
COURTESY OF KENDRA
KRIENKE, CHILDREN'S
ILLUSTRATIONS, NEW YORK.

CLARENCE H. CARTER (1904–)

Sad Pumpkin, *American Weekly*, Oct. 28, 1951, s., watercolor, 11″ × 10.25″.
.... $1,200

RICHARD CASE

Cowboy in Shoot-out in Front of "Wanted" Poster, pulp magazine cover,
"Sonny Tabor," *Wild West Weekly*, June 1, 1940, oil on canvas, 28″ × 26″,
not signed. $3,600

J. ANDRÉ CASTAIGNE (1860–1930)

Anthony and Cleopatra, story illustration, s., d. 1911, oil on canvas en grisaille,
31.5″ × 20.5″. $2,600

EDDIE CHAN

Girl Hugging Record, cover, *American Weekly*, Sept. 7, 1952, s. lower left,
gouache, 18″ × 14″. $950

ALPHONSE CHANTEAU

Madonna and Wrecked Boat, fantasy illus., *Associated Sunday Magazine*, s.,
d., opaque watercolor, 10.5″ × 14.5″. $100

CARLTON T. CHAPMAN (1860–1926)

Naval Battle at Night, c. 1895, s., oil on canvas, 19″ × 25″. $1,500

FRANCIS CHASE

Comprehensive study for *Collier's* cover, s., oil on board, 11½″ × 8½″.
....$150

ERNEST CHIRIAKA

Gouache, reproduced *American Weekly* magazine, s., 17″ × 26½″. $475

EMERY CLARKE

Cowboy Drawing Gun, pulp magazine cover, "King Kolt," *Wild West Weekly*, Mar. 19, 1935, s. lower left, oil on canvas, 31″ × 21.75″. $1,700

ROBERT CONLAN

Group of Four Nudes, figure studies, s., charcoal pencil, 12″ × 20″. ...$20

FRED COOPER (1883–1962)

Colonial Woman in Sedan Chair, advertisement, *Prince George Hotel*, init., brush and ink on paper, 7″ × 12″. $175

FRANK CRAIG (1874–1918)

Couple in Forest, story illus., 1912, s., d. lower right, gouache en grisaille, 15.5″ × 10″. $1,400

WILFRED P. DAVISON

Calendar series, reproduced, (1) dogs pointing pheasants, s., oil on board, 20″ × 16″, (2) pheasants flying off, s., oil on board, 20″ × 16″, (3) dog with pheasant in mouth, s., oil on board, 20″ × 16″. $1,400

ABNER DEAN

Santas Around the Clock, reproduced cover for *Life* humor magazine, s., watercolor, 18¾″ × 13¼″. $350

JOE DE MERS

Gouache, reproduced *Good Housekeeping* magazine, 1951, s., 13″ × 21″. *Note*: Best magazine illustrations of 1957 Award winner, Society of Illustrators show, Jan. 1958. ....$525

PETER DRIBEN

Girl Parachutist, magazine cover, s., oil on canvas, 29″ × 22″. $2,000

ANDRÉ DURENCEAU

Beulah Croaker's Pirate Gold, magazine cover, *American Weekly*, June 6, 1948, oil on panel, 17″ × 15″, not signed. $1,100
Desert Tortoise, magazine cover, *Reader's Digest*, oil on board, 13.5″ × 10.5″, not signed. $650

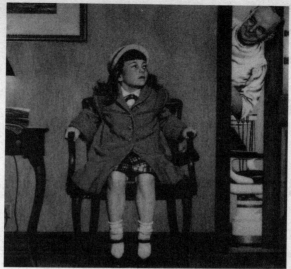

Stan Ekman. "Girl at the Dentist." Reproduced in American Weekly *magazine cover. Oil on board, 18¼ × 19 inches, signed, $475.* PHOTO COURTESY OF GUERNSEY'S.

STAN EKMAN

Cover for *American Weekly* magazine, reproduced, s., oil on board, 15¾″ × 15½″. $400

JOHN FERNIE

Gouache, reproduced *American Weekly*, s., 16½″ × 10″. $175

ANNE H. FISH (1892–1964)

Careers for Our Girls, "The Savage Shingler," *Cosmopolitan*, Nov. 1928, s., pen and ink, red watercolor, 18.75″ × 13.25″. $500

DOROTHY FOX

Two illustrations: (a) Girl at chalkboard, "Real Brain Food At Last," *American Weekly*, Oct. 26, 1947, gouache, 12.25″ × 10″, not signed, and (b) Girl on swing, "Diet for Heartache," *American Weekly*, Dec. 7, 1947, gouache, 15″ × 10″, not signed. $350

A. FRAHM

Blacksmith, reproduced for the Coca-Cola Co., Atlanta, GA, s., oil on canvas, 38″ × 21¾″. $1,600

KELLY FREAS

Kneeling Woman, watercoor on paper, 7½″ × 7″. $175

ALFRED FREDERICKS (?–1907)

The Student, init., black-and-white gouache, 13.5″ × 10″. $350

GWEN FREMLIN

Soda Sipping, reproduced cover for *American Weekly* magazine, s., gouache, 18½″ × 13″. $200

PAOLO GARRETTO (1903–)

Uncle Sam, Donkey, and Elephant, cover painting, "Crystal Ball Politics," probably *Vanity Fair*, s., d. 1935, watercolor, airbrushed, 11.5″ × 10″. $500

ARTHUR GETZ (1913–)

The Saturday Night New York Times, *The New Yorker*, Nov. 22, 1958, s., casein and tempera, 23.5″ × 17.5″. $4,000
End of St. Patrick's Day Parade, *The New Yorker*, Mar. 14, 1953, s., casein and tempera, 23.5″ × 17.5″. $3,000

GEORGE GIGUÈRE

Two Men in a Rowboat, story illustration, oil on canvas, s., 33″ × 25″. $4,500
Garden Dance Performance, story illustration, "Evening Fete," oil on canvas, 33″ × 23.25″, not signed. $4,000

FRANK GODWIN

The Saffron Eel, 20″ × 30″, pen brush and black ink, sepia wash, and gouache on board. $550
Join the Navy, s., illus. for *Redbook* magazine, 19¼″ × 29⅞″, brush, black ink, and ink wash on board. $835

KARL GODWIN (1893–)

Escaping Panther, story illustration, *True*, May 1945, s. lower left, watercolor, 24.25″ × 20″. $1,000

SIMON GRECO

The Black Man in the City, cover painting, *Reporter*, s. lower right, gouache, 16.75″ × 13.5″. $175

WILLIAM C. GRIFFITH

Reproduced *Sportsafield* magazine, s., oil on board, 11¼″ × 20½″. $100

CHARLES GRUNWALD

Couple in Bedroom, Man on Bed, *The Old Photograph*, c. 1905, s., black-and-white gouache on board, 23″ × 13.5″. $400

MICHAEL HAGUE

Rip Van Winkle Surrounded by Little Men, story illustration, 1981, s., d., watercolor and ink, 13″ × 24″ (*Note*: This is one of the largest works executed by Hague.) $2,600

ROBERT HANDVILLE (1924–)

Ski-Mobiles, story illustration, "The Cats that Conquered Winter," *Reader's Digest*, Dec. 1968, s. lower right, gouache, 17″ × 23″. $225

ALICE HARVEY (1894–)

Two Men and a Woman Seated Under a Tree, gag cartoon, "Do you like Kipling?" "Why, I don't know. How do you Kipple?" *Life*, 1924, charcoal pencil, ink wash, 11.5″ × 19″, s. lower left, d., reproduced *The World Encyclopedia of Cartoons*, p. 282. (This cartoon's gag line became famous in the 1920s.) $250

HASSMAN

Civil War Attack in House, story illustration, *Associated Sunday Magazine*, s., black-and-white gouache, 8.5″ × 13.75″. $450

CHARLES HAWES

Winter Birds, *American Weekly* magazine cover, s., gouache, 17″ × 17″.
.... $300

JACK HEARN

Maple Syrup, reproduced as a national ad for General Motors in 1957, s., gouache on ill. board, 13½″ × 31″, the painting was given to the vice-president of GM Truck Division by the artist. $700

ROBERT HILBERT

E-Z Roller Skates, *American Weekly* magazine cover, June 9, 1954, s., gouache, 23″ × 17¾″. $150

POLLY (CLARENCE) HILL

Young Woman Standing Holding Rose, decorative illustration, s., watercolor, 16″ × 11″. $600

HY HINTERMEISTER (1897–)

Black Man Helping Boy on Stilts, calendar illustration, s. lower right, oil on canvas, 25.5″ × 23.5″. $3,000
Fly Fishing, calendar illustration, s., oil on canvas, 21½″ × 32½″. $950

RICHARD HOOK

Woman Carpenter, story illustration, "Do It Herself," s. lower right, gouache, 17.25″ × 21.25″. $600

REA IRVIN (1881–1972)

Internal Combustion Cow, init., ink and gouache, 8″ × 12.75″. $120

LU KIMMEL (1908–1973)

Advertisement, 13½″ × 19″. $440

CHARLES KINGHAN (1895–)

Couple at Fireplace, s., oil on canvas, 27″ × 24″. $700

Earl Oliver Hurst (1895–1958). Left: "Out on the Town." Cover illustration. Watercolor, signed, 20¼ × 13¼ inches, $125. PHOTO COURTESY OF GUERNSEY'S. *Right: "Under the Mistletoe." Cover illustration. Watercolor, signed, 22½ × 15¾ inches, $100.* PHOTO COURTESY OF GUERNSEY'S.

Robert L. Lambdin (1886–1981). Mural study. Watercolor, signed, 8 × 20 inches, $375. PHOTO COURTESY OF GUERNSEY'S.

STANLEY KLIMLEY

Two Women Having Coffee and Salad, story illustration, *American Weekly*, s. lower right, gouache, 18″ × 17.25″. $400
Unfinished Business, Lovers on the Beach, *McCall's* magazine, Oct. 11, 1954, s., gouache, 14¾″ × 21″. $200

WENDALL KLING

Little Boy Who Fell Off Hobby Horse, *American Weekly* cover, Mar. 16, 1952, s., gouache, 21¾″ × 16″. $225

FRANK LACANO

U.F.O. Zapping a Man, story illustration, "Burned by a Flying Saucer," *American Weekly*, Apr. 19, 1953, s., black-and-white gouache, 8″ × 16″. $400

GERALD LEAKE (1885–1975) A.N.A.

The Ice Cream Cone, s., oil on canvas (canvas needs to be relined), 25″ × 39½″. $1,000

RON LESSER

Two Women on Bed, One Smoking, book cover painting, gouache, 14½″ × 8½″, unsigned. $125

JOSEPH WATSON LITTLE

Heroines of the Bible, *American Weekly* magazine, (1) "Sarah and Abraham," s., oil on canvas, 32″ × 23″, (2) "Ruth," s., oil on canvas, 32″ × 23″.
.... $475
Klondike Josie, *American Weekly* magazine, s., gouache on board, 20″ × 19″.
.... $350
Little Boy with Injured Dog, *American Weekly*, Oct. 29, 1944, s., gouache, 15¾″ × 12¾″. $325

Rico Lebrun (1900–1964). Fashion illustration. Travelers on coach.
Watercolor and ink, 10¾ × 15½ inches, signed lower left, $2,600. PHOTO
COURTESY OF ILLUSTRATION HOUSE, INC.

Manning DeVilleneuve Lee (1894–1980). "Pirate's Doom." Illustration for
"Pirate's Doom," The American Boy Youth's Companion, *dated 1930.*
Signed, $150. PHOTO COURTESY OF DU MOUCHELLES ART GALLERIES.

DENNIS LUZAK

Young Woman Wearing Lingerie, s., opaque watercolor, airbrush, 16″ × 21½″. $250

CHARLES MacLELLAN (1885/87-)

Young Woman with Apple Blossoms, magazine cover, "Springtime," *Everybody's*, May 1925, s., d., oil on canvas, 16″ × 13.75″. $7,000

LOUIS MARCHETTI

Girl with Gargoyle, paperback book cover, acrylic, 18″ × 14″, not signed, (Marchetti is considered the originator of the gothic paperback cover). ... $500

ARMAND MARIZON

The Strike, *Outdoorsman* magazine, May/June 1945, s., oil on canvas, 23¾″ × 17½″. $1,200

FORTUNINO MATANIA (1881-?)

Woman of Israel, illustration, s., pencil, 11″ × 9.5″. $250
British and German Military Engagement, WWI, reportorial illustration, probably *London Illustrated News*, s., ink wash, 21.25″ × 35″. $1,100

EARL MAYAN

Safecracker at Work, story illustration, "You Build a Helluva Safe," *Reader's Digest*, June 1972, s., d. lower right, gouache and ink, 10.5″ × 13.5″. ..$450
Madam Forty Four, *Saturday Evening Post*, Oct. 6, 1951, s., egg tempera, 16¼″ × 23½″, copy of tearsheet included in lot. $225

LEW McCANCE

Home Late, man with briefcase, two women, book cover painting, acrylic on masonite panel, 16″ × 17″, unsigned. $50

EMLEN McCONNELL (1872-1947)

Little Girl Blowing Bubbles, magazine cover design, s. verso, gouache on illustration board, 12.75″ × 8.75″. $1,400
Peter Pan, oil on canvas, 15″ × 15″. $800

EDWIN MEGARGEE

The Lost Pup, little lost dog in the rain, *American Weekly*, Sept. 1, 1946, s., oil on canvas, black and white, vignette, 17″ × 19″. $175

ZOE MOZERT

Calendar (Flower Girl series), s., pastel, 32″ × 26″. $3,000

Flower Girl in Pink, s., pastel, 30½″ × 24¾″, one of a series of pastel drawings executed by Ms. Mozert for a series of calendar illustrations titled "The Flower Girls"; Zoe Mozert was one of America's leading pinup artists.
.... $4,000

FRANK A. NANKIVELL (1869–1959)

Maidens Fair Helping the Buxom Novice, *Puck*, 1900, s., brush and ink, litho., pencil, 21″ × 13″. $400

MATHIAS NOHEIMER

Bass in Cyprus, *Outdoor Life* cover, watercolor, 17½″ × 11½″, unsigned.
.... $50

SAMUEL DAVIS OTIS (1889–1961)

New Packard, s., grisaille watercolor, 9¾″ × 14¼″. $925
Chef and Costumed Figures, illustration, s. upper right, ink and watercolor, 17″ × 13″. $1,000

ARTHUR PALMER (1913–)

The Finest and the Swell, s., watercolor, 16.5″ × 12.5″. $3,500

STANLEY PARKHOUSE

Couple in Interior, "Speak No Evil," *Ladies' Home Journal*, Oct. 1940, init. oil on canvas, 27″ × 42″. $850

K. Gunnor Petersen. "Winter Cover." Opaque watercolor. Signed. Cover illustration for Hearst Sunday Pictorial Review, $225. PHOTO COURTESY OF GUERNSEY'S.

K. GUNNOR PETERSEN (1905–1985)

Pretty Girl in Halloween Cat Costume, Hearst *Sunday Pictorial Review* cover, Oct. 26, 1958, s., tempera, 18″ × 12¼″. $150
Halloween Cover, for Hearst *Sunday Pictorial Review*, Oct. 30, 1960, s., opaque watercolor, 16″ × 11½″, tearsheet (cover) included in lot. $125

A. B. PHILLIPS

Five illustrations: 2 fashion panels, init., black-and-white tempera, 16″ × 9″; 3 song titles, init., black-and-white tempera, 16″ × 12″. $30

LESLIE RAGAN (1897–)

Car and Sailboats, advertisement, *Nash Automobile*, s., watercolor, 19″ × 22″. $2,200

MICHAEL RAMAS

Flying Saucers, *American Weekly* magazine, gouache, black and white, 14″ × 19″. $275

BILL RANDALL

American Weekly magazine cover, s., gouache, 19½″ × 17″. $300

F. W. READ

Father Time on a Bicycle, 1898, s., black-and-white gouache, 26.5″ × 14.5″. $430

AL REDMOND

American Weekly magazine cover, s., oil on canvas, 16½″ × 12½″. $275

ROBERT O. REID

The Dieter, *Collier's,* Nov. 26, 1938, s., watercolor, 16.5″ × 15.25″. $1,600
"Oh Come Now—Save that Energy for the War," General Fire Co. Series, *Saturday Evening Post*, Sept. 26, 1942, s., watercolor, 16¾″ × 13½″, tearsheet included in lot. $750

AGNES RICHARDSON

Boy and Girl Holding Hands, illustration, s., gouache on paper, 9″ × 7.5″. $300

BOARDMAN ROBINSON (1876–1952)

Rough Man Carrying Off Woman, story illustration, "Brawl," s., i., Wolff pencil, pen and ink heightened with white, 12″ × 18″. $250

William F. Rose (1909–). American Weekly, 1951. "Strike Up the Band." Tempera, 18 × 26 inches, signed, $500. PHOTO COURTESY OF PRIVATE COLLECTOR. (See *Special Notes* [29] at back of book.)

GENE ROGERS

Preparing to Battle, Revolutionary War, book illustration, s., watercolor on board, 13″ × 11½″. $50

CARL ROHN (1888–1935)

Columbia Bicycles, ad for *Pope Manufacturing Co.*, s., d. 1896, pen, brush and ink, 16″ × 12″. $300

RAY ROHN

Card Game, watercolor, s., black and white, 13″ × 13½″. $125

JEROME ROZEN

Watching Over, s., brown and black oil on canvas, 24.5″ × 20.25″. ... $600
Two Pioneer Women, init., red and black, oil on canvas, 22″ × 16″. ...$450

WALLACE SAATY

Pretty Girl in Red Getting off Airplane, *Woman's Home Companion* cover, June 1938, s., oil on canvas, 28¼″ × 22″. $150

HOWARD SANDEN

Christmas Visitors, s., oil on canvas, 30″ × 39″. $3,250

NORMAN SAUNDERS

Card Gambling Woman, pulp magazine cover, s., oil on board, 29.5″ × 19.5″. $1,100
Woman in Black Lingerie, pulp illustration, s., oil on board, 28″ × 19.5″. $1,800

JOHN SCHOENHERR

Swans and a Turtle, magazine cover study, *Reader's Digest*, oil on board, 7″ × 6.5″, not signed. $450

ALEX SCHOMBURG

Future Magazine Cover, c. 1954, acrylic on board, 18″ × 24″, publication included. $1,600

CHARLES SHELDON (1894–1961)

Hour of Sorrow, cover illus., s., oil on board, 23½″ × 17½″. $550

Pencil drawing of George S. Kaufman, producer/ director/playwright. First published in the New York Herald Tribune, Sept. 7, 1941. Drawn from life by Ben Solowey, $1,500. © 1990 THE STUDIO OF BEN SOLOWEY, BEDMINSTER, PA.

FRANK O. SMALL (1860–)

A Freshly Picked Blossom, s., oil on board, 12″ × 14″. $1,200

W. B. SMITH

Woman in White Bathing Suit and Red Cape, magazine cover, *American Weekly*, pastel on board, 27.5″ × 22″, not signed. $400

WILLIAM A. SMITH (1918–1989)

Lighting the Cigar, story illustration, *Life*, Apr. 8, 1946, p. 107, s., tusche on gesso panel, 18″ × 23″. $450
Bread-Making, s., d. 1907, oil on canvas, 20″ × 30″. $8,200

WUANITA SMITH (1866–1959)

Sand Dune, s., d. 1923, pastel on sandboard, 8.5″ × 10.5″. $250

FRANÇOIS C. SOMM (1844–1907)

Fox Barking at Hiding Elf, story illustration, s., d. 1897, pen and ink on paper, 6″ × 9.75″. $50

PAUL STAHR (1883–)

Woman Beseeching Stern Librarian, story illustration, s., oil on canvas, 30″ × 20″. $850
Elegant Couple Sitting on Lawn, *Saturday Evening Post*, 1910, s., watercolor, black and white, 20½″ × 26¾″. $350

PETER STEVENS

Woman Weeping, Cowboy on Floor, story illustration, "It was all so foolish," *American Weekly*, Jan. 14, 1951, oil on canvasboard, 18″ × 22.75″, not signed. $400
Treasure, *American Weekly* magazine, s., oil on board, 18½″ × 17½″. . $125

ROBERT W. STEWART

Couple on Veranda, story illustration, s. lower left, oil on canvas, 34″ × 30″, exhib. Society of Illustrators, 1920s. $5,000

GILBERT STONE (1940–1984)

Cale Yarborough at the Daytona 500, story illustration, *Sports Illustrated*, 1970, s. and d. center right, acrylic, 24″ × 25.5″. $800

RICHARD STONE

Woman in a Crowd, story illustration, watercolor and ink, 11.5″ × 27″ not signed. $300

The Swimming Hole, s., watercolor, blue and white, 17″ × 13½″, Society of Illustrators Annual Award Winner. $125

FRANK STREET (1893–1944)

Man Hauling Sled in Snow, story illustration, *Saturday Evening Post*, s., oil on canvas, 24″ × 34″ (Street was a student of Harvey Dunn). $3,200

TH. SUNDQUIST

Couple Lying on the Grass, s., tempera, 18″ × 25″. $400

RICHARD TAYLOR (1902–1970)

Pianiste Extraordinaire, a typically bizarre Taylor character, s., oil on panel, 15″ × 18″. $850

MARVIN F. THOMPSON

War Savings Stamp Poster, WWI poster composition, soldier and dog, lettering and borders hand-painted, picture in center is a print of some kind; the composition was the original work for this poster. $400

THURE DE THULSTRUP (1848–1940)

Funeral Procession in Recolita Cemetery, Asuncion, Paraguay, story illustration, ''Funeral of an Angelito,'' s., black-and-white gouache, 14.25″ × 20.75″. $350

GEORGE TOBIN (1864–1956)

Nude with Arm Raised to Head, drawing, s., i., colored pencil, 7″ × 11″. $550

HERB TOUSS (1929–)

Beach Embrace, s., oil on board, 7¼″ × 11″. $150

STUART TRAVIS (1868–1942)

Farm Visitor, *Puck*, May 1903, s., d., gouache, 27″ × 19.5″. $450

JAMES TREMBATH

The Glorious Fourth, reproduced cover illus. for *Judge* magazine, s., opaque watercolor, 23½″ × 17½″. $1,100

CLARENCE F. UNDERWOOD (1871–1929)

Enchanted, s., opaque watercolor vignette, 24″ × 18″; Underwood executed hundreds of covers for *The Saturday Evening Post* and others from 1900 to 1920. ....$900

*Saul Tepper. This illustration was done for Chesterfield cigarettes, 1928.
"At the Masquerade." Oil on canvas, 32 × 37 inches, signed, dated,
$6,000.* PHOTO COURTESY OF ILLUSTRATION HOUSE, INC. (See *Special
Notes* [30] at back of book.)

*Edna Ganzhorn Unsworth .
(1890–). "He Dealt His Last
Hand." Oil on board, 23 × 17
inches, $2,200.* PHOTO
COURTESY OF BUTTERFIELD &
BUTTERFIELD, SAN FRANCISCO.

GEORGE VAN WERVEKE

Three editorial headings: (a) Chaotic medieval scene and two other drawings, "When Every Robber Baron Was His Own Troubador," *New York Times Book Review*, 1920s, s., pen and ink, c. 8″ × 22″, (b) Coleridge, (c) Pushkin.
.... $400

WILSON F. VAUX

Norma Shearer and Wallace Reid, c. 1931, s., d. 1931, charcoal on paper, 22″ × 13½″. $150

FRANK VERBECK (1858–1933)

Bears gathering honey, swarming bees, s., ink and watercolor, 11.25 × 13.5″.
.... $1,100

VINCINTINI

Watercolor, reproduced, *Photoplay*, Sept. 1938, s., d.'38, 21″ × 18¾″.
.... $300

EDWARD A. WILSON (1886–1970)

Sailing, "Stay as You Are!" s., black and green watercolor, 12″ × 24″.
....$475
French Court Dance, init., black watercolor wash, 12.5″ × 14″. $250

EUGENIE WIREMAN

Girl with flowers, magazine cover, s., oil on canvas, 20″ × 16″. $3,500

GEORGE ZIEL

Girl in pool, man on horseback, paperback book cover, 1980, s., d., acrylic on board, 23″ × 15.5″. $700

PART VII

MAGAZINE COVER ART
AND ARTISTS

EVALUATING MAGAZINE
COVER ART

For the TV generation of today's adults, who grew up in the 1950s, 1960s, and 1970s, it is difficult to understand the importance of magazine cover art. But to the average American growing up in the early 20th century, magazine covers offered a type of art they could understand— and afford. Indeed, at many an estate and garage sale, it's not unusual to find those old covers behind expensive frames. They had been respectfully hung as art—and why not? The covers were treated as something special by the magazine editors, as were the artists they hired, for high wages, to create them. The cover was an important sales tool to sell the contents inside.

Around the turn of the century, American magazines enjoyed phenomenal growth, and many changes were brought about by technology and public taste. For the most part, magazines were small in size, the covers generally used for titles and a table of contents. With the advent of larger magazines, editors gradually realized that a colorful cover, with art done in a particular format, would build reader interest. A stable of cover artists, selected from the most important illustrators of the day, was consistently used. J. C. Leyendecker and Norman Rockwell were joined by Harrison Fisher, Stevan Dohanos, John Falter, Amos Sewell, and many others as cover artists for *The Saturday Evening Post*.

During the 1920s, the favorite cover subject was the pretty girl. Among the artists who did pretty-girl portraits were Charles Chambers, Neysa McMein, Coles Phillips, F. Sands Brunner, Penrhyn Stanlaws, and Guy Hoff.

It was the cover artist who pictured the idealized, sometimes folksy image of the "American Dream." Norman Rockwell comes to mind first, but genre studies and street scenes also were done by John Falter, Mead Schaeffer, and Melbourne Brindle. Others are less well known these days: J. F. Kernan, who, like Rockwell, combined humor with classic touches of Americana, along with E. M. Jackson and Revere F. Wistehuff. Unforgettable were the changing faces of American life mirrored in the 1950s and 1960s by Stevan Dohanos.

Sophisticated humor erupted on the covers of *The New Yorker* magazine, represented by the work of Constantin Alajalov, Ralph Barton, Peter Arno, and Garrett Price.

Collier's, a rival of *The Saturday Evening Post*, took a different approach with their cover art. Artists like Edward Penfield and Herbert Paus used a poster-type technique.

The growing group of women's magazines, such as *Good Housekeeping*, *Ladies' Home Journal*, and *Woman's Home Companion*, used a wide range of subjects and art styles, covering more than women's fashions. Quite a contrast were the covers for the women's fashion magazines such as *Vogue* and *Harper's Bazaar*. Very sophisticated, they often used French artists. An exception was "Eric," Carl Oscar August Erickson, an American who had studied and practiced fashion drawing in Paris.

Children's magazine covers offer yet another collecting category. Among the most popular of the early-20th-century children's magazines were *St. Nicholas*, *Story Parade*, *Jack and Jill*, and *Youth's Companion*. Early artists were Rose O'Neill, Fanny Young Cory (Cooney), Jessie Willcox Smith, and Lucile Patterson Marsh.

These are only a few of the cover categories. Others include sports, wildlife, and adventure. There are doubtless many examples of cover art and artists still awaiting discovery.

What makes one cover worth more, when both are by the same artist? Many times, one subject is more appealing. Another consideration would be the stature of the magazine. A *Post* cover would have a higher value than an *American Weekly* or *Good Housekeeping* cover. Name recognition is an important factor, too. The names of Norman Rockwell, Joseph Leyendecker, and Harrison Fisher are well known even to the general, noncollecting public. But how many collectors are familiar with Adolph Treidler, who did poster-style covers for *Harper's*, *Collier's*, *The Saturday Evening Post*? Or Charles Buckles Falls, who did many magazine covers?

There are many affordable covers among lesser-known artists; sometimes they sell for as little as $1,000. Buying at auction can be risky for a beginning collector. Auction fever can put a cover far beyond its actual value simply because of determined bidders. On the other hand, a fine cover by one of the less currently popular artists can be a true bargain.

Other factors to consider are condition and restoration. A well-restored cover loses little of its value. If you buy "as is," you have to consider that the cost of restoration may be as high as the sale value.

If a cover piece isn't signed but appears to be in the style of a top cover artist, should you pay the probably steep price? It can be an expensive decision unless you are offered good provenance. Over the decades, popular artists have been copied, not always with the intention to deceive. Add to that the students of famous illustrators, who may not have become famous but chose to copy "the master." A dealer or museum curator who is knowledgeable about specific artists should be consulted.

NORMAN ROCKWELL

by Judy Goffman

Some twenty-five years ago, Judy Goffman started her career as an art dealer/collector with her early recognition of the value and significance of American Illustrators in the art market as a whole. Judy began collecting posters, magazine covers, sketches, and memorabilia of the greatest illustrators of the period, now known as the Golden Age of American Illustration. *From this modest beginning, she branched into a wide-ranging search for the original paintings used for the covers and illustrations of the most successful and popular magazines, such as* The Saturday Evening Post.

In the 1960s, Goffman was actually besieged by friends and neighbors to share her findings with them and slowly realized that she was in fact becoming a professional art dealer (her background had been fine arts with a bachelor's degree in fine arts from the University of Pennsylvania).

In 1983, from having had an "appointment only" gallery in her home and a part-time gallery in shared space in New York, the Judy Goffman Fine Art Gallery officially opened its doors.

In 1988–89, the gallery sponsored and curated traveling exhibitions to six museums and the New York World Financial Center and is currently organizing the first major international tour of American illustrators to Italy and Japan. A Norman Rockwell exhibit was held October 1, 1990, in the National Gallery of Modern Art in Rome.

What has always attracted me to Rockwell's art is the warmth and humor of his subject matter. As he said, "I'm not a historian. I just painted the things I saw around me. I was showing the America I knew and observed to others who might not have noticed." Truly, Rockwell reflected the currents of American life and times, from his earliest drawings to the patriotic themes of World War II to American life and times. His genius was in being able to capture the essence of what is now a vanished America. Before the media revolution, "the television age," people looked forward to and identified with magazine covers. The Rockwell covers captured the emotions of the times, not only what was but what people would have liked life and America to be and to have been.

Not only did he do covers, but he also painted for advertising campaigns, calendars, posters, books, and magazine story illustrations.

Unfortunately, many know the look of Norman Rockwell art only from reproductions, the cartoon-like figurines, bells, and other licensed reprographics of the American phenomenon that I call "Rockwell commercialism." It is necessary to see his original works to fully understand Rockwell's place as an important American artist. His thorough technique, ability, and sensitivity are readily apparent.

Rockwell's early inspiration to draw and paint certainly came from his father, an avid Sunday painter, and also from his grandfather's canvases of bucolic barnyard scenes of animals and outbuildings, which were an exercise in definition of detail.

Born in New York City in 1894, Rockwell spent his childhood and adolescence there, with significant summer excursions into the country. There he felt a strong sense of connectedness, not only with nature but with the people who had chosen to live "on nature's terms." After dropping out of high school at sixteen, he attended classes at the National Academy School, which he found stifling and restrictive. He shortly moved from there to the newly formed Art Students League. It was while he was enrolled at the League that he was taught an anatomical approach to drawing by George Bridgeman and learned composition from Thomas Fogarty. The fashionable illustrators—N. C. Wyeth (Andrew Wyeth's father) and Howard Pyle—were powerful influences in Norman Rockwell's development as an artist and impressed him with the need to give serious attention to historical reference and detail.

In 1915, after completing his studies in New York, Rockwell moved to New Rochelle, New York. Shortly thereafter, he married Irene O'Connor, whom he subsequently divorced in 1929. In 1930, he married Mary Bartow and began his family of three sons, who would become part of his stable of models and a ready source of inspiration. Early on, his internal art of "storytelling" became integrated with his external skills as an artist; what emerged was what we know today as an incredible facility in judging the perfect moment, when to stop the action, snap the picture . . . when all the elements that define and embellish a total story are in place.

At twenty-two, Rockwell caught the "brass ring." He sold his first piece to be used as a cover for *The Saturday Evening Post*—the prized position for an illustrator—with a distribution of millions. His distinctive style and sensitivity to subject matter were evident then and were what *Post* editor George Horace Lorimer responded to in 1916. It was the beginning of a 324-cover relationship between Rockwell and the *Post*. Beginning with his earliest drawings, Rockwell followed in the footsteps of the 19th-century genre painters such as J. G. Brown and Thomas Waterman Wood and consequently painted "slices of life." Rockwell had not yet fully developed his style in the drawings done in those New

Rochelle days, such as the 1915 charcoal portrait of his father as a boy delivering a letter, commissioned for *St. Nicholas* magazine.

However, by 1918, in "Boy with Buttons," which was his first *Literary Digest* cover, he had developed his distinctive and recognizable style, capturing a specific moment and feeling. (Rockwell was enlisted in the navy at this time, and these covers featured servicemen and their families, with an emphasis on off-duty life, not vivid scenes of war.) This painting later became a WW I poster for the Fourth Liberty Loan campaign and depicts a young boy proudly showing off his Boy Scout, YMCA, and War Savings Stamps and favorite theme buttons, a war bond in his pocket. This became a famous image and helped raise substantial amounts of money for the war effort. In a sense, Rockwell was the last of the 19th-century genre painters but one who came into his creative powers at a time when a new audience and a new market were opening up through the mass-circulated national magazines, whose popularity catapulted certain artists into millions of households weekly.

As late as 1919, four-color printing was still very expensive, and most popular storytelling magazine covers were reproduced in limited color. Like his predecessor, Frederic S. Remington, whose chronicles of Western life were printed in black and white, Rockwell met the editorial requirements by painting the early originals without color, reproduced from fully executed paintings. Even today, Rockwell is mainly known from prints and graphics, which, in many cases, are themselves merely reproductions. Unfortunately, the originals were and are rarely seen.

In the 1920s and 1930s, Rockwell's work developed more breadth and greater character. His use of humor, which had already been developed in the character of "Cousin Reginald," became an important part of his work. It was a technique he used effectively to draw the viewer into the composition to share the magic of the moment with the artist. Not immediately recognizable as a Rockwell is "Love Ouanga," completed in 1936 for *American Magazine*. In this uncharacteristic painting, Rockwell filled the entire canvas with a masterful composition making a pointed political and social statement.

In 1936, George Horace Lorimer retired from *The Saturday Evening Post*, and the second of two successive editors, Ben Hibbs, altered the circular format of the cover. In fact, Hibbs permitted Norman Rockwell to create with more freedom within a different cover layout. The new mood of both the magazine and the country was reflected in Rockwell's work, as he used the entire cover, unconfined by borders and logos, to express himself. In the 1940s, Rockwell moved to Arlington, Vermont, where he started to paint the full-canvas paintings that are increasingly treasured by collectors today. With Grandma Moses as a friend and neighbor and local townspeople as his models, Rockwell became a living part of Americana—a national treasure. During his Vermont years he flourished but always, as he realized, within the framework of being an illustrator. Norman Rockwell was acutely aware of his goals as an artist and his critical acceptance. In 1962, Rockwell was quoted in *Esquire* magazine as saying: "I call myself an illustrator but I am not an illustrator. Instead I paint storytelling pictures which are quite popular but unfashionable." "Unfashionable" was a misnomer; his works were, in fact, very popular, but he was extremely sensitive to the way the art world as well as the public judged him.

Rockwell was constantly seeking new ideas and new faces in his daily life. He wrote that everything he had ever seen or done had gone into his pictures. He painted not only the scenes and people close to him but, in a quest for authenticity, would approach total strangers and ask them to sit for him.

During World War II, Rockwell joined the legion of artists and writers involved in the war effort to help boost the sale of savings bonds on behalf of the U.S. government. His 1944 painting, "Soldier and U.S. Savings Bond," became a symbol to all Americans of patriotism and sacrifice. Rockwell tried to explain, through his art, what the war was all about. The result of his effort was "The Four Freedoms," at first rejected by the government and then printed in millions of copies as war bond posters. Seen by millions of people, these posters raised $132 million in war bonds in a six-month period.

In the 1960s, from his home in Stockbridge, Massachusetts, Rockwell struck out in a new direction. Though by then his reputation was rooted in the evocation of nostalgia, he boldly tackled political issues. "The Problem We All Live With" confronted America's racial tensions. "The Peace Corps in Ethiopia" captured the idealism of the Kennedy years in realistic, contemporary settings. He painted portraits not only of Kennedy but Presidents Eisenhower and Johnson. Portraits of other world leaders included Nehru of India and Nassar of Egypt.

Since his death in 1978 and with the passing of the America he loved and painted, it is now possible to view Rockwell's work more objectively and place him among this century's finest American artists. His work has proved that, to be enduring, a commercial project assignment—with limitations, a deadline, size parameters, and assigned subject matter— must be rich in creativity, aesthetics, and expression. Through his personal vision and execution, illustration today is finally beginning to be accorded the stature it deserves. Indeed, not only in America but in Europe is there an acceptance of the American illustration as a collectible art form. This burgeoning international market will, of course, influence prices in America as well. Don't be surprised if the current highs of $275,000 for a Norman Rockwell *Saturday Evening Post* cover and

Norman Rockwell. Ladies' Home Journal. Oil on canvas. Signed, dated 1921, $90,000. Copyright © 1921 Estate of Norman Rockwell. PHOTO COURTESY OF ILLUSTRATION HOUSE, INC.

$60,000 for a J. C. Leyendecker *Saturday Evening Post* cover are surpassed in the coming years. This is only the beginning of an exciting new era for collecting not only cover art but the many other examples of illustration art, with Norman Rockwell leading the way.

NORMAN ROCKWELL (1894–1978)

Norman Rockwell

Girl Sitting in Grandfather's Lap, "100 Neediest Cases," 1950s, s., i., etching, 9″ × 8.5″. (This etching belongs to the small group of works Rockwell did "for Art's sake." The size of the edition is probably fewer than 10. He used the same image he had drawn for the *New York Times* some years before.)
....$2,000
Santa with Coke, s., with artist's initials NR, lower right, also i. "A cheerful Start/for a Merry Xmas/A drink for busy people/A cheerful start/for a wonderful job/after a job well done/drink Coca Cola" on reverse; oil on canvas, 24¼″ × 20″ (62.9 × 50.8 cm); painted c. 1935, unused sketch for Coca-Cola.
.... $33,000
The Long Shadow of Lincoln, s. and dedicated to Clarice and Walt Squires on a piece of the original mat, oil on photographic paper, 15″ × 11⅛″; preliminary sketch for the painting that illustrated Carl Sandburg's poem "The Long Shadow of Lincoln"; final version (collection Lincoln Shrine) reproduced in *Saturday Evening Post*, Feb. 10, 1945; prov. Tilting at Windmills Gallery, Manchester, VT; *Literature*: Laurie Norton Moffatt, *Norman Rockwell: A Definitive Catalogue*, Hanover, NH, 1986, vol. 2, p. 790, no. S642a. $7,700
The Wishbone, s., Norman Rockwell, lower left, oil on canvas, 18¼″ × 16½″ (46 x 42cm), used as the cover illus. for *Country Gentleman*, Nov. 19, 1921. .... $88,000
Have You Lips That Make Good Resolutions? and Hot Toddy, two drawings, both s. Norman Rockwell, lower right, charcoal on board, unframed; the first, 10″ × 8½″ (25.4 × 21.5cm); the second, 15¼″ × 13″ (38.7 × 33cm), used in Schenley Cream of Kentucky Whiskey advertisements in 1937–38; the first was reproduced in *Life*, Mar. 22, 1937. .... $5,720
Countdown to Takeoff, s., Norman Rockwell, lower right, charcoal and colored pencil on board, unframed, 11⅜″ × 12¼″ (28.8 × 31.1 cm), used in a Schenley Cream of Kentucky Whiskey advertisement in 1938. ....$11,000
Getting Ready to Eat, s., Norman Rockwell, lower left, oil on canvas, 14″ × 15″ (35.6 × 38.1cm), executed for use in an advertisement for Swift Baby Products, Swift & Company, featured in *Woman's Day* magazine, April 1955.
.... $22,000
Man Holding a Mint Julep, Schenley Whiskey advertisement, 1939, s., charcoal pencil with red and green conté pencil, 12″ × 14″. $9,000
The New Tavern Sign, unpublished version for *Saturday Evening Post*, Feb. 22, 1936, s., oil on canvas, 21″ × 38.5″. $195,000
Vacation, *Saturday Evening Post*, June 30, 1934, s., preliminary drawing in charcoal, 31″ × 23.25″. $25,000

Norman Rockwell. Bob Cratchit with Children from A Christmas Carol.
Preliminary drawing for Hallmark Cards, 1948. Charcoal on tracing vellum,
14 × 12 inches, signed in red, $10,800. PHOTO COURTESY OF
ILLUSTRATION HOUSE, INC.

What Shall I Do? *Saturday Evening Post*, Oct. 1, 1936, s., i., preliminary study in oil and pencil, 23.25″ × 20″. $42,000

Give Me a Boy, oil sketch, s. Norman Rockwell, i., 14½″ × 9¼″, oil and pencil on paper. $3,300

Study for Picasso vs. Sargent, s., 14″ × 11″, oil on paper laid down on board. $8,800

The Auto Repairman, Want to Know Why I Use It? s. Norman Rockwell, lit., illus. for a Raybestos brake service advertisement in *Saturday Evening Post*, Feb. 4, 1922, 11⅞″ × 17″, oil en grisaille on canvas. $8,800

The Right to Know, drawing, final study for oil of the same title, illus. for *Look* magazine, Aug. 20, 1968, prov., lit., 38¼″ × 59⅝″, pencil on paper. $9,900

Stop Here for Gas 23, unfinished, 30″ × 20″, charcoal. $192

The Magician, s. Norman Rockwell, reproduced on cover *Popular Magazine*, Nov. 20, 1916, lit., 29″ × 20″. $63,250

Don't Say I Said It, s. Norman Rockwell, prov., lit., also called "Two Women Gossiping," used as the illus. for *Life* cover, March 23, 1922, p. 1922, 30⅛″ × 26″. $66,000

Russian Schoolroom, s., illus. on catalog front cover, 15″ × 37″. .. $70,400

Christmas, s., *Saturday Evening Post* cover, Dec. 6, 1930, 44¼″ × 34¾″. $77,000

Abraham Lincoln, s. Norman Rockwell, reproduced as cover illus. for *McCall's*, July 1942, lit., 49″ × 36″. $77,000

Braced for a Feud, s., dedicated, 18″ × 15″, oil on illustration board. $14,300

The Ship, illus. for an article by C. S. Forester in *Ladies' Home Journal*, s., prov., 15″ × 22½″. $14,850

Study for Yankee Doodle Mural, s. Norman Rockwell, i., study related to the 13-foot mural titled "Yankee Doodle," p. 1937, prov., sight size 34″ × 25½″, charcoal on paper. $17,600

Kaynee Blouses and Wash Suits Make You Look All Dressed Up, inits. NR, reproduced in *Boy's Life*, Nov. 1919, p. 49, prov., lit., 21″ × 20⅛″. $26,400

Fishing, s., p. for Brown and Bigelow, 1952, for summer calendar, prov., exhib., 15½″ × 13″. $27,500

Portrait of Jackie Kennedy, s. norman rockwell, p. 1963, prov., lit., from the collection of Andy Warhol, 14″ × 11″, oil on canvasboard. $28,600

Fall: Preliminary Drawing, 1948, s. Norman Rockwell, i. on mat, prov., from "The Four Seasons, Man and Boy" illus., on catalog cover, 25″ × 21″, graphite on paper. $34,100

New York Central Diner, s. Norman Rockwell, i. on mat, study for cover illus., *Saturday Evening Post*, Dec. 7, 1946, prov., lit., sight size 11″ x 10″, oil on paper. $44,000

The Expert Salesman, Refrigerator and Eskimo, s. Norman Rockwell, t., reproduced in Brown Bigelow's 1964 Four Seasons Calendar, prov., lit. $44,000

While the Audience Waits, s. Norman Rockwell. prov., lit., painting also called "Performer Bandaging Paw," used as cover illus. *Literary Digest*, Oct. 28, 1922, p. 1922, 23¼″ × 20¼″. $60,500

Samson Tearing Down the Temple: Portrait of Victor Mature, 1949, s., lit., probably commissioned by DeMille or Paramount Studios in connection with promotion of movie of the same name, from the estate of Cecil B. DeMille, 69″ × 36″. $82,500

Love Letters, s. Norman Rockwell, p. 1919, appeared as cover illus. *Saturday Evening Post*, Jan. 17, 1920, prov., 26" × 23". $132,000

And Every Lad May Be Aladdin, Crackers in Bed, s. Norman Rockwell, prov., exhib., lit., advertisement for Edison Mazda Lampworks, in *Saturday Evening Post*, Apr. 17, 1920, p. 77, 49" × 28". $242,000

Me and My Pal: Rivals, s., dedicated "My best to Van sincerely," pencil on paper, 13" by 10½", prov. John H. Surovek, Palm Beach. $7,150

ADDITIONAL
COVER ARTISTS

WLADYSLAW THEODOR BENDA (1873–1948)

W. T Benda

Benda, who was born in Poland, had achieved an international reputation before coming to America. As an illustrator, he gained additional fame with his beautiful girls. They graced many a magazine cover, along with the other pretty-girl illustrations of the era. His work appeared in most of the major magazines. In his later years he designed beautiful masks for ballet and theater.

The Shakespearean Players, s., charcoal, 18″ × 20¾″. $1,200
Palm Trees, s., watercolor, 9½ × 8½″. $200

Wladislaw T. Benda. Charcoal and watercolor, 23 × 18¾ inches, signed, $15,000.
PHOTO COURTESY OF ILLUSTRATION HOUSE, INC.

Howard Chandler Christy. "Fifth Avenue to the Footlights." Oil on canvas. Reproduced in McCall's magazine cover, May 1922, 25½ × 17½ inches, signed lower right, $10,000. PHOTO COURTESY OF ALAN M. GOFFMAN AMERICAN PAINTINGS.

WALTER APPLETON CLARK (1876–1906)

Walter Appleton Clark

Walter Appleton Clark began a short but successful career as an illustrator while still a student at the Art Students League. His first assignment was for *Scribner's* magazine. In addition to his magazine and book illustrations, he painted a series of large oils for a mural project based on *The Canterbury Tales*. They were published in 1904 in a book for Fox Duffield & Co. Clark died early in his career from complications resulting from typhoid fever.

Dining Together, 1904, s., d., black watercolor, 9.75″ × 9.75″. $700
Tinkling the Keys, s., d. 1903, exhib., illus. for George Buchanan's story, "A Proffered Herion," *Scribner's*, June 1903, 11½″ × 17½″, brush and black ink on board. $495

STEVAN DOHANOS (1907–)

Stevan Dohanos

Stevan Dohanos studied at the Cleveland School of Art, and after an apprenticeship as a letterer, he worked as an artist for an art studio.

An assignment for the Treasury Art Project in the Virgin Islands in

Stevan Dohanos.
Reproduced
illustration for the
100 Neediest Cases
Charity, New York
Times. *Gouache*, 16 ×
20 inches, $1,600.
PHOTO COURTESY
OF GUERNSEY'S.

1936 led to a variety of mural commissions around the country. His illustrations were used on *Saturday Evening Post* covers for several years, and his work appeared in almost all of the important magazines. This versatile illustrator has also designed over forty stamps for the U.S. Postal Service and contributed designs for many charitable causes.

Shackle House, s., 11″ × 7¼″, pen and ink and watercolor on paper. ..$330

Pacific War Surplus, *Saturday Evening Post*, cover, Dec. 1, 1945, s., gouache on masonite, 11⅛″ × 10⅞″. $4,500

Busy Marina, preliminary study for unpublished cover, *Saturday Evening Post*, s. lower right, gouache, 25.5″ × 19.5″. $1,500

Christmas Decorating, cover for *Medical Times*, Dec. 1960, 28″ × 30″.
....$3,250

Man Lost, reproduced, *Saturday Evening Post*, Nov. 2, 1940, s., gouache, green and black, 15″ × 17½″. $375

Illustration for 100 Neediest Cases Charity, *New York Times*, s., gouache, 16″ × 20″. $1,600

No-Cal, oil painting, boatyard scene of two workmen sprucing up the ''No-Cal'' for the boating season as three onlookers watch, s., 25″ × 25″. $3,500

Couple with Rifles, Dead Soldier, story illustration, "Mountains of the Morning," *Saturday Evening Post*, s., gouache, 31.5″ × 24.5″. $1,500
Rifle and Bullets on Book Jacket, editorial illustration, "In Cold Blood," *Famous Writers*, s., gouache, 21″ × 12.5″. $3,600
Avocados, s. Dohanos, d. 1936, i. with t. verso, prov., 10¼″ × 14″, gouache, watercolor and pencil on paper. $990
No Passing, s., cover for *Saturday Evening Post*, Oct. 9 1954, 26⅛″ × 20″, gouache on board. $8,800

JOHN FALTER (1910–1982)

John Falter

Although John Falter is primarily known for his more than 200 *Saturday Evening Post* covers, his career in illustration began with the pulps. Born in Nebraska, he studied at the Kansas City Art Institute, at the Art Students League in New York, and at the Grand Central School of Art in New York. When only twenty, he sold his first slick illustration to *Liberty* magazine.

John Falter. "After Home Leave." Oil on canvas, 33½ × 29½ inches. Reproduced Wave recruiting poster, signed twice, $550. PHOTO COURTESY OF GUERNSEY'S.

During his career, he sold his work to most of the magazines, advertising agencies, and over forty books for *Reader's Digest*. Other noteworthy assignments were portraits of celebrities and famous and important Americans. In 1976, during the Bicentennial, he did a series of historical subjects for the 3M Company.

Gary Cooper and Signe Hasso, s., c. 1944, based on a true World War II story (Gary Cooper played the heroic Dr. Wassel), from the estate of Cecil B. De-Mille, 35″ × 26″. $7,150
Trick or Treat, reproduced, ad for Goodyear Tire Co., 1962, s., oil on board, 17½″ × 15″. $1,700
Boy in Car with Mother, story illustration, "Little League," *Reader's Digest*, s. lower left, gouache, 7″ × 5″. $650

J. F. KERNAN (1878–1958)

J. F.
KERNAN—

Many magazine covers were done by J. F. Kernan in a style similar to Norman Rockwell—Americana with a light touch. His characters offered a realistic "slice of life," with old characters or young boys. His special interests, hunting and fishing, were put to good use illustrating outdoor subjects for such magazines as *Outdoor Life* and *Liberty*.

Story of the Shipwreck, *Saturday Evening Post*, May 31, 1924, s., oil on canvas, 22″ × 20″. $9,000
Man Painting Duck Decoys, magazine cover, *Country Gentleman*, c. 1927, s. lower right, oil on canvas 30″ × 20″ $6,200
Hunters with a Quail, *Outdoor Life*, c. 1945, s., oil on canvas, 20″ × 20″. $6,500
Taxidermist, s., oil on canvas, 25″ × 20″. $6,000
Breaking into the Season, Apr. 1933, s., oil on canvas, 28″ × 22″. . $6,800

FRANK XAVIER LEYENDECKER (1877–1924)

F. X. Leyendecker

Frank Leyendecker, like his older brother, was a talented illustrator. Born in Germany, he came to America with his brother as a child. His work appeared in such magazines as *Collier's*, and he did both covers and editorial illustrations. He also worked for advertising clients such as the Howard Watch Company. Throughout his career, he was surpassed by his brother Joseph's more flamboyant style.

The Kiss, s., gouache on paper, 20″ × 13½″, prov. purchased by the present owner's father at the Collier estate auction (Collier's Publishing Co.). .. $7,975

*J. F. Kernan. Man
painting duck decoys.
Magazine cover,
Country Gentleman,
c. 1927. Oil on
canvas, 30 × 20
inches, signed lower
right, $6,200.* PHOTO
COURTESY OF
ILLUSTRATION HOUSE,
INC.

*F. X. Leyendecker. "Rachel
Peace." Collier's magazine
cover, May 1903. Tempera
on board, 22¼ × 15⅝
inches, signed lower right,
$15,000.* PHOTO COURTESY
OF AMERICAN ILLUSTRATORS
GALLERY/JUDY GOFFMAN FINE
ART, NEW YORK.

Timing the Experiment, s. FXL, oil on canvas, 23″ × 21½″, one of a series of illustrations done for the Howard Watch Co. $3,250

The Blacksmith, reproduced, *Collier's Illustrated Weekly* cover, Sept. 6, 1902, s. lower left, gouache on illustration board, 18½″ × 15″. $15,000

The Greek Athlete, s., 36″ × 26″. $4,125

The Mirror, s., prov., sight size 21¼″ × 14″, gouache on paper. $7,975

The Letter, s., prov., sight size 20½″ × 14½″, gouache on paper. ... $7,700

Stopping for a Chat, inits., 10¾″ × 8½″, watercolor, Chinese white, and pencil on paper. $935

The Juggler, s. indistinctly, cover for *Collier's* magazine, Vol. 27, No. 6, 13″ × 8½″, gouache on board. $990

Pirate, illustration, s., 24″ × 16 ″. $1,925

JOSEPH C. LEYENDECKER (1874–1951)

Joseph Leyendecker began his career as an illustrator in a Chicago engraving company at the age of sixteen. In the evenings after work, he studied at the Chicago Art Institute. After saving his money for five years, he traveled to France, where he did further studies at the Paris Academie Julian. Upon his return to America, he was successful in doing illustrations for both major magazines and advertising clients. He did over 300 covers for the *Post* over a forty-year period. His annual New Year baby series are among the most popular. His successful advertising illustrations included the Arrow Collar man, and Hart, Schaffner & Marx.

The Gentleman, 34″ × 21″. $770

Kuppenheimer Good Clothes, 1876, 26″ × 20″. $6,600

A Sunday Job, s. J. C. Leyendecker with inits. conjoined, 26″ × 21½″. $9,350

Kuppenheimer Good Clothes, 1926, 27″ × 19¾″, oil on canvas laid down on board. $12,100

Flowers for the Lady, 27¼″ × 19¾″, oil on canvas laid down on board. $13,200

A Player in the Marching Band, mono. inits., cover for *Saturday Evening Post*, 1921, 27½″ × 20½″. $14,300

At Your Service, s. JCLeyendecker, with inits. in monogram, lower right, oil on canvas, 21½″ × 20″ (54.6 × 50.8cm), an advertisement for Kuppenheimer men's clothing. $28,600

Spring Cleaning, preliminary studies for a *Saturday Evening Post* cover, Apr. 1, 1939, oil on canvas, 22″ × 30″, not signed. $4,000

Chinoiserie, *Saturday Evening Post*, Sept. 21, 1907, s., oil on canvas, mounted, 25″ × 20″. $26,000

Joseph C. Leyendecker. "Victorian Lady at the Opera," c. 1905. Success magazine cover. Oil on canvas on board. Signed lower left, 26 × 18 inches (oval), $35,000. PHOTO COURTESY OF AMERICAN ILLUSTRATORS GALLERY/JUDY GOFFMAN FINE ART, NEW YORK.

Easter, *Saturday Evening Post*, Apr. 10, 1909, s., oil on canvas, 26″ × 20″.
.... $24,000

Francis Scott Key, oil on canvas, 22″ × 23″ calendar, date 1945 (approx.).
.... $1,100

Bass Drummer, reproduced, *Saturday Evening Post* cover, Sept. 24, 1921, s.
lower right, oil on canvas, 27½″ × 20½″. $35,000

Two Oil Paintings on One Canvas, 32″ × 25″; monogrammed, Independence
Hall and the Capitol building, illus. for "The Challenge to Liberty" by Herbert
Hoover, *Saturday Evening Post*, Sept. 8, 1934. .... $3,250

Thanksgiving Baby, comprehensive study for *Saturday Evening Post* cover, Nov.
25, 1922, oil on canvas, 11″ × 9″, unsigned; copy of cover included in lot.
.... $3,200

Football, s., oil on canvas, 27″ × 19¼″. $5,500

Richard Barthelmess, comprehensive study for a House of Kuppenheimer clothing ad, *Saturday Evening Post*, Mar. 26, 1927, oil on canvas, 23½″ × 19¼″,
unsigned; ad copy included in lot. $3,250

Clothing Studies—Face, Arms, Cane, Overcoat, preliminary studies for advertisement, "Welcome Home," Kuppenheimer Clothes; oil on canvas, 20″ ×
27″, not signed. $2,600

Minute Man Astride Brooklyn Bridge, editorial illustration, "Consequences
to Liberty," by Herbert Hoover, *Saturday Evening Post*, Sept. 15, 1934, oil on
canvas, mounted, 25″ × 12″, monogrammed lower right (this article by Hoover
was his first public affairs statement since expiration of his term as president).
.... $5,400

Portrait of Young Girl, preliminary study, oil on canvas, 19.5″ × 15.5″ oval,
not signed. $650

Man Mowing Lawn, magazine cover, "Getting in Shape," *Saturday Evening
Post*, Aug. 6, 1910, s. lower right, oil on canvas, 26″ × 21″. $21,000

Woman at the Wheel of Her Car, magazine cover, "Automobile Number,"
Collier's, Jan. 6, 1917, s. lower right, oil on canvas, mounted, 28″ × 19.25″.
.... $26,000

The Start of a Race, s., oil on canvas, 26″ × 21″. $16,500

Maxfield Parrish. Study for Collier's *magazine cover. Colored marker on paper. Initialed lower right: M.P., 17 × 12½ inches, $4,950.* PHOTO COURTESY OF BUTTERFIELD & BUTTERFIELD, SAN FRANCISCO. *Note:* This is a good opportunity to study the two styles of Parrish.

Maxfield Parrish. "Morning" oil on panel. Life magazine cover, April 6, 1922, 19⅝ × 15 inches, $175,000. PHOTO COURTESY OF AMERICAN ILLUSTRATORS GALLERY/JUDY GOFFMAN FINE ART, NEW YORK.

Edward Penfield. "Thanksgiving Harvest." Gouache on artist board. Signed lower left with monogram, 17⅜ × 14⅝ inches, $9,500. PHOTO COURTESY OF ALAN M. GOFFMAN AMERICAN PAINTINGS.

EDWARD PENFIELD (1866–1925)

Edward Penfield was a master of the poster, whose style influenced American illustration. His coaching subjects were among his personal favorites. His illustrations for his book *Holland Sketches* were published in 1907 by *Scribner's*. He did both covers and editorial illustrations for *Collier's* and other magazines. He also did a series of calendar illustrations, redrawn from the 1843 *Old Farmer's Almanack* for the Beck Engraving Company. His works were either signed with a monogram or his name in letters.

We Passed Many Boats, *Holland Sketches*, gouache, 14″ × 9″, monogram. $2,250

Steeplechase, *Collier's*, May 16, 1903, watercolor, 13.25″ × 11.75″, monogrammed. $8,500

Ray Strang (1893–1957).
"Prairie Fire." Cover for
book, The Boy Pioneer or
Strange Stories of the
Great River, *by Johnston*
Grosvenor. Oil on
canvas. Signed lower right,
36 × 32 inches, $4,400.
PHOTO COURTESY OF
BUTTERFIELD & BUTTERFIELD.

HENRY J. SOULEN (1888–1965)

H.J. Soulen

Born in Milwaukee, Wisconsin, Soulen studied first at the Chicago Academy of Fine Arts and later with Howard Pyle. He is known for his vibrant colors and patterned work. Because of his use of color, his illustrations, especially his covers, were used in many of the top magazines in color.

Moroccan Scene, "Surprising Grace," *Saturday Evening Post*, Nov. 2, 1918, oil on board, 16″ × 23″, not signed. $450
Surprising Grace, *S.E.P.*, 11/2/18, oil on board, 16″ × 23″, not signed.
....$650

CHARLES LESLIE THRASHER (1889–1936)

Thrasher was a forerunner of Norman Rockwell in style and subject matter and did many covers for *The Saturday Evening Post* early in his career. He developed relationships with many of Howard Pyle's students, and as a result, when Norman Rockwell refused *Liberty* magazine's request to contract for a cover illustration a week, Thrasher was contacted and agreed to the arrangement. From 1926 through the early 1930s Thrasher did a cover a week.

Leslie Thrasher. "House Call."
Oil on canvas. Reproduced in
Liberty magazine, Nov. 24,
1928. Signed lower right, 19½ ×
15½ inches, $3,500. PHOTO
COURTESY OF BRANDYWINE
FANTASY GALLERY.

Father Bathing Baby, magazine cover, *Liberty*, Sept. 19, 1928, s., oil on canvas, 17″ × 14″ (this is one of the famous series of *Liberty* covers Thrasher executed weekly, showing a couple courting, marrying, and raising a family in the 1920s). $3,600
Late from the Lodge, cover illus., *Liberty* magazine, Oct. 8, 1927, s. lower right, oil on canvas, 19½″ × 15½″. $3,500
Father's Touch, cover illus., *Liberty* magazine, June 16, 1928, s. lower right, oil on canvas, 19½″ × 15½″. $3,500

REVERE F. WISTEHUFF (1900–1971)

*Revere F.
Wistehuff*

Wistehuff was part of the New Rochelle school of illustrators that included his friends Norman Rockwell, Coles Phillips, and J. C. Leyendecker. He did covers for most of the major magazines, including *The Saturday Evening Post* and *Collier's*.

Coast to Coast or Bust, *The Country Guide*, Nov. 15, 1929, s., oil on canvas, 29″ × 23.5″. $4,800
Tiger Tamer and Mouse, *Liberty*, July 1, 1933, s., gouache on board, 24″ × 19″. $2,800
Love's Delight, 1930s, s., oil on canvas, 22.5″ × 17″. $3,800
Girl with Basket, Boy with Fish, calendar illustration, "Jimmie Loves Mary," s., oil on canvas, 29.25″ × 22.75″. $3,000
Radio Jazz Fan, *Collier's* cover painting, s., oil on canvas, 19.5″ × 15.5″. $3,800
Waiting for a Train, sketch for *This Week*, Sept. 10, 1939, s., oil on board, 11″ × 10.5″. $500
After the Party, s., gouache, 23″ × 18″. $3,500

Leland R. Gustavson. "The Church Supper." Reproduced in Country Gentleman *cover, Sept. 1947. Oil on canvas. Signed, 34 × 31 inches, $1,200.* PHOTO COURTESY OF GUERNSEY'S.

Walter Beach Humphrey. Country Gentleman *cover. New Year, 1922, signed, $1,100.* PHOTO COURTESY OF GUERNSEY'S.

PART VIII

CONTEMPORARY
ILLUSTRATION

INTRODUCTION

I had a hard time defining *contemporary illustrators* since many of the artists who classify as "currently working" were just as active in the '70s and '80s as now. In fact, names like Bernie Fuchs and Leo and Diane Dillon, well-established, respected illustrators, are covered elsewhere in this book. Nonetheless, I surveyed a group of experts that included a magazine art director, several artists' representatives, and the wife of a late, great illustrator. The same names turned up: Brad Holland, Mark English, Malcolm (Skip) Liepke, Robert Peak, Braldt Bralds, among others. These illustrators, they believe, represent the most collectible illustrator art of the next decade.

However, finding prices for and sometimes information about these illustrators is not so easy. One of the problems is that although contemporary illustrators retain the rights to the original art as well as the published art, they apparently haven't investigated the secondary market, such as galleries and auctions. In fact, many of the people I talked to had a hard time putting a price on work already sold once to be reproduced. By now the word has probably spread that there is a growing secondary market.

On Saturday, November 10, 1990, many of these important contemporary illustrators came to market at an Illustration House auction. While some were "buy-ins," not reaching their reserves, others did extremely well. These had often been done for big name publications such as the *Post* or *Time* or had an especially appealing subject. Or the illustrator's name was the draw.

NAMES TO LOOK FOR

BRALDT BRALDS (1951–)

Crowd Reaching up to Bird, magazine cover, *U.S. News*, s. lower center, acrylic on board, 14.5″ × 11″. $250

MARK ENGLISH (1933–)

Women Playing a Flute, s. lower right, painting, oil and pastel, 19″ × 17″ (did not sell but has estimated value of .... $3,500–$4,500).

BRAD HOLLAND (1943–)

Man with Hands on Hips, "California C," story illustration, *Playboy*, Nov. 1980, s. verso, acrylic on canvas, 30″ × 24″ (did not sell but has estimated value ....$6,000–$8,000

MEL ODOM (1950–)

Heads of Couple about to Kiss, book cover, *Going Wrong* by Ruth Rendell, 1980, init. lower center, pencil, dyes, and gouache, 6.25″ × 6″. $1,800

ROBERT PEAK (1928–)

Study, Male Head, charcoal on board, 13.5″ × 9″, not signed. $300

Some additional names are Paul Giovanopoulos (1939–), David Grove (1940–), Richard Sparks (1944–), Walt Spitzmiller (1944–), and Ross Barron Storey (1940–).

COLLECTING CONTEMPORARY ILLUSTRATION

How can collectors discover new potential illustrator artists? The easy way is to start a scrapbook with the reproduced art you see, whether it's a book cover (Xerox it) or magazine editorial or advertising illustration. Keep tabs on your choices by reading the Society of Illustrators' *Annual of American Illustration*. It showcases the best illustrator art in editorial, book, advertising, and institutional categories. In their 1990 (31st) edition, you'll find many of the same names my experts suggested: Brad Holland, Skip Liepke, and some names only a few years out of college or art school.

Another source of what's happening is *Step-by-Step Graphics*, published seven times a year. Not only does it feature articles by top illustrators but also discusses trends in graphic art and presents interviews with important contemporary illustrators. One example is Gary Kelley, who is known for his pastel illustrations for advertising and editorial clients. Background information appears here before anywhere else.

Many times contemporary illustrations will be donated to various charitable auctions. Familiarize yourself with the artists of interest to you and just keep on looking.

PART IX

APPENDIXES

APPENDIX A: MUSEUMS WITH PERMANENT COLLECTIONS OF ILLUSTRATOR ART

The only museum devoted solely to American illustrator art is the Society of Illustrators' Museum of American Illustration, 128 East 63rd Street, New York, NY.

The following museums have permanent collections of American illustrator art:

New Britain Museum of American Art, New Britain, CT

The Brandywine River Museum, Chadds Ford, PA

The Delaware Art Museum, Wilmington, DE

The Library of Congress, Washington, DC

Examples are also found in such major museums across the country as the New York Metropolitan Museum, the Art Institute of Chicago, and the Los Angeles County Museum of Art, as well as the Amon Carter Museum of Western Art, Fort Worth, TX, the Collection of Buffalo Bill Historical Center, Cody, WY, the National Art Museum of Sports, Indianapolis, IN, and the Norman Rockwell Museum in Stockbridge, MA.

APPENDIX B: SOURCES/
CONTRIBUTORS

Beverly Saks, Sacks Fine Art, 50 West 57th Street, New York, NY 10019; (212) 333-7755

Walt and Roger Reed, Illustration House, Inc., 96 Spring Street, New York, NY 10012; (212) 966-9444

Robert Benney, illustrator, 50 West 96th Street, New York, NY 10025; (212) 222-6605

American Illustrators Gallery/Judy Goffman Fine Art, 18 East 77th Street, New York, NY 10021; (212) 744-5190

Terry Booth, Brandywine Fantasy Gallery, 750 N. Orleans, Suite 205, Chicago, IL 60610; (312) 951-8466

Alan Goffman/American Paintings, 264 East 78th Street, New York, NY 10021; (212) 517-8192

Rick Marschall, 850 Maple Avenue, Glenside, PA 19038; (215) 659-7557

Carl Sciortino, military illustrations, 8515 East Via Del Sol, Scottsdale, AZ 85255; (602) 585-5210

Frederic B. Taraba, Curator, 498 Henry Street, #3, Brooklyn, NY 11231-3010

Leo and Diane Dillon, illustrators, 221 Kane Street, Brooklyn, NY 11231

Les Mansfield, fine American illustrative art, P.O. Box 3033, Cincinnati, OH 45201

J. N. Bartfield Galleries, 30 West 57th Street, New York, NY 10019; (212) 245-8890

Kendra Krienke, children's illustrations, 230 Central Park West, New York, NY 10024; (212) 580-6516

Benjamin Eisenstat and Jane Sperry Eisenstat, artists, 3639 Bryant Street, Palo Alto, CA 94306; (415) 424-9505

Mort Walker, Studio Court, Stamford, CT 06903

David Leopold, archivist, c/o the Margo Feiden Galleries, Ltd., 75 University Place, Greenwich Village, NY 10003

Pam Sommers, The Illustration Gallery, 330 East 11th Street, New York, NY 10003; (212) 979-1614

Every Picture Tells a Story Gallery, 836 N. La Brea, Los Angeles, CA 90038; (213) 962-5420

APPENDIX C:
AUCTION HOUSES

Butterfield & Butterfield
220 San Bruno Avenue
San Francisco, California 94103
(415) 861-7500

Christie, Manson & Woods International Inc.
502 Park Avenue
New York, New York 10022
(212) 546-1000

Christie's East
219 East 67th Street
New York, New York 10021
(212) 606-0400

William Doyle Galleries
175 East 87th Street
New York, New York 10128
(212) 427-2730

Du Mouchelle Art Galleries
409 E. Jefferson
Detroit, Michigan 48226
(313) 963-6255

Samuel T. Freeman & Co.
1808 Chestnut Street
Philadelphia, Pennsylvania 19103
(215) 563-9275

Morton M. Goldberg Galleries
547 Baronne Street
New Orleans, Louisiana 70113
(1-800) 882-7422
(504) 592-2300
FAX (504) 592-2311

Guernsey's
136 East 73rd Street
New York, NY 10021
(212) 794-2280

Robert W. Skinner, Inc.
Route 117
Bolton, Massachusetts 01740
(508) 779-5528

Sotheby Parke Bernet Inc.
1334 York Avenue
New York, New York 10021
(212) 606-7000

Sotheby's Arcade Auctions
1334 York Avenue
New York, New York 10021
(212) 606-7409

SPECIAL NOTES

Note 1. Santa Claus has been the favorite subject for many illustrators. And, each has given him their own interpretation. Thomas Nast gave us our modern "Santa" in the 1860s. Other illustrators who have depicted St. Nick are Everett Shinn, Norman Rockwell, J. C. Leyendecker, and Haddon Sundblom. *(See p. 28)*

Note 2. During the Golden Age of Illustration, it was a must for every illustrator to have dexterity in the use of pen and ink. Before the use of halftones, pen and ink gave the most effective results, and the most talented illustrators could produce many different effects within this limitation. *(See p. 36)*

Note 3. Boileau specialized in beautiful, fashionable women and did some *Saturday Evening Post* covers as well as magazine illustrations. His original art rarely comes to market, but the prints of many of his illustrations abound. *(See p. 35)*

Note 4. These dramatic illustrations, though both employing Becher's allegorical themes, have a totally different look. The oil has a softer approach to death, war, and peace. The pen and ink have a bold interpretation. *(See pp. 58–59)*

Note 5. The print was subsequently reproduced in *The Northwest under Three Flags* by Charles Moore (1920), in Merle Johnson's great *Howard Pyle's Book of the American Spirit* (1923), and in the 1941 *New York Times Book Review* in connection with the review of several fur trade histories.

Pyle, like his contemporary and good friend Frederic Remington, produced a substantial amount of illustrator art in black and white form. This reflected both the reality that prior to roughly 1900 technical limitations did not allow publishers to use color, and the desire of the better artists to maximize their control over the way their work would appear in print. Pyle was a master of the medium because of his incredible detail and the subtlety of his shading, which frequently (a sin in this case) were less than fully captured by the engraver. *(See p. 62)*

Note 6. There have always been good opportunities for women in the field of illustration. As early as the 1870s, Mary Hallock Foote (1847–1938) not only raised three children but helped to support her husband by writing sixteen novels and doing illustrations for such magazines as *Scribner's*, *The Century* magazine, and others. Other women illustrators include Alice Barber Stephens (1858–1932), Elizabeth Shippen Green (1871–1954), Charlotte Harding (1873–1951), Florence Scovel Shinn (1869–1940), and Sarah S. Stilwell Weber (1878–1939), to name a few. *(See p. 69)*

Note 7. "Ten feet of hardwood protruded in front of them, a compelling ram, and there was no jeering from the defenders when it bore down on them."

Prize pupil of Howard Pyle, Harvey Dunn passed on Pyle's teachings to a new generation of artists, combining forcefulness and great sensitivity with a brilliant sense of color. He himself lived an adventurous life as an official World War I artist, living in the fighting trenches of Europe. *(See p. 74)*

Note 8. Albert Beck Wenzell (1864–1917), one of the founders of the Society of Illustrators, was primarily known for his drawing room subjects of the 1890s and 1900s. "Danger Man" marks a departure for him. *(See p. 93)*

Note 9. Rudolph Belarski did a great deal of work for the pulps, including covers for *The Phantom Detective, Mystery Book,* and *Black Book Detective* in the 1930s.

Belarski's images were also frequently used by paperback publishers, notably Popular Library, beginning in 1948. In fact, many of his pulp covers were reused in the paperback format. *(See p. 95)*

Note 10. Unquestionably one of the true masters of the pulps, Walter Baumhofer also illustrated for a number of the slicks, yet never lost the sensibilities of the pulps. *(See p. 95)*

Note 11. Here is another trademark example of what made Baumhofer great, showing the bold dramatic approach that characterized the best of the pulp era. *(See p. 96)*

Note 12. "At last Fitch saw in the dimness a man and a girl on a spirited horse riding toward him. Pio Pico had kept his promise."

Matt Clark's use of dry brush over strong ink compositions made his illustrations reproduce exceptionally well. When magazines such as *American Weekly* wanted to depict adventure, he was a natural choice to fill the bill. *(See p. 97)*

Note 13. A versatile illustrator, William Smith enjoyed working in a wide variety of mediums. This example conveys a feel of adventure without blazing pistols or drawn swords. *(See p. 98)*

Note 14. John McDermott spent World War II as a combat artist with the Marines. The powerful images he created during wartime led to a peacetime job with *Blue Book*. Contributor to many major magazines, he also became interested in film and wrote the script for *Loving*, probably the only general release film highlighting the day-to-day work of professional illustrators. *(See p. 98)*

Note 15. Loran Wilford (1893–1972) got his start in the newspapers like many adventure illustrators who were affected by the sense of the immediacy of action. He is best known for his use of dry brush. *(See p. 99)*

Note 16. Joseph Clement Coll, who also got his start in newspapers, was a virtuoso with pen and ink. His unusual and vivid imagination was a perfect match to the stories of Arthur Conan Doyle and Sax Rohmer, for which he is best known. *(See p. 100)*

Note 17. The dramatic composition and meticulous rendering of this piece is typical for Mario Cooper. His work of this vintage shows well the blending of a bold sense of line found in the pulps with sensibilities aimed at the mainstream slick magazines. *(See p. 101)*

Note 18. Frederic Gruger got his start in the newspaper business. It was there that he developed the idea of using the cardboard newspapers used to mount silver prints as a drawing surface; hence, "Gruger board." He felt that "[Illustration] deals with the spirit." It is the spirit showing in the subjects' eyes at the breathless moment that makes this a fine example of adventure art. *(See p. 105)*

Note 19. Leland Gustavson was one of the cornerstones upon which the very successful *Blue Book* was built. Though he worked for a wide variety of magazines, including many top "slicks," he was particularly fond of the pulps because they allowed him to "kill a staggering number of people in all the diabolical ways an author can dream up." *(See p. 106)*

Note 20. In the best adventure tradition, Louderback's characters and heroics seem larger than life. *(See p. 107)*

Note 21. Yet another student of Harvey Dunn, Mead Schaeffer was master at presenting "romantic, swashbuckling theatricality." *(See p. 109)*

Note 22. Noel Sickles began his career in the newspapers and created the "Scorchy Smith" comic strip. A remarkably prolific illustrator, his clients included *The Saturday Evening Post*, *National Geographic*, *Life*, and *This Week*. *(See p. 110)*

Note 23. Noel Sickles's (1911–1982) work, particularly his pen and inks, show his forthright approach to composition. His strokes are reduced to their most expressive minimums. *(See p. 110)*

Note 24. By knowing what magazines and books your favorite illustrator appeared in, you can develop a secondary collection of reproduced work. Old *TV Guides*, practically throwaways, become important when the covers were done by Bernard Fuchs. *(See p. 116)*

Note 25. Hundreds of illustrators studied Brangwyn's work in books, but one other of the few who crossed the ocean to study directly with him was Peter Helck. Helck assisted him with commissions and, following F. B.'s dictum "Go to Nature," he traveled across Europe, painting landscapes. Helck was influenced by Brangwyn's monumental treatment of architectural and industrial subjects in powerful oil paintings and etchings. *(See p. 118)*

Note 26. Jessie Willing Gillespie was born in Brooklyn. She worked around 1915 in Philadelphia, then New York. An illustrator artist, she was known for her satirical touch. *(See p. 185)*

Note 27. "Deep down in the bowels of the earth, under the capitals of the nations involved, are to be found the government offices." Clayton Knight (1891–1969) joined the U.S. Army Air Service in World War I, and throughout his career, specialized in aviation subjects. *(See p. 207)*

Note 28. Some artists didn't always sign their own names. Herbert Morton Stoops, for instance, signed many of his black-and-white dry-brush illustrations with his pen name, Jeremy Canon. Collectors should learn to recognize the artists' style, rather than pass up a good illustration because the name is unfamiliar. *(See p. 212)*

Note 29. The fact that the subjects are Judy Garland and Mickey Rooney add to the value of the illustration. *(See p. 266)*

Note 30. Historian Walt Reed refers to Saul Tepper (1899–1987) as "one of the last of the titans, a member of that elite group that had a direct link to Howard Pyle through the tutelage of Harvey Dunn. His contribution was colored by his origins in the Lower East Side of New York." *(See p. 270)*

GLOSSARY

Definitions used by various auction houses in catalogs and terms relating to illustration art:

after a copy of the work of the artist

attributed to a work of the period of the artist that the auction house considers to be in whole or part the work of the artist

bears date in the opinion of the auction house was executed at about that date

bears signature has a signature that, in the opinion of the auction house, might be the signature of the artist

circle of a work of the period of the artist that, in the opinion of the auction house, is closely related to his or her style

dated was executed at that date

estate-stamped documentation that the work is by the artist but not signed by the artist; may also be stamped by a dealer who has documentation

estimate price range given by an auction house of a probable selling price on an individual work; usually based on previous selling prices at auction

executed ____(date) when the date of the work of art is known, though it does not bear a date

foxed, foxing usually brownish spots caused by fungus, dampness, paper impurities, or any combination, the amount and seriousness of which can affect the value of a work

initials letters of an artist's name rather than his or her full signature

inscribed something other than a signature written by the artist on a picture

known as popularly accepted name rather than given name

manner of a work that the auction house considers to be in the style of the artist but possibly of a later period

monogram a character composed of two or more letters interwoven, the letters usually being the initials of a person's first and last name

N.A. National Academy of Design

painted in ____(date) when the date of the painting is known, though it does not bear a date

school of a work that, in the opinion of the auction house, is by a pupil or follower of the artist

signed has a signature that, in the opinion of the auction house, is the signature of the artist

studio of, workshop of a work that, in the opinion of the auction house, possibly has been executed under the supervision of the artist

verso reverse side of a work, where signature, initials, or monogram sometimes appear

Wolff pencil compressed carbon that gives drawings a rich, velvety black; a more refined product than charcoal; used by illustrators such as Frederic Rodrigo Gruger

ABBREVIATIONS USED IN LISTINGS

d. dated
i. inscribed
s. signed

BIBLIOGRAPHY

CHILDREN'S SUBJECTS

Bader, Barbara. *American Picture Books from Noah's Ark to the Beast Within*. New York: Macmillan, 1976.

Brandywine River Museum. *The Art of Rose O'Neill* (exhibition catalog). Preface by James H. Duff, essay by Helen Goodman. Chadds Ford, PA: The Brandywine River Conservancy, 1989.

———. *A Child's Garden of Dreams* (exhibition catalog). Preface by James H. Duff, essays by Justin G. Schiller and Betsy B. Shirley. Chadds Ford, PA: The Brandywine River Conservancy, 1989.

Goff, Diane M., and Margaret Dowling. "The Life and Art of Grace G. Drayton: Part 1." *Doll News*, Spring, 1988.

Mahoney, Bertha E., Louise Payton Latimore, and Beulath Folmbee, comps. *Illustrators of Children's Books, 1744–1945*. Boston: The Horn Book, 1947.

McClintock, Inez. "Kewpies: The Invention of Rose O'Neill (1874–1944)." The Antique Toy Collectors of America, Inc., *The Toy Chest*, Vol. 16, No. 1, April 1982.

Meyer, Susan E. *A Treasury of the Great Children's Book Illustrators*. New York: Harry N. Abrams, 1983.

The Museum of Cartoon Art. *Childhood Enchantments* (exhibition catalog). Introduction by Kendra Krienke, essay by Brian Walker. New York: The Museum of Cartoon Art, 1989.

Nudelman, Edward D. *Jessie Willcox Smith—a Bibliography*. Gretna, LA: Pelican Publishing, 1989.

Petteys, Chris. *Dictionary of Women Artists*. Boston: G. K. Hall, 1985.

Santa Barbara Museum of Art. *Enchanted Images* (exhibition catalog). Essay by Judy L. Larson. Santa Barbara, CA: Santa Barbara Museum of Art, 1980.

Schnessel, S. Michael. *Jessie Willcox Smith*. New York: Thomas Y. Crowell, 1977.

Skeeters, Paul W. *Maxfield Parrish: The Early Years, 1893–1930*. Los Angeles: Nash Publishing, 1973.

FANTASY AND SCIENCE FICTION

Feldman, Mark A., and John A. Taylor. *The Brothers Hildebrandt*. Published in honor of their exhibition July 9, 1978. Maryland Funnybook Festival.

Sackmann, Eckart. *Great Masters of Fantasy Art*. Berlin: Taco, 1986.

Summers, Ian. *The Art of the Brothers Hildebrandt*. New York: Ballantine Books, 1979.

Weinberg, Robert. *A Biographical Dictionary of Science Fiction and Fantasy Artists*. Westport, CT: Greenwood Press, 1988.

HISTORY

Hodgson, Pat. *The War Illustrators*. New York: Macmillan, 1977.
Sears, S. W. *The American Heritage Century Collection of Civil War Art*. New York: McGraw-Hill, 1974.

OTHER CATEGORIES

Allen, Douglas, and Douglas Allen, Jr. *N. C. Wyeth, His Collected Paintings, Illustrations and Murals*. New York: Crown, 1972.
Annuals of American Illustration, 1959 through 1983. Published for the Society of Illustrators. New York: Hastings House and Madison Square Press.
Delaware Art Museum. *The Golden Age of American Illustration 1880–1914* (exhibition catalog). Introduction by Rowland Elzea. Wilmington, DE: Wilmington Society of Fine Arts, 1972.
Duff, James H., Andrew Wyeth, Thomas Hoving, and Lincoln Kirstein. *An American Vision, Three Generations of Wyeth Art*. Boston: New York Graphic Society/Little Brown, 1987.
Eggenhofer, Nick. *Horses, Horses, Always Horses: The Life and Art of Nick Eggenhofer*. Cody, WY: Sage, 1981.
Ellis, Richard Williamson. *Book Illustration: A Survey of Its History and Development*. Kingsport, TN: Kingsport Press, 1952.
Elzea, Rowland, and Elizabeth H. Hawkes, eds. *A Small School of Art: The Students of Howard Pyle*. Wilmington, DE: Delaware Art Museum, 1980.
Falk, Peter Hastings, ed. *Who Was Who in American Art*. Madison, CT: Soundview Press, 1985.
Glenbow Museum. *American Illustration, 1890–1925: Romance, Adventure and Suspense* (exhibition catalog). Text by Judy L. Larson. Calgary, Alberta, Canada: Glenbow Museum, 1986.
Graphic Artists Guild Directory 1981–1982. New York: Annuals Publishing Company.
The Grunwald Center for the Graphic Arts. *The American Personality: The Artist-Illustrator of Life in the United States, 1860–1930* (exhibition catalog). Foreword and introduction by Maurice Bloch. Los Angeles: The Grunwald Center for the Graphic Arts, UCLA, 1976.
Holme, Bryan. *Advertising: Reflections of a Century*. New York: The Viking Press, 1982.
Hutchinson, W. H. *The World, the Work and the West of W. H. D. Koerner*. Norman, OK: University of Oklahoma Press, 1978.

Hyland, Douglas K. S., and Howard P. Brokaw. *Howard Pyle and the Wyeths: Four Generations of American Imagination*. Memphis, TN: Memphis Brooks Museum of Art, 1983.

Johnson, Fridolf, ed. *Treasury of American Pen & Ink Illustration, 1881–1938*. New York: Dover Publications, 1982.

Kery, Patricia Frantz. *Great Magazine Covers of the World*. New York: Abbeville Press, 1982.

W. H. D. Koerner, Illustrator of the West (exhibition catalog). Los Angeles: Los Angeles County Museum of Natural History, 1968.

McConnell, Gerald, ed. *Twenty Years of Award Winners*. Published for the Society of Illustrators. New York: Hastings House, 1981.

Meyer, Susan E. *America's Great Illustrators*. New York: Harry N. Abrams, 1978.

Morse, Willard S., and Gertrude Brinckle. *Howard Pyle, A Record of His Illustrations and Writings*. Wilmington, DE: Wilmington Society of Fine Arts, 1921.

Pitz, Henry C. *Howard Pyle*. New York: Clarkson N. Potter, 1975.

_____.*Norman Rockwell's People*. New York: Harry N. Abrams, 1981.

Reed, Walt. *Great American Illustrators*. New York: Abbeville Press, 1979.

_____. *Harold Von Schmidt Draws and Paints the Old West*. Flagstaff, AZ: Northland Press, 1972.

Reed, Walt, and Roger Reed. *The Illustrator in America, 1889–1980*. The Society of Illustrators. New York: Madison Square Press, 1984.

Schau, Michael. *"All-American Girl," The Art of Coles Phillips*. New York: Watson-Guptill, 1975.

_____. *J. C. Leyendecker*. New York: Watson-Guptill, 1974.

Schnessel, S. Michael. *Jessie Willcox Smith*. New York: Thomas Y. Crowell; Toronto: Fitzheary & Whiteside Ltd., 1977.

Schoonover, Cortlandt. *Frank Schoonover, Illustrator of the North American Frontier*. New York: Watson-Guptill, 1976.

Schoonover, Frank E. *The Edge of the Wilderness, A Portrait of the Canadian North*. Secaucus, NJ: Derbibooks, 1974.

Tarrant, Dorothy, and John Tarrant. *A Community of Artists: Westport-Weston, 1900–1985*. Westport, CT: Westport-Weston Arts Council.

Traxel, David. *An American Saga: The Life and Times of Rockwell Kent*. New York: Harper & Row, 1980.

200 Years of American Illustration. Text by Henry C. Pitz, foreword by Norman Rockwell. Published in association with the Society of Illustrators. New York: Random House, 1977.

Who's Who in American Art. Washington, DC: American Federation of Arts; New York and London: R. R. Bowker, 1936 to present.

Wyeth, Betsy James. *The Wyeths*. Boston: Gambit, 1971.

INDEX